THE SOVIET MILITARY EXPERIENCE

'Roger Reese utilises an impressive range of archives, military publications and personal accounts to show how persistently peacetime deficiencies, crime, corruption, incompetence, training and leadership affected battlefield performance from the Civil War to Afghanistan'

John Erickson, University of Edinburgh

'Roger Reese's *The Soviet Military Experience* is a clear and persuasive narrative of the Red Army's history from its founding to its demise. He has made excellent use of recent disclosures from the Soviet archives to shed new light on all the major periods in the Army's development. Professor Reese's keen instinct as a social historian allows him to capture from the documentary record what service was like for officers and soldiers during each period, but he also has a welcome sense of the Army as a political and military institution, and the importance of war for such an institution. Finally, Reese stresses the distinctive features of the Red Army throughout its history and compares it to the experiences of other armies; he thereby helps the reader to place the experience of the Soviet Army in the broader context of Imperial and post-Soviet military life'

Mark von Hagen, Columbia University

From its revolutionary inception in 1917, to its counter-revolutionary demise in 1991, the Red Army played a crucial role in all aspects of Soviet life. *The Soviet Military Experience* is the first general work to place the Soviet army into its true social, political and international contexts.

Focusing on the Bolshevik Party's intention to create an 'army of a new type', the army's aim was both to defend the people and propagate Marxist ideals to the rest of the world. Lenin believed that this new people's army would be a tool for social transformation and cohesion. But *The Soviet Military Experience* shows that by the end of the cold war and collapse of the USSR in 1991, Russian society once again saw their army as the elitist and callous organization which its Bolshevik founders had tried so hard to avoid. This timely account of the Soviet military experience includes discussion of the:

- origins of the Workers' and Peasants' Red Army
- effects of the Civil War
- Bolshevik regime's use of the military as a 'school of socialism'
- effects of collectivization and rapid industrialization of the 1920s and 1930s
- Second World War and its profound repercussions
- ethnic tensions within the army
- effect of Gorbachev's policies of *Glasnost* and *Perestroika*.

This up-to-date account is organized chronologically and thematically within chapters, and includes a comprehensive bibliography.

Roger Reese is Associate Professor of History at Texas A & M University, USA.

Warfare and History

General Editor
Jeremy Black
Professor of History, University of Exeter

THE SOVIET MILITARY EXPERIENCE

A History of the Soviet Army, 1917–1991

Roger R. Reese

London and New York

First published 2000
by Routledge
11 New Fetter Lane, London EC4P 4EE

Simultaneously published in the USA and Canada
by Routledge
29 West 35th Street, New York, NY 10001

Routledge is an imprint of the Taylor & Francis Group

© 2000 Roger R. Reese

Typeset in Bembo by
BC Typesetting, Bristol
Printed and bound in Great Britain by
Clays Ltd, St Ives plc

British Library Cataloguing in Publication Data
A catalogue record for this book is available from the British Library

Library of Congress Cataloging in Publication Data
Reese, Roger R.
The Soviet military experience: a history of the Soviet Army,
1917–1991/Roger R. Reese.
p.   cm. – (Warfare and history)
Includes bibliographical references and index.
ISBN 0–415–21719–9. – ISBN 0–415–21720–2 (pbk.)
1. Soviet Union.   Sovetskaia Armiia–History.   I. Title.
II. Series.
UA772.R434   1999
355'.00947–dc21   99-14259
                                                         CIP

ISBN 0–415–21719–9 (hbk)
ISBN 0–415–21720–2 (pbk)

TO MY BELOVED CHILDREN,
EMILY, ALEXANDER AND HELEN

CONTENTS

ACKNOWLEDGEMENTS

I would like to acknowledge the help I received from Julia Blackwelder who helped arrange departmental funding and allowed me the flexibility necessary to conduct research. I thank Texas A&M University for funding a year off of teaching and providing a grant for a summer salary to research and write. My thanks go to the staff of the European section of the Library of Congress for their help in uncovering sources and securing valuable materials. I am indebted to the Kennan Institute for Advanced Russian Studies of the Woodrow Wilson Center for International Scholars in Washington DC for their financial and institutional support.

I would also like to gratefully acknowledge: the use of text from *Notes of a Red Guard*, copyright 1993 by the Board of Trustees of the University of Illinois, used with permission of the University of Illinois Press, and Isaac Babel, *1920 Diary*, Yale University Press, copyright 1995; and the University Press of Kansas for its permission to reproduce extracts from *Stalin's Reluctant Soldiers*, copyright 1996. Extracts have also been taken from *The Military Writings and Speeches of Leon Trotsky*, Volumes 1 & 2 (1979), by kind permission of Mehring Books.

LIST OF ABBREVIATIONS

DRA	Democratic Republic of Afghanistan
GKO	State Council of Defense
GlavPUR	Main Political Administration
KGB	Committee for State Security
KOMUCH	Committee of the Constituent Assembly
NCOs	noncommissioned officers
NKO	People's Commissariat of Defense
NKVD	Peoples' Commissariat of Internal Affairs
PUR	Political Administration of the Red Army (also PURKKA)
RKKA	*Raboche Krest'ianskaia Krasnaia Armiia* (Workers' and Peasants' Red Army)
RKP	Russian Communist Party
RVS	Revolutionary Military Council
RVSR	Revolutionary Military Council of the Republic
SRs	Socialist Revolutionaries
URVS	Ukranian Revolutionary Military Soviet
VTsIK	All-Union Central Executive Committee

LIST OF RUSSIAN WORDS
AND PHRASES

Cheka	secret police
chistki	membership purges
dedovshchina	the rule of the grandfathers, hazing
edinonachalie	one-man command
Ezhovshchina	terror purge
glasnost	openness
inogorodnie	non-cossacks
istrebitel'nyi	fighting battalions
krasnoarmeitsy	Red Army men
kulaks	wealthy peasants
mladshie leitenanty	junior lieutenants
opolchenie	citizens militia army
Osoaviakhim	Society for the Advancement of Aviation and Chemistry
otriad	detachment
partizanschchina	partisan mentality
perestroika	restructuring
pomeshchnik politruk	assistant political instructor
raions	districts
samokritika	self-criticism
shtrafnyi	penal combat battalion
Sovnarkom	Council of Peoples' Commissars
stariki	soldiers in their last six months of service
terrarmeitsy	territorial soldiers
Tsaritsa pole	queen of battle
uezd	sub-county level military commissariats
voenspetsy	military specialists, former tsarist officers serving in the Red Army
volost	county level Soviet military commissariats
Vsevobuch	Universal Military Training Administration
zamestitel' politruk	deputy commander for political affairs

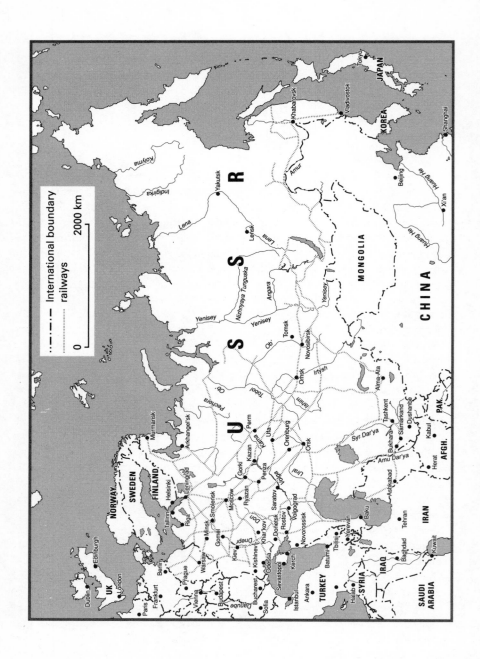

INTRODUCTION

This book is a history not so much of an army, but of a phase an army went through. We can neither treat the Soviet Army as an institution *sui generis*, nor as phenomenon isolated in time and space that has come and gone, but must seek to understand the Soviet military experience as a distinct phase on the centuries old continuum of Russian military history. This is to assert that the Soviet phase of Russia's military history exhibits continuities as well as discontinuities from its tsarist roots and has put its mark on Russia's emerging new national army. In a sense this book is a case study of the Soviet military experience particularly focusing on the Bolshevik Party's attempt to create a distinctly different military, distinct not only from the imperial military heritage, but from the evolved Western military model as well. What the Bolsheviks loathed in particular about the former tsarist army and planned to avoid were: its class nature, in which elites ruled and the oppressed served; the physical violence inflicted on soldiers; often abysmal conditions of life, especially poor food and housing; the lack of political and civil rights for soldiers; and the lack of accountability of officers for their men. In some aspects the Soviets achieved temporary success, and in others complete failure. This work, then, is a study in contrasts between what was attempted and what was achieved, and how the Red Army evolved from its revolutionary inception in 1918 to its counterrevolutionary demise in 1991.

Even before the October 1917 Revolution and the eventual founding of a soviet army, Bolshevik leaders intended to create an "army of a new type." Two factors conditioned their views on this new type army: Marxist ideology, and their impressions of the Imperial Russian Army – none of the Bolshevik elite had performed military service. In the months before the October Revolution the Bolshevik Party openly addressed the question of the form a future socialist army should take. The June–July 1917 Conference of Bolshevik Organizations resolved to eliminate the standing army and replace it with a popular militia. This resolution reflected a widespread and deep-seated distrust of standing armies held not only by Bolsheviks, but by most Russian leftist parties. The purpose of this army would be different from armies of the old type, this army would serve the people, defending

1

them from foreign and class enemies, and carry Marxist revolutionary ideals and freedoms to the enslaved nations of the world. In short, Lenin proposed to found a new army from scratch and in so doing radically change, if not abolish, three hundred years of Imperial Russian military heritage.

Creating this new army was a tall order based on intense idealism and gross naivete. Yet, it was a necessary stance given their revolutionary goals and rejection of all things feudal or bourgeois. Unaware of the enormity of what he proposed, Lenin purposely followed a path that led to the destruction of the old army and necessitated a new army in its place. What Lenin failed to appreciate was that Russian society was completely unprepared to create the type of army necessary to establish and maintain Bolshevik power in the manner he dreamed of. Furthermore, the Bolsheviks had begun to create conditions that would force them to sacrifice core ideology in founding an army that could not, despite self-delusional rhetoric, reflect the values on which they based their revolution. Thus, during the period 1917–21 the Bolsheviks' army proved to be a complete improvisation lacking clear long-term vision and direction, which translated into *ad hoc* organizational decisions made by people who either did not consider or care how those decisions would affect the army in the long run, or who hoped to create a military institution not accepted as appropriate by many.

Before the 1917 October Revolution the Bolsheviks understood that the old Imperial Army had to be done away with. They saw that the Provisional Government was unable either to control the generals or win the loyalty of the common soldiers. Lenin suspected too, that the Bolshevik Party, though making inroads, was in no position to take over and control this army of several millions. The Bolsheviks would have had to compete with other revolutionary parties for influence, and contend with reactionary tendencies of some soldiers, apathy and war weariness to the point of mutiny of others. Therefore, the Bolsheviks directed their military efforts before the October seizure of power toward mobilizing armed workers' detachments (Red Guards) to their cause, and undermining the ability of the army high command to use the army against them.

The destabilization of the old army began without Bolshevik participation. Order Number One of the Petrograd Soviet, issued in March 1917, encouraged the front-line soldiers to elect committees to represent themselves against the authority of the officers and, among other things, not to surrender their arms to their officers. Soldiers thereupon refused to obey orders unless approved by their committees as the army, in the midst of a world war, became a democratic institution. The officers' hold on their men became tenuous, discipline deteriorated, and desertion skyrocketed – all of which facilitated the Bolsheviks' disorganizing propaganda and agitation work. At the time the October Revolution succeeded in deposing Kerensky's Provisional Government, the army did not answer to the Bolsheviks, but neither would it serve Lenin's opponents.

2

The Bolsheviks' new army, which they called the Workers' and Peasants' Red Army (*Raboche Krest'ianskaia Krasnaia Armiia*, RKKA) did, surprisingly enough, start out nearly as Lenin had envisioned. Based on Red Guard detachments the Bolsheviks' first military force was completely voluntary, drawn from the working class, and determined to defend the revolution. It soon became apparent to even the most idealistic of revolutionaries, however, that groupings of Red Guards did not constitute an army. The civilian leadership also quickly realized that the tasks at hand, such as preserving an empire threatened by independence movements and defending their fledgling Bolshevik government from a counterrevolutionary civil war and foreign intervention, required a real army and all it entailed. In March 1918 Lenin assigned Leon Trotsky the task of creating a true army.

Trotsky wisely dropped most of his Marxist utopian preconceptions of what an army ought to look like and immediately began forming an army along traditional lines. This included creation of a hierarchy of officers and enlisted men and provisions for military discipline and organization. Initially recruitment was limited to the working class, but this soon proved to be inadequate and the gates were flung open to all comers except rich peasants, the clergy, bourgeoisie and, with exceptions, the nobility. Manning the army on a voluntary basis also went by the wayside rather quickly; the regime instituted conscription early in 1918. The most controversial aspect of Trotsky's new army was his reliance on former tsarist officers to train and even lead units of the Red Army. Such dependence on the avowed class enemy was anathema to the average Bolshevik and caused considerable turmoil in the party. This army, which swelled to nearly five million men at its peak, successfully fought a civil war preserving Bolshevik dominance, though it failed to restore Russia's pre-1914 borders.

Demobilization of the Red Army began in late 1920 and the debate resumed on the form the peacetime armed force would take. Once again Marxist idealists resurrected the idea of a citizens' army but were now challenged by those Bolsheviks desiring a professional standing army. A compromise resulted. In 1921, the party accepted the need for a standing army but insisted that the bulk of the country's military force would be its reserve, the citizen army. The compromise was viewed differently by the two opposing camps: the socialist idealists accepted the standing army as a temporary but necessary evil, expecting that once the conditions for true socialism were achieved the standing army would be done away with. Those in favor of a large and permanent standing army accepted the small active army and large territorial militia as a temporary expedient that would eventually result in a large standing army and small reserve once the economy became strong enough to support it.

The Communist Party still insisted that the standing army reflect the revolutionary ideals that guided the party's transformation of civilian society. It would not be a replica of the old tsarist army. The political and military leadership, despite their abandonment of a fundamental tenet of socialist philosophy, honestly attempted to create an army of a new type in officer-enlisted relations, discipline, war-making doctrine, and quality of life in contrast to the Imperial Russian Army. The regime believed their army could be a tool of social transformation for the masses. Some military theorists even believed that socialism would be the basis of a new method of warfare. Ultimately the idealism waned, and by 1941 the Red Army in many ways, both intentionally and unintentionally, resembled the reviled and much maligned imperial army. Between 1945 and 1991 the Red Army completely fell away in practice from its founding revolutionary vision and resembled the tsarist army of the nineteenth century more than it did the Soviet Army of the 1920s. The process of this transition and the attendant ramifications are major themes of this book.

The early history of the Red Army is the story of the Soviet regime's attempts to create an army that not only treated its soldiers well, but also tried to elevate their consciousness. It is the story of perhaps the world's first political army in the sense that the military leadership of the Red Army shared decision-making responsibility with a political party. The Communist Party's values became so intertwined with those of the military that the two became virtually indistinguishable. This union of party and army seemed logical and necessary to the party and was never seriously challenged by the army, yet proved to be the source of some of the weakness of the armed forces.

The Second World War shows the Red Army at both its nadir and pinnacle of effectiveness. The war began with the catastrophe of German invasion and ended with the Soviet conquest of Eastern Europe. In between, the army reverted to many Civil War practices that proved costly in lives but also developed new methods of manning that promoted cohesion and morale. The leadership of the army matured under fire ultimately rising to the occasion. Soviet society temporarily became wedded to the army in the way Lenin envisioned in 1917, and the army temporarily became a trusted and respected institution by most.

The history of the Soviet Army during the cold war is one of slow degeneration. The heroic traditions of the Great Patriotic War replaced revolutionary idealism and the faded legacy of the Civil War. In the post-Stalin era generals and the interests of the armed forces became entrenched in the highest decision-making circles of the party and government. The apparent pre-eminence of the army in society was its undoing, however. The military leadership ensconced on its lofty perch adopted the mentality of the former tsarist officer corps – that of elitism and self-assumed feeling of superiority divorced from their humble origins – which created a chasm in the relationship with their enlisted men. The officer corps lost touch with the men and allowed the human environment to once again become a harsh unpleasant one dominated by sergeants and senior enlisted men who brutalized their underlings. Training, discipline, and cohesion once again began to suffer. The military and its needs dominated the political economy of the USSR, much to the detriment of the whole country. Because of its institutional amalgamation with the party and government, the army could not help but share the stagnation and decline suffered by the rest of the Soviet polity and economy. By 1991, when the Soviet Union collapsed, society once again saw the army as a callous and uncaring organization brutal to its enlisted members and divorced from society.

For the most part this book is arranged chronologically into seven chapters. Within each chapter the material is treated thematically. The salient themes of 1917–21 treated in Chapter One are the origins and organization of the Workers' and Peasants' Red Army. Special attention is paid to the military–political aspects of the Civil War especially the development of the Political Administration of the Red Army and its commissars, the dependence of the Red Army on former tsarist officers recruited or impressed into Bolshevik service for technical and tactical expertise, and the dependence for manpower on non-Bolshevik peasant conscripts. Chapter Two examines the performance of the Red Army in the Civil War, and the war against Poland. Of particular importance is the Red Army's adaptation for warfare in the period of civil war.

The major themes of Chapter Three, which covers the interwar years 1922–39, are the resurrected standing army versus citizens' militia debate and its resolution at the Tenth Party Congress; the subsequent compromise of the mixed system of regular army and territorial militia, and the Frunze reforms of 1924–25, which finally created a sense of normality in the Red Army. Here also is illustrated the Red Army's initial attempts to deal with the enduring legacies of the old army in the daily life and training of the individual soldier and officer. Other major topics are the regimes' abandoning of the territorial forces and creation of an all regular army, and the debate over doctrine that was part of a new vision for the armed forces that emerged in these years. These coincided with the initial expansion of the army and the many problems this caused such as a shortage of officers and housing.

In Chapter Four, which also covers the interwar years, the regime's use of the military as a "school of socialism," is highlighted as a major theme. Collectivization and de-kulakization, rapid industrialization, and the army's role in those programs and the effects those programs had on the army are presented as important turning points in the development of the army, as was the army's turn to more traditional officer-enlisted relations. Important themes of the immediate prewar years are, the continuation of rapid expansion in which units were created so rapidly that the quantity of manpower assembled outstripped the ability of industry to provide equipment and the leadership's ability to train the men, the purge of the officer corps and the accompanying re-introduction of dual command, and the decline in efficiency and discipline in the units.

Chapter Five chronicles the Red Army's ordeal in the Second World War beginning with the Soviet invasion of Poland in September 1939. On the heels of its success in Poland the Red Army initiated a more significant armed engagement with Finland in the winter of 1939–40 in which the RKKA suffered grievous casualties and failed to conquer the country forcing the civilian leadership to settle for a negotiated peace. This little war exposed the Red Army as a hollow shell. In the two years before the German invasion the army began to mechanize and adapt its doctrine accordingly, but not in a consistent methodical way, rather by fits and starts with numerous changes in organization that served to confuse instead of promote the incorporation of new technology and ideas. The chapter includes an assessment of the Red Army in all its capabilities and lack thereof on 21 June 1941, the day before the Nazi invasion. The second major topic is the German invasion and the failure of the Red Army to stem the onslaught. The third theme is the changes wrought by the Second World War, especially the social changes that the army underwent, the changes in party–army relations, and shifts in the interaction of army and society.

Chapter Six delves into the history of the Cold War Soviet Army 1946–91. The overarching theme of this chapter is that of the final transformation of the Soviet Army into a traditional army very much in the mold of the old Imperial Russian Army as the culmination of Stalin's social policies of the 1930s, the experience of the Second World War and the ever present influence of Russia's military culture, and how this changed the relationships between officers and men, army and party, and army and society. Other important themes are hazing and ethnic tensions in the units, and their effect on morale.

Chapter Seven has two major themes. The first is the war in Afghanistan, which serves as a vehicle to illustrate how the peacetime shortcomings of the Soviet Army affected it in wartime, in particular conditions of service in Afghanistan are highlighted and their effect on the morale and discipline of the soldiers. The second theme is the effect on the army of Mikhail Gorbachev's (the last Party General Secretary) attempts to end the arms race, reduce the size of the army, and withdraw from Eastern Europe and the Baltic states, and his policies of *glasnost* and *perestroika*.

1

THE BIRTH OF THE RED ARMY

Following the successful destruction of the Provisional Government, Lenin highjacked the Second Congress of Soviets from the moderate left and shifted his focus from revolution to consolidating and retaining power. He first moved to assert control over the old tsarist high command at the beginning of November 1917, by sending a mere ensign in the army, Nikolai V. Krylenko, to Mogilev, to take command of the army in the name of the Revolution and Bolshevik Party. Krylenko's missions were first to prevent reactionary generals from mounting a counterrevolutionary attack, maintain the defense against the Central Powers, and finally prepare for the eventual demobilization of the old army.

Next Lenin sought peace with the Central Powers. He considered it impossible to consolidate power with the ongoing distraction of the war that continued to devour Russia's resources and victimize the population. Despite the respite that an end to the war might bring to the suffering population, many in the party – for nationalistic and political reasons – opposed his peace initiative, but Lenin prevailed. The Germans granted a truce in December and talks began in January 1918.

With the front quiet Lenin made his third move; he began the process of abolishing the old army while creating a new army that would serve the Bolshevik Party. He created a People's Commissariat for War in December 1917 by appointing Nikolai I. Podvoiskii to take over the former Ministry of War. Under Podvoiskii the Commissariat concerned itself largely with administering the old army and trying to keep track of its rapidly depleted personnel and its vast materiel that would be crucial to arming a new Red Army. Within the Commissariat of War, Podvoiskii also headed the All-Russian Collegium for the Organization of the Workers' and Peasants' Red Army created on 20 December 1917. Lenin intended for the Collegium to create a new army, a Red Army, for the obvious purpose of defending the Bolsheviks' grasp on power from all comers on the left or right.

With some ideological trepidation, the Collegium took their first steps that reflected the idealistic, yet fundamentally unworkable, democratic principles first articulated in Order Number One. Soldiers still elected their unit commanders and soldiers' committees continued to represent the collective interest of the enlisted men. In those first heady days after October the Bolsheviks expected the multitudes to flock to their cause and so confidently declared that the Red Army would be a volunteer army open only to "the most conscious workers and peasants." Local soviets would do the recruiting for the army and were entrusted with the task of keeping out class alien elements. The Collegium considered that these conditions would safeguard the party and the people from Bonapartism (military dictatorship) and supposed inherent reactionary tendencies of military institutions.

The first steps to forming an army included strengthening the numbers and armament of Red Guards, reorganizing them as Red Army units, and consolidating Bolshevik control over them. Eliminating the Red Guards as independent bodies and transforming them into an army turned out to be a complicated task. The central governing apparati definitely intended to end the Red Guards, but local leaders and groups often wanted to keep them. The transition to a regular army began in March 1919 and lasted until October 1919 because of deliberate foot dragging by independent-minded soviets, factory committees or Red Guards. Sometimes whole Red Guard detachments volunteered for Red Army service, while others disbanded and then individual members chose for themselves whether to join the army. Occasionally, Red Guard detachments became the kernel for Red Army units and transmitted their *esprit* to the new non–Red Guard recruits, becoming some of the more reliable units throughout the war.[1]

Several problems cropped up in short order. First, the democratic–anarchic tendencies left over from the disintegrating Imperial Army caused problems of central control over units. Locally raised units fought conscientiously in defense of their homes but did not do well very far from their districts. They also attached their loyalty to the local soviet rather than the emerging but unfamiliar central government. Second, rifts emerged due to the elitism of former Red Guards who considered themselves superior to former soldiers and new worker and peasant volunteers. Third, few volunteers appeared, dealing the Bolsheviks a psychological blow. In the first call for volunteers in February 1918 Podvoiskii had expected some 300,000 class conscious workers to come forward but only 20,000 – many of them of very low moral character – did so. Fourth, and the most compelling problem, the new army failed in battle.

The first test of Bolshevik military prowess came in mid-February 1918 after a breakdown in peace talks. Podvoiskii's mostly Red Guard army, in their working clothes, lightly armed with rifles and handguns clashed with German troops advancing through Estonia. The Germans intended to force the Bolsheviks into accepting Berlin's peace terms. Germany's disciplined and battle-tested soldiers thoroughly routed their Red adversaries. The most serious casualty of this defeat was Lenin's cherished notion that the voluntary efforts of a handful of class-conscious proletarians could uphold the revolution. Others in the party would not so easily be stripped of their delusions. The defeat, however, finally enabled Lenin to get the party to accept the Treaty of Brest–Litovsk in March 1918. Its terms cost Russia the entire Ukraine, Poland, the Baltic provinces, and some of the Caucasus. The simultaneous mass desertion of soldiers from the old army helped Lenin sway the Central Committee with his famous statement to the effect that "The soldiers have voted for peace with their feet." As of March 1918, millions of men had drifted home from the front and rear and the old army ceased to exist.

Lenin responded to the Brest–Litovsk disaster and continuing fear of Germany by moving Leon Trotsky into military affairs with instructions to create a hierarchically and centrally controlled army. Here, then, begins the actual organization of a new *regular* army and a profound break with revolutionary socialist ideology regarding military establishment. Until 4 March 1918 the Bolsheviks had made no serious attempt to coordinate under one command resources to address the military threat to the fledgling Soviet Republic. On that date Lenin's government, the Council of Peoples' Commissars (Sovnarkom), created the Supreme Military Council. Former tsarist General Bonch-Bruevich and two commissars headed the Supreme Military Council's staff of mostly former officers.

Before the end of hostilities Bonch-Bruevich had created a series of defensive screens comprising improvised units of Red Guards, former soldiers and officers and miscellaneous party members. Because the screens defended against the Germans and Austro–Hungarians some 8,000 former tsarist officers willingly put themselves at the disposal of the Soviet Republic out of feelings of patriotism – not support for the revolution. The two most important screens were the northern – controlled from Petrograd and directed against German forces in the Baltic States – and the western – controlled from Moscow and directed against German and Austro–Hungarian forces in the Ukraine and Belorussia. The Bolsheviks reinforced and maintained the screens even after concluding peace with the Central Powers because of uncertainty over how long the Peace of Brest–Litovsk would actually hold up. Behind these screens Trotsky went to work creating and molding an army from scratch.

Before reviewing Trotsky's work, the institutional structure within which he worked must be outlined to appreciate the complexity of his task, and to illustrate the regime's uncertainty and ignorance in governing military affairs. There came to exist, during 1918, three parallel structures of bureaucracy designed to enable the government and Bolshevik Party to oversee and control the armed forces. This triple structure was far from efficient and fostered competition and misunderstanding between competing organizations. One structure was the Bolshevik-controlled government, the aforementioned Council of Peoples' Commissars with Lenin as its chairman. Subordinate to the Sovnarkom was the Peoples' Commissariat for Military and Naval Affairs (Narkomvoenmor) first under Podvoiskii then Trotsky. Narkomvoenmor supervised the work of both the All-Russian Collegium for the Organization of the RKKA and the All-Russian Supreme Staff. The Staff, headed by a former major general of the Imperial General Staff Aleksandr A. Svechin, had responsibilities for administration, mobilization and training and manning the fronts.

In May 1918, Trotsky created the post of Commander-in-Chief of the Red Army. The first Commander-in-Chief was Mikhail A. Muravev, a former tsarist lieutenant colonel and member of the Left Socialist Revolutionary Party (Left SR), followed in July 1918 by Ioakhim I. Vatsetis, a former tsarist colonel, subsequently replaced in 1919 by Sergei S. Kamenev, also a former tsarist colonel. Trotsky, to rationalize the system, had Svechin's All-Russian Supreme Staff absorb the All-Russian Collegium for the Organization of the RKKA. The next lower levels of bureaucracy were provincial, district, and soviet military commissariats, and the Operations Department (of the Moscow Military District). Subordinate to the provincial and district military commissariats were the *uezd* military commissariats. Beneath them were the *volost* soviet military commissariats. The military sections of local soviets constituted the lowest organs of government involved in military affairs.

Political organs of supervision and control existed parallel to the government organs. At the top was the All-Russian Central Executive Committee (VTsIK) of the Congress of Soviets. Subordinate to the VTsIK in late 1918 was the Council of Workers' and Peasants' Defense of the Congress of Soviets (usually referred to as the Council of Defense). The initial membership of the Council of Defense included Lenin, Trotsky, Stalin and three others. Next in descending order came the Supreme Military Council, headed by Trotsky with former tsarist general Bonch-Bruevich as Chief of Staff, followed by the Revolutionary Military Soviet of the Republic (RVSR) established on 2 September 1918, also headed by Trotsky. The RVSR actually supervised the conduct of the Civil War.

Within the RVSR was the Field Staff that directed combat operations. Trotsky headed this body that included the Commander-in-Chief of the Army and a commissar. Also included in the RVSR's structure was the Political Department of the RVSR, which in May 1919 became the Political Administration of the Workers' and Peasants Red Army (PURKKA). The RVSR, answered to the Central Committee of the Communist Party, the VTsIK and the Sovnarkom.

The third element of bureaucratic control over the army was the Russian Communist Party (RKP). At the top was the Politburo, chaired by Lenin, which included Trotsky and Stalin and others. Lenin occasionally gave Politburo members special military assignments. Subordinate to the Politburo was the party Central Committee that debated, approved and helped supervise military policy and governed the activities of all subordinate party committees. The Central Committee supervised the activities of the Political

Administration and its commissars, and arbitrated conflicts between commissars and commanders. Finally, periodically convened party conferences or congresses debated and decided the most important military policies.

One can appreciate that there were actually few clear lines of authority and responsibility in the civil–political military bureaucracy. The confusing array of organizations and spheres of responsibility made Trotsky's work all the more difficult, but was perhaps unavoidable given that men with no working experience in large-scale hierarchical bureaucratic organizations, who did not trust soldiers and military organizations, created the structure. Historian Francesco Benvenuti observes that the consensus of equality between party members and lack of hierarchy within the pre-Revolution Bolshevik Party greatly hindered the plethora of leading Bolsheviks from assuming subordinate roles to other Bolsheviks – especially late comers such as Trotsky who had been in the party only a matter of nine months before taking over military affairs – and all but precluded their submission to non-Bolsheviks.[2] Therefore, fitting party members into a structured military organization requiring obedience, loyalty, and submission would prove to be an arduous and frustrating task.

That the party would be the driving force behind the military in its organization, training, and supply, and would define its strategic and operational goals was understood by all. In a report to the Moscow City Conference of the RKP on 28 March 1918, in which he referred to the need to create an army as a question of life and death, Trotsky said: "But we cannot create an Army through an administrative mechanism alone – which is in our case at present as bad as it could possibly be. If we do possess a powerful mechanism, this is an ideological one, namely, our Party. The Party will create the Army, comrades . . .".[3] From the outset, until it ceased to be the Soviet Army in August 1991, the Red Army would be the party's army.

That the Red Army was the party's army shaped virtually every facet of its development. Recruitment, retention, and promotion would all take on political as well as military overtones. The party's civil–political values would take precedence over strictly military values. The very notion of military professionalism would be held suspect for nearly two decades, not only because of connotations of class and elitism that went along with it, but also because of the fear that a soldier's primary loyalty might shift to the army rather than the communist regime. The army became drawn so tightly to the party that its fortunes would rise and fall with those of the party.

Trotsky's first practical steps to creating an efficient and reliable fighting force reflect a recognition that internally the army needed clear lines of authority, responsibility, and iron discipline. Therefore the democratic practices adopted in the February to October 1917 period had to be suppressed. To this effect, in March 1918, he abolished the election of officers and ordered soldiers' committees to disband. In the companies and battalions the commanders would possess all authority, at the regiment, brigade, and

11

division levels the commander would share responsibility with an appointed commissar, and at the army and front levels a Revolutionary Military Council (RVS) of at least three men would wield power. Sergei Gusev, one time head of PUR, made a reasonable point that the army needed RVSes during the Civil War, not so much to keep an eye on the former tsarist officers serving in the Red Army, but because so many issues had to be dealt with in the course of the war, such as forming units, dealing with emergent local party and government organizations, issues of supply, insurrections in the rear, organizational questions and "thousands of questions" that a commander would have been unable to deal with individually.[4] Within the units and the Bolshevik Party some protested Trotsky's method as anti-democratic and counter to socialist ideals. Trotsky, however, backed by the VTsIK, ran roughshod over protesters. Conformity with his orders and decrees was uneven and well into 1919 some units maintained their committees. Some units still elected officers in 1920.

Given the poor turnout, numerically and qualitatively, under the volunteer system the VTsIK decreed compulsory military training and conscription in April 1918. Without good reason VTsIK created the Universal Military Training Administration (Vsevobuch) rather than let the army create its own training apparatus, establishing another layer of bureaucracy and creating a turf war that would last until Vsevobuch was abolished in 1923.[5] The Bolsheviks did not subject the entire population to the draft. Only workers and toiling peasants (distinct from the rich peasants – kulaks) were allowed the privilege of serving in the Red Army. Getting the men into uniform was another question altogether. The recruiting apparatus had to be built from the ground up. Draft evasion was widespread for a variety of reasons from war weariness, political disinterest or hostility to the Bolsheviks, and economic necessity.

The Red Army's first conscription drive of 12 June through 29 August 1918 mobilized, in Moscow, Petrograd, Vladimir and Nizhni–Novgorod provinces some 540,000 men. Slowly but surely as the military apparatus grew and gained experience they gathered in tens then hundreds of thousands of men. By the end of 1918 the army had grown to 800,000 men. In the course of 1919 the size of the army increased to three million men, most of whom were peasants.

Not until the very end of the Civil War and suppression of anti–Bolshevik uprisings had been completed did the army reach its peak of five million men. Even then, the rosters always included names of deserters not actually present for duty. At any given time between 1918 and 1921 hundreds of thousands of men were absent without leave from their units. The number of registered deserters for the whole of the Civil War period was 3,714,000. Untold tens of thousands or more deserters went unregistered. An especially devastating byproduct of desertion was an exacerbation of the supply problem because deserters, in most cases, took their uniforms, equipment, and weapons with them for personal use or for sale.[6]

The army adopted a number of measures to address the desertion problem. On the one hand, Trotsky threatened dire consequences for desertion and for those who aided deserters. His Order Number 65 to the troops and soviet institutions on the Southern Front dated 24 November 1918 is typical of his hard-line approach:

1   Every scoundrel who incites anyone to retreat, to desert or not to fulfill a military order, is to be shot.
2   Every soldier of the Red Army who voluntarily deserts his post is to be shot.
3   Every soldier who throws away his rifle or sells part of his uniform is to be shot.
4   Battle-police units are to be stationed along the entire front-line zone, in order to catch deserters. Any soldier who tries to offer resistance to these units is to be shot on the spot.
5   All local soviets and Committees of the Poor, are obligated, on their part, to take all measures to catch deserters. Deserter-hunts are to be carried out twice in every 24 hours, at 8 am. and 8 pm. Captured deserters are to be handed over to the headquarters of the nearest unit or to the nearest military commissariat.
6   Persons guilty of harboring deserters are liable to be shot.
7   Houses in which deserters are found are to be burnt down.[7]

Commanders seldom enforced such draconian measures. Most often, when deserters were apprehended they were simply assigned to duty in a different unit.

The most successful technique in mitigating the effects of desertion was the general amnesty. Periodically the army would announce an amnesty week. Men who turned themselves in would be returned to duty and exempt from punishment. Presumably no questions would be asked of the whereabouts of his kit. The first amnesty week was 3–9 June 1919 during which 98,000 men turned themselves in. Because of its success Trotsky extended the amnesty one week and another 34,000 men surrendered themselves.[8]

Once the men began reporting for duty and units began forming, the army faced the challenges of clothing, equipping, arming, housing, feeding and paying its soldiers. To an extent the army never overcame these challenges, but diverted a disproportionate amount of time, effort and manpower to address them. It has been estimated that as many as 70 percent of army personnel devoted their time to procuring food and supplies. Historian Orlando

Figes relates one aspect of the Red Army's manpower problems to its supply problems in that Lenin created an army that proved to be too large for the war-torn economy to sustain. A vicious circle of problems in supply and training led to mass desertions which necessitated wider conscription that led to greater supply problems.[9] Lenin recognized from the beginning that the military effort would much depend on the success of its provisioning so he included the Commissar of Food and the Chairman of the Extraordinary Commission for Producing Supplies on the Council of Defense.

Economic problems began before the October Revolution and the advent of "war communism" – the creation of central government control over the entire economy dating from June 1918. The demands of the First World War had done much to disrupt the Russian economy, skewing production to war materiel and taxing rail transport to the limit. The tsarist government's granting itself a monopoly over the grain trade and consequent peasant resistance created a situation of food shortages which the Bolsheviks compounded by affirming the monopoly and doing everything they could to prevent smuggling of food into the urban areas. The Treaty of Brest–Litovsk denied the Bolsheviks vital raw materials to keep factories running from March to November 1918. Workers' committees disrupted production as they challenged owners and management for control of the workplace. Suffice it to say these were poor economic conditions in which to conduct war, especially when the new regime running the economy had no experience and only a utopian Marxist mindset to guide them.

The supply situation in 1919 and 1920 was so bad that many soldiers went without uniforms. Sometimes units could not even leave their barracks or encampments because they lacked adequate footwear. At times units went without issues of food for weeks causing men and horses to die. Malnutrition contributed to the death toll from disease among soldiers. The main killers were typhus, influenza, smallpox, cholera, typhoid and venereal disease. As material conditions worsened desertion and discipline problems increased. When units did not receive adequate food supplies they invariably resorted to supplying themselves locally at the expense of soviet organs and civilians. Sometimes independent procurement turned into looting and violence against civilians, particularly non-Russians. In other instances soldiers mutinied against their officers and commissars, arrested them and elected new commanders and refused to march until material conditions improved.

Of course not all cases of material hardship led to dramatic mutinies, but many led to passive resistance. Unit commanders sometimes used the lack of supplies and consequent lowering of morale to beg off of further combat operations. Trotsky knew full well the extent of shortages and their impact and made every effort to shore up units in critical operations by personally delivering urgently needed supplies from boots to borsch with his personal train. Even so, Trotsky would not let the material situation become a crutch or standing excuse for inactivity and decried, in November 1918:

Some commanders reply like this to military orders: "My unit won't march . . . My unit is tired and won't advance . . . My soldiers have not received, when they should, their pay or an issue of warm underwear: they won't go forward until they get what is due to them." A commander who is capable of giving such replies is either a fool or a criminal.[10]

Indeed, Trotsky had a well-deserved reputation for not accepting excuses, no matter how compelling. Many commanders not involved in critical battles had the unenviable and nearly impossible task of placating and motivating masses of often cold and hungry troops to stick with the colors.

Acquiring sufficient amounts of food had been a problem for all Russia since 1916 and this motivated a good many desertions, not only so the soldier could find food, but also to help his family – particularly with the sowing and harvest. Naturally the party preferred workers over peasants and not just for ideological reasons. In practical terms workers were fairly self-motivated to resist the Whites and the political, economic, and social reaction they represented. Peasants, on the other hand, were more concerned with their land and usually only a direct and immediate threat to their ownership stirred them to action. Lenin considered that the more peasants the Red Army had the less stable it was.

Nevertheless, workers simply did not exist in sufficient numbers, nor were they all willing to bear arms in support of the Bolsheviks. Therefore, reluctantly, Lenin had to turn to the peasantry for manpower in overwhelming numbers. In 1920, 75 percent of the Red Army were peasants. The integration of peasants and workers proceeded awkwardly. Often proletarian soldiers, noncommissioned officers (NCOs), and officers felt hatred and contempt for their peasant comrades. Informally it was permissible to punish peasant soldiers with a rifle butt stroke to the teeth, though officially Trotsky deplored and inveighed against such practice.[11]

The general unreliability of peasants hampered their acceptance by the party and workers. Eduard Dune, a young assistant commissar, tells of his first assignment to a regiment consisting exclusively of peasants.

The Nizhegorod division, made up of newly mobilized troops and well staffed with former tsarist officers, had surrendered as soon as they arrived at the front. The particular regiment I had joined had just moved to strengthen a neighboring division, and in this way they escaped the fate of the rest of their division. Having learned that the Nizhegorod division had given itself up, this regiment also began to kick up a row. They held rallies with the demand, "Down with the war – long live peace!" On the order of a newly arrived commander, the soldiers formed up their units, but they still refused to occupy their positions. Finally, when persuasion had failed, the

15

regiment was surrounded by a battalion of sailors, formed into ranks with the commander at the head and stripped of their weapons without opposition. Now without rifles, with the muzzles of machine guns pointing at them, they again refused to obey the order to go to the front. Only under individual interrogation did one unit agree to go to the front, "if everyone goes," but the majority still refused. In this way the regiment was divided into two parts, and from those who still refused, the authorities began to single out every tenth man. Each of those who was pulled out was shot in front of the others and of course after these executions the regiment adopted a new resolution: to go to the front.[12]

Dune's peasants acted typically, and yet, counter to expectations, some completely peasant units fought with distinction from the earliest days of the Civil War. Some voluntarily formed peasant brigades had tremendous military cohesion and enthusiasm but were initially motivated and established to defend their own villages and soviets, not the Bolshevik government. In general, during the Civil War, the army as a whole never did achieve a high degree of cohesion or enthusiasm, but was held together by threats and intimidation, and loyal communists and dedicated workers.

Isaac Babel, a Red Army military correspondent who accompanied the 1st Cavalry Army (Konarmiia) during the Soviet–Polish War of 1920, had a generally low opinion of the rank and file as human beings but often admired their fighting qualities. He loathed the pervasive anti-semitism, boorishness, and sexual depravity of the men – and some officers – but, like Lenin, seems to have understood that the use of the unenlightened and politically ignorant masses was an unfortunate but necessary evil to preserve the revolution. It comes through clearly in his diary that Babel remained unconvinced, even skeptical, that the participation of the dregs would advance socialist revolution. He described the Russian infantryman as, "not just unmodernized, but the personification of 'pauper Russia,' wayfaring tramps, unhealthily swollen, bug-ridden, scrubby, half-starved peasants." He even describes soldiers as "cavemen."[14]

Though most were uncultured and uneducated it must not be forgotten that a great number of men stuck with their units and comrades to fight and die in the Red Army. Babel describes the opening battle for the Galician town of Brody during the war with Poland in August 1920:

> Our infantry in trenches, it's remarkable, young lads from Volhynia, barefoot, semi-idiotic – Russian peasants, and they are actually fighting against Poles, against the gentlemen oppressors. They're short of rifles, the cartridges don't fit, these boys have to skulk in heat-flooded trenches, they get shunted from one forest edge to another."[15]

What Babel seems to have found most remarkable was that the Russian peasants were beating the Poles. Months later, when the Poles began to beat the Russians, Babel found the scenes of panic and retreat were equally notable.

The Red Army used the services of thousands of women in the civil war years, all of whom were volunteers. Often wives and sweethearts joined their men's unit in official and semiofficial capacities. Most women served in administrative roles or as nurses, but some fought as ordinary infantry. Babel noted in his diary that:

> A whole volume could be written on women in the Red Army. The squadrons go into battle, dust, din, bared sabers, furious cursing, and they gallop forward with their skirts tucked up, covered in dust, with their big breasts, all whores, but comrades, whores because they're comrades, that's what matters, they're there to serve everybody, in any way they can, heroines, and at the same time despised, they water the horses, tote hay, mend harness, steal from the churches and from the civilian population.

Babel came into contact with the nurses of his headquarters commandant frequently and had little good to say about them. His impression was that they slept around entirely too much which impaired morale because of the rivalries it created.[16]

Integral to politicizing, manning and supplying the army was Trotsky's drive to centralize the Red Army for political as well as practical military purposes. Like many aspects of the Red Army's growth and maturity the effort to centralize control and development of the army came as a reaction to its failed utopian origins. That the army would be controlled centrally rather than locally had to be spelled out as official policy by the Fifth Congress of Soviets in July 1918 as vital to the creation and maintenance of discipline in the army. Centralization entailed control over all aspects of the military and conduct of the war by the Council of Defense and the RVSR, by the Peoples' Commissariat of Military and Naval Affairs, and the Politburo. In terms of personalities this meant central control by Leon Trotsky who sat on all these bodies and headed two of them, and Vladimir Lenin who sat on three of the bodies heading the two Trotsky did not. The main goals of centralization were to achieve obedient subordination and to end independent or autonomous policy making of subordinate military and military-related bodies while not squashing their use of initiative. Lenin and Trotsky never fully realized their aim of centralization but its necessary pursuit consumed an inordinate amount of their time and energies.

The main obstacles to centralization were: geography; poor communications; *"partizanshchina"* or partisan mentality on the part of locally raised formations; bull-headed high-ranking party members, and conflicting socialist ideals among Bolsheviks; conflicting outlooks of non-Bolsheviks serving in the Red Army, such as cossacks, peasants, Left SRs, left communists, and anarchist peasant armies (Greens) allied to the Reds; lack of a true and respected state structure and infrastructure; questions of the political legitimacy of Bolshevik rule; and questions of practical legitimacy because under the circumstances of revolution and civil war the new regime could not fulfill the normal functions expected of a state. Throughout the Civil War, control, over the army by the party and government, and within the army by each level of command over the one below, remained tenuous.

The very first practical acts of assembling soldiers into military formations under Moscow's control initiated the contest of central versus local control of military units. Before Moscow's urging local soviets had raised military formations in order to complete and then defend the revolution in their locale. As the central authorities began to gather in these units resistance and outright defiance sometimes cropped up. This kind of independent mindedness lasted well into 1919 hindering cohesive, large-scale operations. Trotsky slapped the label "*partizanshchina*" on commanders of locally raised and controlled troops as well as those commanders of regular units who insisted on always adapting operations to local conditions rather than strictly adhering to the orders of the appropriate RVS. Eventually Trotsky felt compelled to arrest and even execute a few high ranking commanders and commissars in an effort to put a stop to their adaptations. Trotsky's use of the term *partizanshchina* tends to confuse the issue because many guerilla detachments joined the Red Army en masse keeping their local identity, commanders and attitudes.

Two of the largest and most notorious partisan bands to temporarily come into the fold of the Red Army were those of Nikifor Grigorev and Nestor Makhno. Grigorev, a self-styled liberator of the Ukraine with vague ambitions to rule some or all of the Ukraine, created his own army in 1918 which ranged in numbers from a few thousand to tens of thousands depending on circumstances. Grigorev volunteered his services to the Red's Vladimir Antonov-Ovseenko who had in November 1918 been put in charge of seizing the Ukraine in the wake of Germany's withdrawal. Antonov-Ovseenko accepted the offer, expecting Grigorev to fully subordinate his forces and amalgamate them into the Red Army. Grigorev led a great number of men to victories in southwest (right bank) Ukraine first against German then allied troops (French and Greek), but refused in the long run to completely subordinate himself to the authority of the Red Army. He was no Bolshevik, had his own agenda and considered his army to be his own property. His personality was so strong and his successes so vital that for a period he actually had Red Army units under his command, mainly because some key subordinates of Antonov-Ovseenko were more afraid of Grigorev than of Antonov-Ovseenko.

Antonov-Ovseenko had to delay plans to rein in Grigorev in March 1918 because at the time Red Army units were beginning to fall apart and it was the partisans who were doing most of the fighting. In May 1919, Grigorev rebelled against the Bolsheviks refusing to follow orders or acknowledge Bolshevik authority. The Red Army promptly attacked and destroyed his forces in a short campaign which greatly complicated Red operations in the Ukraine and eventually made them susceptible to a successful White counteroffensive.[17]

Nestor Makhno, an anarchist, formed his guerilla bands and got his first military experience in 1918 operating against the Austrian occupiers of south Ukraine. He began cooperating with the Red Army in 1919 though he never really trusted the Bolsheviks nor they him. For him the Whites were the immediate threat to his vision of a peasant socialist Ukraine. Makhno's Order no. 1, of 5 August 1919 established his army's enemies as, the rich bourgeoisie, those who upheld an unjust social order of a bourgeois nature which included Bolshevik Commissars, the *Cheka*, or members of punitive detachments. He tried to create a well ordered army without former tsarist officers, allowing no pogroms, no drunkenness, no looting, and demanded respect for local populations, and disciplined behavior in general. At its peak in late 1919 Makhno's army may have had as many as 55,000 men.[18]

The Bolsheviks turned on Makhno in January 1920 for resisting the sub-ordination of his army to the Red Army. The campaign against Makhno lasted eighteen months including a brief intermission. There was bitter, ruth-less fighting which saw mass murders of peasants by the *Cheka* and execution of all Makhnovite prisoners taken in the fighting. For their part, Makhno's men killed all Bolshevik Party activists they could lay their hands on, all *Cheka* members, and all officials of grain procurement detachments. The Makhnovites usually shot all captured officers unless the Red rank and file strongly interceded for them, and sent home those of the rank and file who chose not to serve with Makhno. Operations against Makhno were generally unpopular with Red Army men. Between 26 and 30 November Makhno routed three Red Army divisions and attracted many soldiers to his side. He finally escaped to Romania at the end of August 1921.[19]

In both cases the partisan bands supplied the Reds with thousands of armed and organized men for the struggle against Denikin and made vital contributions to operations, yet remained essentially independent armies – an intolerable situation in the long run. Both leaders, however, fell out with the Reds and in so doing brought serious harm to the Bolsheviks. Grigorev's defection opened the way for Denikin's advance on Moscow, and Makhno's attacks on the Red rear prevented the Bolsheviks from eliminating the Whites early in 1920. Fighting against these purely peasant bands further discredited the Bolshevik movement in the eyes of the peasantry.

The practice of front mobilizations hampered central control of manpower distribution. A front mobilization consisted of the impromptu conscription of military aged males in the front-line areas by army and front RVSes. Rather than send the conscripts to Vsevobuch for training and subsequent assignment, the men were sent directly to combat units. Very often they were sent into the front-lines with little or no training at all. Sergei Gusev estimated that two-thirds of the Red Army was formed or reformed in the vicinity of the front by the armies themselves. Nearly half a million men were taken into the army through front mobilizations in 1919. Not until late 1919 did the central conscription and training organs produce decently trained and organized divisions for the front in quantity.[20] Prior to this the divisions Vsevobuch organized in the rear were of very poor quality and as many as a third or more of a unit might desert on the way to the front. Feeling let down by the central authorities the fronts opted to fend for themselves and maintained a degree of independence in their control of manpower.

Red Army leadership

The leadership of the Red Army consisted of a variety of types of people – some of them amazingly incompatible – who despite great odds managed to work together well enough at critical times to win the Civil War (but not the war with Poland). All told, the Red Army, throughout the Civil War period, relied on a few thousand qualified, dependable, talented, and energetic individuals to hold the masses of unqualified, undependable, mediocre, and unenthusiastic leaders and men together. Trotsky often shifted the able from front to front, between armies and crises because the army's pool of talent and reliability was so shallow.

Trotsky understood only too well the shortcomings of the Bolsheviks in military matters and decided his only recourse was to tap the reservoir of tsarist professional military expertise despite the loathsome noble or bourgeois class origins of most officers. Trotsky's decision to rely on former tsarist officers, whom he termed "military specialists" (*voenspetsy*), stirred up a hornet's nest of protest within the party. Only a minority of party members supported the use of military specialists and a vocal opposition faction of "left communists" arose to fight the decision. Lenin, who had thought of using officers of the old army as early as December 1917, gave his personal support to Trotsky on the use of military specialists, yet even that was not enough to quiet dissent.

The "left communists" thought an army generaled by tsarist officers and based on wide conscription would soon lose the necessary proletarian class character and become unable to support the revolution's goals or the Russian proletariat in international revolution. They argued for the hasty creation of a proletarian reserve officer corps (ironically to be trained by military specialists) and conscription only of workers and poor peasants. The "left communists" feared that Trotsky, by his appointment of former officers, was recreating the officer corps and command structure of the Imperial Army.[21]

Trotsky was not foolish and did not trust all military specialists – although he trusted them far more than any of his party peers – and was content to rely on a system of dual command in which commanders at regiment, brigade and division level were watched over by an appointed commissar. In July 1918, the Fifth Congress of Soviets, with Lenin's and Trotsky's urging, formally accepted the institution of commissars in the army. At the army and front level the commander shared power in an RVS troika of himself, a chief of staff and a commissar. Chiefs of staffs were often Bolsheviks to boot. Under this system orders became valid only when signed by the commissar in addition to the commander. Trotsky's stubborn insistence on using military specialists and support of individual officers under personal attack from party members earned him many lifelong enemies in the party.

The most famous incident over the issue of the use of military specialists was the "Tsaritsyn Affair," of September–October 1918. Tsaritsyn (later renamed Stalingrad) was, in the summer of 1918, important as a manufacturing center and communications hub on the lower Volga. The commander of forces in Tsaritsyn was Kliment Voroshilov who was simultaneously a member of the Southern Front RVS along with former tsarist general Pavel Sytin – personally appointed by Trotsky – and commissar S. K. Minin. Sytin had his headquarters 350 miles away at Kozlov. The geographic distance between the Bolsheviks and Sytin is perhaps symbolic of their poor personal relationship. Sytin, it is said, was hard to get along with. Nevertheless, all was well until Joseph Stalin entered the picture in May. He was on his way to the North Caucasus as a special plenipotentiary to take charge of food supplies but ended his journey in Tsaritsyn because White forces had cut off the North Caucasus for the time being. Rather than return to Moscow, Stalin stayed on in Tsaritsyn and invited himself to join the Southern Front RVS, which was quite irregular as membership was centrally controlled. Using his plenipotentiary powers (not given for this particular purpose) Stalin took over personal supervision of affairs in Tsaritsyn from Voroshilov who seems not to have complained. Before long, Sytin formally disapproved of several military measures which Stalin refused to reverse. In a personal confrontation in September, Sytin insisted that as military specialist he had the final word on military questions, not the Bolshevik trio. On 31 September, Stalin, Minin and Voroshilov dismissed Sytin and cabled their decision to the RVSR in Moscow. Stalin asked that Voroshilov be named military commander of the Southern Front. Outraged, Trotsky and Commander-in-Chief Vatsetis took the case to Lenin who, in conjunction with the Central Committee, supported them and recalled Stalin to Moscow the following week.

In the short term Trotsky won; however, the Tsaritsyn Affair in part forced the issue of military specialists out of Trotsky's hands and into the hands of the party. In March 1919, after much debate, the Eighth Party

Congress ordered that military specialists continued to be used and watched over by commissars. Neither Trotsky nor the party intended to rely on former officers indefinitely and had begun training a new cadre of "Red commanders" in early 1918.

In the larger picture we might view the Tsaritsyn Affair as a struggle over principle in the question of who controlled the army, the party or government bureaucracy. Given the revolutionary context of the creation of the army and the ideological ramifications of using *voenspetsy* Stalin had a valid point in questioning if a government commissariat would be able to operate without the oversight of the Central Committee. Was this the party's army or not? Trotsky had made the decision to use military specialists in his capacity as Commissar of Military Affairs, under the authority of the Sovnarkom. Yet, Stalin referred the question to the party, so in the end Stalin actually won. The party resolved the question, not the government. Thereafter, Trotsky understood that he needed to be on firm ground with the party hierarchy regarding controversial military policies and that even Lenin's backing would not decide an issue.

In the course of the Civil War the Red Army used the services of over 300,000 military specialists – most by compulsion. Military specialists were called to service by decree of the Commissariat of Defense in July 1918 and any who refused to serve were arrested as deserters. Those who did serve often faced great hostility from the rank and file, and communists who worked with them. Lenin too, though he backed Trotsky on the issue of *voenspetsy*, was not about to put undue faith in any particular officers. In July 1918, Lenin nominated former colonel Ioakhim Vatsetis for the post of Commander-in-Chief and in the same breath told Trotsky not to hesitate to shoot him if he failed "to obtain rapid and decisive success."[22] A minority of former officers did turn traitor going over to the White forces at opportune moments. Others who may have been tempted to switch sides were dissuaded by the reprisals that would befall their families. The whereabouts of all officers' families were supposed to be kept on file so they could be arrested if the need arose.

Former officers provided vital expertise for the successful building up of the Bolshevik military establishment, particularly its administrative arm. Without such figures as former General Bonch-Bruevich, and colonels Ioakhim Vatsetis and Sergei Kamenev, the Red Army never would have achieved the organization and capacity it did. Former officers below the rank of lieutenant colonel also contributed mightily in the areas of training, organization, administration and tactical leadership. The vast quantity of expertise these men contributed could not have been provided by the small number of leftist officers who naturally gravitated to the Red cause. The party's dependence on these men is reflected in the state decree that every military commissariat from local to national level had to include a former officer – hence the huge numbers employed. Perhaps the pervasive presence of former Imperial officers is responsible for the subtle appearance of a caste mentality among some of the new Red commanders – an attitude forewarned of by left communists. The abuse of material privileges by commanders, their abuse of right to leaves, alcohol use (forbidden of all servicemen) and fraternization with women at a time when the rank and file existed in materially and socially deprived conditions grew so flagrant that difficulties cropped up between leaders and men and warranted an official condemnation by Trotsky in October 1920.[23]

The Imperial Army also made its presence felt in the new army through its NCOs. Some NCOs joined the Red Army out of conviction, but many more were conscripted by decree. On 2 August 1918, the Sovnarkom called up workers of birth cohorts 1893, 1894, and 1895 who had served as NCOs in the old army, but from only five of the major provinces controlled by the Bolsheviks. This call up yielded nearly 18,000 former NCOs. Later, as Bolshevik territorial control spread, more former NCOs would be called up. The next day Trotsky, as Commissar of Military Affairs, promoted all former tsarist NCOs currently serving in the Red Army to platoon commanders. By this means the army eventually acquired several hundred thousand experienced junior level leaders for the front-line units. It was in response to this call that Georgi Zhukov reported for duty in the Red Army and Semion Budenny joined the ranks of officers. In only a few months Budenny would be commanding a cavalry division and Zhukov a cavalry squadron. Both would eventually become Marshals of the Soviet Union.

Despite their lack of military credentials and because the Red Army was the party's army, Bolshevik revolutionaries such as Joseph Stalin, Sergei Kirov, Valerian Kuibyshev, and Grigori "Sergo" Ordzhonikidze who fulfilled military-political functions, and Nikolai Podvoiskii, V. A. Antonov-Ovseenko, N. V. Krylenko, and Mikhail Frunze who performed military-operational duties, wielded paramount political power and influence in the army. A few new Bolsheviks, such as Trotsky, who joined the party after the February Revolution also rose to great prominence. Minor party members, such as Vasilii Bliukher, who on their own formed Red partisan detachments that the army eventually absorbed, also rose to positions of great responsibility. The army for a time welcomed into its ranks and relied on Left SRs such as M. A. Muravev – the first commander-in-chief of the Red Army – and a smattering of anarchists as well. Others who came to have great influence in the army were radical former officers such as Mikhail Tukhachevskii. Far more acceptable in the eyes of the party and soldiers than *voenspetsy* were the temporary junior officers, commissioned by the tsarist army for the duration of the First World War, who for the most part had held radical views before their service in the Imperial Army. These men formed much of the backbone of company and battalion level military leadership in the Red Army.

The army continuously searched the ranks of conscripts for promising officer candidates to be sent to the newly founded schools for Red Commanders. Volunteers were always welcome but had to pass the scrutiny of attestation committees first established in April 1918. Special officer training courses produced 2,000 company grade Red Commanders in 1918, 11,000 in 1919, and 25,000 in 1920. Their numbers represented but a drop in the bucket compared to the number of *voenspetsy*.

Leadership ability and style varied tremendously. For their part *voenspetsy* often kept a low profile confining their efforts to tactical planning. They certainly had no desire to lead by example thereby increasing their chances of being killed for a cause they had wanted no part of in the first place. One of the most vaunted leaders of the Civil War, Mikhail Tukhachevskii, led from the rear with inspiring pronouncements but few personal appearances. Other "amateur" leaders such as Budenny, Chapaev, Timoshenko, and even the much maligned Voroshilov, always went to the front-lines in critical situations.

Isaac Babel gives colorful first hand accounts of Timoshenko, Budenny and Voroshilov at the front that show their dedication to the cause. In an episode during the war with Poland, Timoshenko, when confronted with a brigade whose leaders were hesitant to attack,

> starts using his whip on the regimental commanders, including Kniga [regimental commissar], he shoots at the commissar, to horse you bastards, charges at them, 5 shots. I'll show you, shoots himself through the hand. He electrifies the Cossacks, a Budenny man – go up forward with him and if the Poles don't kill you, he will.[24]

Budenny was not much for theatrics; his motivational technique was just to threaten to shoot his subordinates for failure. Such threats – and their fulfillment – were unheard of in the old army, but unfortunately became entrenched in the habits of the generation of new Red Commanders who got their start in the Civil War. Babel described Budenny and Voroshilov during a critical attack in the Konarmiia:

> Voroshilov is short, graying, wears red breeches with silver stripes, always hurrying people up, tense . . . Budenny says nothing, smiles occasionally, showing his dazzling white teeth. The regiment parades for Voroshilov and Budenny. Voroshilov pulls out an enormous revolver – "show the Polish gents no mercy," his harangue is received with approval.[25]

The norm, however, may have been closer to Trotsky's depressing observation made in 1919:

After a few successes commanders and commissars often start to rest on their laurels. Training is not carried out in units that have been pulled back into reserve. Regulations are not observed. As soon as a firm military regime slackens and fades in the units, disintegration sets in: the scoundrels desert and the middle peasants lose heart.[26]

In general Bolsheviks normally attempted to play the role of revolutionary leaders rather than military commanders.

To their credit, in the span of a year, the Bolshevik Party had created a functioning army adequate to its purposes – though it appeared and behaved like a ragtag gang at times – in the face of striking material, social, and ideological obstacles.

2

THE CIVIL WAR, AND POLISH–SOVIET WAR, 1917–21

PUR, commissars, communist soldiers, and the party and the Army

In addition to martial expertise, political supervision and control were fundamental building blocks of the Red Army. The Red Army was to be an army of a new type, a revolutionary peoples' army which would become a school of socialism only with the direct participation of the party on a daily basis in every unit. The practical manifestation of this thinking was first the commissar and then the Political Administration of the Red Army (commonly referred to as PUR). The Bolsheviks assigned commissars at all levels down to the most important front-line unit, the regiment.

On the one hand it looks as though the Civil War and use of *voenspetsy* caused the creation of PUR, yet on the other hand one must consider that under all circumstances if the army of the Bolshevik state were to be the party's army it would need an appropriate administration to train it up in the ways of Marx and Lenin. Therefore, the presence of a *voenspets* did not determine the presence of a commissar; every regiment and higher unit had a commissar regardless of whether it was commanded by a military specialist or not. Likewise with RVSes. Not until 1919 did the Eighth Party Congress formally delineate the powers of commissars. In the meantime a multitude of power struggles between commanders and commissars ensued with Trotsky firmly backing the commanders, yet ascribing a good deal of authority to commissars as well. He strongly urged commissars to use initiative to assist commanders in every way, even tactically, and charged them with responsibility for a unit's success or failure along with the commander. Informally, Trotsky assigned commissars responsibility for unit logistics.

Trotsky established the precedent of punishing commissars for the military failure of a unit in 1918. He issued an order in August of that year which read in part, "I issue this warning: if any unit retreats without orders, the first to be shot will be the commissar, and the next the commander."[1] By the end of 1921 hundreds of commissars, commanders, and soldiers had been executed by military tribunals for their crimes and failures. Simultaneously, the Sovnarkom authorized "Special Sections" (*Osobyi Otdely*) of the *Cheka* to operate inside the army with wide powers to combat espionage, malfeasance, and the "forces of counterrevolution."

While on the one hand the Eighth Party Congress in March 1919 affirmed the use of *voenspetsy* it simultaneously enhanced the authority and functions of the commissar. The Congress declared commissars to be party function-aries, thus reducing the authority of the military apparatus over them. The party would hereafter also have more of a say in the selection of military commanders through the introduction of attestation committees. According to Francesco Benvenuti, this resulted in the reduction of the influence and freedom of maneuver that Trotsky and his group in the Commissariat of Military Affairs had possessed prior to the Congress, and accentuated the structurally contradictory elements that made up the Red Army. The party's supervisory role had been vastly increased at the expense of the Red Army's internal autonomy. Trotsky sought not to comply with the resolutions of the Congress for as long as they remained unpublished.[2] He firmly believed in the powers of formal military hierarchy and discipline, and considered inter-ference from commissars and party organs to be undermining and potentially disastrous.

PUR

The establishment of the Political Administration of the RKKA followed the introduction of commissars. PUR expanded its role from recruiting com-missars to include organizing communists in the army into primary party organizations (cells), recruiting soldiers into the party, conducting political education of the soldiers, providing literacy instruction, supervising activities of party cells, in short, doing whatever it could to turn the army into a school of socialism. That the army could become a training ground for socialists greatly appealed to the party leadership. In the short-term crisis of civil war, political education would presumably bolster the loyalty of non-Bolsheviks to the party's cause, especially the peasants', because, according to the party's understanding, it was only out of ignorance and the influence of kulaks that they resisted conscription and requisitioning. In the long term, it would render the military incapable of becoming a reactionary force in society and further the political education of the nation's young men. The process would wed the army to the party.

Perhaps the two most important tasks PUR had during the Civil War were to sufficiently control party members in the army in order to get the most out of them for the war effort, and to indoctrinate non-party soldiers to secure their loyalty to the Bolshevik regime. The keys to success in these tasks were the commissars and their assistants in the division political sections and regimental political bureaus, sanctioned formally in January 1919. One of the first tasks they undertook was to exert their authority over party cells and squash their independence. Ironically, rank and file party members, in defense of their independence and democratic views, for the first year or so, often proved as uncooperative to PUR officials as did non-party men.

The existence of party cells dates back to at least December 1917, if not to the Red Guard. Whether their creation was ordered or spontaneous is unclear. Whatever the case, before the political hierarchy was firmly established cells began organizing and taking care of party business on their own, which of itself seems good, except that these cells acted like the revolutionary soldiers' committees of the post-February Imperial Army. They elected their own commissars and formed political bureaus that almost always interfered with operational and command decisions not just at regiment, but even at division and army level. Most troublesome was that they continued to do so even after the center had organized the political landscape in the units by formal orders. The Instruction on Party Cells issued in January 1919 specifically outlined the subordinate status of cells to commissars and political sections. To overcome these obstinate and independent tendencies the party did two things: issued a New Instruction on Party Cells in December 1919 that clearly made chiefs of division political sections exclusively responsible for all party and political work in their units, and granted party membership to some 35–40,000 soldiers. This influx, according to historian Dmitrii F. White, destroyed the cohesion of the extant cells, which had become rather tight, by flooding them with men whose political consciousness was likely to be less developed than the longtime communists or worker masses. The new communists were more likely to follow the lead of the commissars than that of the cells.[3]

The root of the problem lay in the mindset of the mobilized communist. These men saw their military service as only a temporary party assignment. Therefore, they tended to identify with and answer to the local party committee that mobilized them (and to which they expected to return) in the name of the ruling party, rather than subordinate themselves to the military commissar. Additionally, as historian Mark Von Hagen points out, there was an element of personal frustration for mobilized communists who had ambitions in civilian party work – a sure route to social advancement – and here they found themselves in the army, in a subordinate position taking orders from some commissar who might not even be a communist. Experienced communists often considered themselves perfectly qualified to decide their tasks without unwanted direction from their military authorities. In essence they sought to maintain a civilian, rather than adopt a military identity. Ironically, some of these loyal Bolsheviks became so disaffected with their situation that on their own they left the army and went back to their civilian posts. They interpreted their departures as self-authorized changes in duty; the Central Committee interpreted it as desertion and ordered wayward communists rounded up and sent back to the army.[4]

In the course of the battle for Kazan in August–September 1918 the Eastern Front RVS incorporated several thousand hastily mobilized communists into the fighting units as emergency replacements. The presence of disciplined and motivated Bolsheviks galvanized the rest of the troops, very likely providing the margin of victory in what at first promised to be a disastrous defeat. From this experience Trotsky concluded that hereafter party members would by necessity be the backbone of the fighting units. From mid–1918 to the end of the war the army, in times of its greatest need, consistently turned to the party to produce levies of the conscious and dedicated to bolster the indifferent and unreliable masses. The first widely enforced special mobilization of party members, trade unionists and skilled workers lasted off and on from September 1918 to April 1919, but yielded only tens of thousands of Bolsheviks and class conscious workers, rather than the hundreds of thousands sought. A major effort in November 1918 garnered 40,000 Bolsheviks. By December 1919, 180,000 communists served in the Red Army; most of them had been in the party before being mobilized, but tens of thousands were soldiers who joined the party while in the ranks.

The massed use of party members had some drawbacks. Communist soldiers in the army in 1919 acted as though they were a privileged minority. They did not always take a comradely attitude toward their fellow non–party soldiers. Old Bolsheviks in the rank and file particularly resisted taking orders from purely military persons or organizations. They considered themselves subordinate only to party organs and officials. They viewed postrevolution party members as lesser Bolsheviks. Trotsky appreciated the threat such attitudes posed to discipline and morale and responded accordingly with an order in December 1918 that proclaimed:

> The Communist soldier has the same rights as any other soldier, and not a hair's breadth more: he only has incomparably more duties. The Communist soldier must be an exemplary warrior, he must always be in the forefront of the battle, he must try to lead others to the places of greatest danger, he must be a model of discipline, conscientiousness and courage. At the front and in the rear he must offer others an example of careful treatment of public property in general and army property in particular. [He thought] Only such a model soldier has the right to the name of Communist . . .[5]

The idea that communists bore a special responsibility as role models remained until 1991.

Just how effectively PUR used the army as a school of socialism is a matter of debate. Certainly instances of successful agitation exist, agitation that turned neutral or anticommunist soldiers into pro–Bolsheviks or even party members. Objective conditions of the Civil War, however, mitigate against too confident a reading of PUR's influence. PUR experienced shortages of lower level commissars and political workers throughout the war. Consequently PUR employed many non-Bolshevik functionaries who could not be counted on to faithfully present the party line as dictated. In general, PUR did not train its workers thoroughly so the quality of political instruction varied widely.

PUR faced a daunting task: to convince peasants to give up the free market and to deliver their harvest to the cities in exchange for promises of future payment in kind; to convince nationalists to give up nationalism; to convince workers to give up their committees and worker control; to convince socialists of other parties to relinquish the right of their party to political participation; to convince anarchists to trust a Bolshevik one-party state; all in the name of a workers' paradise that at the present arrested and executed without trial, stole crops and nationalized factories in which Bolshevik bosses ruled with dictatorial powers. In the absence of both political legitimacy and "Soviet patriotism," coupled with the near death of Russian patriotism, people tended to cling to the identities they had before entering military service. For the peasants this was the powerful communal or village identity. For non-Russians the identity could combine national or ethnic and village identities. For the worker his factory and its politics, which may have been Menshevik, Popular Socialist, Socialist Revolutionary or Left Socialist Revolutionary, provided an identity that Bolshevik political education would be forced to reckon with.

Eduard Dune serves as an example of how PUR conducted business. Dune answered the call for communists to volunteer for the front in autumn 1918. The army promptly assigned him to assist a regimental commissar. Of his assignment Dune wrote, "I did not ask any questions about what kind of work I was being sent to do: this was understood; I was going not as a commander or commissar but as a member of the party – as a Bolshevik." He assumed that the army RVS "must have known best, to assign an eighteen-year old kid to conduct political work."[6] His blind faith in the party did not stand the test of time however.

A class-conscious worker and Bolshevik, but untrained in methods of political instruction, Dune had a hard row to hoe in trying to indoctrinate the men of his regiment. He observed that:

> There was not one volunteer in the regiment; they were all young men drafted from the peasantry of Nizhegorod province. Men from the same village stuck together in small groups – this is how they were mobilized, and so they wound up together in this or that platoon. There were very many among them who could not read or could barely read . . . They talked among themselves only about their villages, their streams, their sweethearts. They were obsessed with land . . . They were interested only in "my" or "our"

village. Red–White, revolution–counterrevolution, nationalization–socialization, all this was for them gibberish, about as interesting to them as a sermon from a church pulpit. All of this began to make me feel very uncomfortable, very alien: I had nothing to talk about with the Red Army soldiers, and it was even worse with the commanders – former tsarist officers.[7]

The soldiers regarded Dune with hostility, as an outsider. He overheard talk of them wanting to kill him.

The peasantry posed a special problem to PUR's efforts because of fundamentally different values. While ordinary peasants might report for conscription, few would tolerate and certainly would not aid and abet the victimization of their own kind by the Bolshevik regime no matter what face the commissar put on it. Forced grain requisitioning caused scores of mutinies by soldiers and several all-out peasant rebellions supported by Red Army men. One of hundreds of such uprisings occurred in the middle Volga around Samara in March 1919. It was caused in part by harsh requisitioning and a political struggle between the party apparatus and village soviets. The army itself had been grossly insensitive to the needs of the local peasants. It had mobilized more men than called for, indiscriminately confiscated farm produce, and imposed what amounted to corvée labor. Large numbers of soldiers from the local garrison deserted and went home to help organize the revolt. It took regular Red Army troops armed with artillery and machine guns and battalions of party loyalists and a regiment of workers to finally suppress the revolt. The army suffered heavy casualties as would be expected when taking on 150,000 peasants, 20,000 of whom bore arms in defense of their way of life.[8]

Rather than desert to support insurrection, sometimes whole field units turned against the regime despite their indoctrination. Sapozhkov's revolt is one example. Sapozhkov, a peasant who had been in the Imperial Army from 1914, joined the SRs in 1917 and served in the Red Army from 1918. In early 1920 he was relieved of command of the 22nd Division for opposition to forced requisitioning. Despite this black mark he was assigned to form a new division in May 1920. He subsequently led this division into anti-Bolshevik revolt. The main grievances propelling him and his men into revolt were: the requisitioning of grain, the suppression of the free market, the Bolshevik subversion of the local soviets, and the use of military specialists. They adopted as their slogans "Down with the commissars, the specialists, and the regional provisions committees!" "Long live free trade!"; "Down with Tsarist officers, who hold commanding positions in the Red Army!" Again, loyal troops had to be employed to suppress this revolt.[9]

Like peasants, cossacks came to the Red Army as a community with a firmly established identity that proved a formidable obstacle to Communist ideology. Isaac Babel never failed to be dismayed by the low culture of the cossacks and soldiers and the failure of PUR to overcome it. He lamented the failure of political education to mitigate the anti-semitic feelings of the cossacks and of the leadership's inability to prevent pogroms. In his diary Babel wrote, ". . . same old story, the Jews have been plundered, they expected the Soviet regime to liberate them, and suddenly there were shrieks, whips cracking, shouts of 'dirty Yid'." As soldiers, Babel idolized the Red Army's cossacks but as revolutionary examples he despaired, writing: "We are the vanguard, but of what? The population await their saviors, the Jews look for liberation – and in ride the Kuban Cossacks . . ."[10] The average representative of the Soviet regime was far from the enlightened revolutionary desired by the intellectual Bolshevik elite.

One must also appreciate the caliber of men PUR was trying to educate. The Red Army took just about anybody who could walk and carry a rifle. Intellectual capacity was no issue, but one needs some intellectual capacity to understand the rudiments of Marxist philosophy, no matter how crudely presented, and then to internalize it. Again Babel's diary gives a down to earth vignette of real Red Army men: "Cherkashin . . . insolent, gangling, depraved, what sort of citizen of communist Russia will he make, Matyash, the Ukrainian, infinitely lazy, a womanizer, always limp and listless, with his shoelaces untied, indolent movements, Sokolov's dispatch rider Misha . . . handsome, slovenly."[11] Without a doubt, to raise these men's consciousness posed a challenge to the best prepared commissar.

The commissars, were, however, often not prepared for their posts at all. Babel described the 6th Cavalry Division's division commissar Yakovlev as: "a Moscow workingman, obtuse but with the rough edges rubbed off," and "a sly peasant, rough, sometimes insolent and muddleheaded." Yakovlev's assistants were, "limpy Gubanov the terror of the regiment, a reckless rough-neck, a youngster of 23, then there's modest Shiryaev and crafty Grishin." Of another of the division's many commissars Babel said, "Vinokurov is a typical military commissar, he sticks to a line of his own, wants to reform the 6th Division, the struggle with the partisan mentality, slow-witted, bores me to death with his speeches, rude at times, addresses everyone familiarly."[12]

Perhaps the most damning evidence for the corporate failure of PUR to politically educate and thereby gain soldiers' adherence to the Bolsheviks' cause were mutinies in May 1919 by the 1st Regiment of Red Cossacks and in September 1920 by the 6th Cavalry Division of the 1st Cavalry Army.

In May 1919 the 1st Regiment of Red Cossacks mutinied in the Ukraine during the brief campaign to suppress Grigorev. Elements of the regiment attacked *Cheka* units (one of the more hated arms of Soviet power) and stopped passenger and freight trains to rob, rape, loot, and destroy. *Cheka* units attacked it in turn. The cossacks occupied the town of Lubny which they freed from Bolshevik control by disarming the *Cheka* and local militia, driving out soviet workers, looting state property, and liberating the prisoners from the local prison. Members of the regimental staff organized a pogrom shouting "Death to the Jews and Communists." Finally, sane heads in the chain of command prevailed and ended the troubles by executing several men after courts-martial. The commissar blamed the whole affair on a few troublemakers and the regimental staff for not having taken stern measures from the beginning. Certainly poor leadership played its role, but no doubt the ambivalence of serving the Bolsheviks must be considered contributing factors.[13]

The mutiny of the Konarmiia is even more revealing of PUR's failure to indoctrinate soldiers because from its creation in 1919 the Konarmiia, led by Semion Budenny, was one of the Red Army's most effective fighting forces. Contrary to Babel's impression, Stephen Brown shows that the Konarmiia was not a Cossack army. Instead, a 1920 military census revealed that it consisted of 62 percent peasants, 14 percent Cossacks, 20 percent workers and 4 percent intelligentsia. Most of the peasants were non-cossacks (*inogorodnie*) from North Caucasus Cossack lands, the Don, the Kuban, and Stavropol'.[14] In contrast to other Red Army armies, the Konarmiia had few military specialists and even fewer Jews.

It was a powerful striking force of four cavalry divisions and undefeated on the battlefield from November 1919, when it was formed, until the Polish Army forced it into bloody retreat in August 1920 so one would naturally assume that the men were completely loyal to the Soviet regime, as were most of the more effective divisions. Nothing could be further from the truth – which was suppressed for some seventy years. The retreat and temporary collapse of morale in August–September, however, cannot be blamed for the mutiny. The potential for revolt was actually inherent in the make-up of the Konarmiia, and commanders and commissars recognized the failure of its political education to reduce the potential months earlier.

A sample from the summary of the Konarmiia's revolutionary tribunal's investigation into the mutiny reveals the basic instincts of the Konarmiia's soldiers at work:

> 2 October. [1920] In Priluki, twenty-one Jews killed and twelve wounded. In Oveche, drunken Red Army men raped almost every woman. Soldiers broke into the offices of the special department [*Cheka*] and the deserters commission, demanding to know who was a Communist or a commissar. In Vakhnov, eighteen homes were burnt, twenty men killed, women raped in the streets in full view of the townsfolk and the younger women taken away like slaves in transports. Events of this kind took place in Annopol, Berezdovo, Krasnostav, Tarashcha and other places.[15]

Soldiers likewise hunted down and murdered Jews. The Konarmiia commander had more than one hundred men executed in the course of putting down the mutiny.

The aim of the uprising was not to vent frustration and satisfy animal lusts of the men, that aspect of the mutiny was merely symptomatic of the deeper problem the men had with the Bolshevik regime. In their minds the soldiers associated Jews and Communists not only as the source of the front-line soldiers' misery, but also as the primary threat to their fulfillment of the goals of the revolution. The slogans of the soldiers, were to "kill the Jews, Communists and commissars," "clear the rear of Jews" and "unite with Makhno." Joining with Makhno meant substituting the peasant anarchist vision of revolution for that of the Bolsheviks' proletariat version, which at the time was being constructed at the expense of the peasantry. The leadership of the 6th Cavalry Division was no better in that they took few or no steps to stop the violence. The tribunal subsequently accused the commanders of sympathizing with the mutineers.

Perhaps raising the collective consciousness of the 1st Cavalry Army was doomed from the start. It is clear that the *inogorodnie* were not especially fertile ground for Bolshevik politics. They were land hungry, having been shut out of land ownership by the Cossacks for the past sixty years. They did not want communes, but private land and feared that the Bolsheviks would cheat them out of their chance at it. The party's preference for state and collective farms raised suspicions that *inogorodnie* would end up as mere agricultural laborers, rather than independent farmers. Like most peasants, they resented grain requisitioning, conscription and the general violence perpetrated against the village by the Soviet regime.

Not only were most of the Konarmiia predisposed to resist communist indoctrination, the more than 800 political workers sent to educate them in 1920 were not a promising lot. Few had been in the party more than two years and some for only a matter of months. Some were quite idealistic, but most were not well versed in Marxism. Because around 20 percent of the soldiers were illiterate and most of the rest barely literate, the plethora of propaganda pamphlets and tracts were quite useless to the education effort. The political workers overwhelmingly hailed from urban areas making it doubly hard to relate to the cossacks and *inogorodnie* who served alongside fellow villagers and viewed the commissars with a suspicion reserved for outsiders. Commanders, many of whom rose from the ranks of peasants, often found themselves at odds with their commissars. The lack of progress in the Konarmiia's assimilation of political education is shown in a July 1920 report of the 4th Cavalry Division's political department: "The attitude to Communists and commissars is for the most part completely negative . . . At present political and cultural work has come to a full stop. Communist cells do not function." According to I. Vardin, the head of the Konarmiia political department from June 1920, the soldiers of the Konarmiia "fought not for socialism, about which they had only the vaguest idea, but to right past injustices." In other words, they fought for revenge against a system that

34

had oppressed them for generations. Yet they also fought for "Soviet power," but their interpretation of Soviet power was that of independent, locally elected and controlled soviets, not the soviets of the Bolshevik government that merely carried out Moscow's instructions.[16] In most respects the 1st Cavalry Army mirrored PUR's problems with the entire Red Army and its overall failure to convert the average soldier into a loyal Leninist.

Historian Arthur Adams sums up one of the psychologically troublesome aspects of the Civil War for soldiers, and one that troubled the Red Army for years to come, that of identity:

> Individual men, small bands, and whole units, caught up in the turmoil and forced to decide for themselves where they stood politically, found that they were not sure; accordingly, peasant groups, military sections, regiments, and entire towns swayed back and forth from one side to the other in what was a commander's nightmare and sheer agony for the men and families involved.[17]

The presence of non-Bolsheviks and anti-Bolsheviks in the ranks tremendously inhibited a clear "Red" identity arising in the ranks of the Red Army.

In addition to political education, military discipline fell under the auspices of PUR and the commissars. Indeed, it was natural that true military leadership, especially in combat, would devolve on the commissars because of the soldier's hatred for the *voenspetsy*, and because the *voenspetsy* had no vested interest in personal heroics or going out of his way to motivate soldiers for a cause the officers did not believe in. Therefore, it quickly fell to the commissars – and the few Red commanders – to lead, inspire, and discipline the soldiers. Leadership quality varied widely among commissars, mostly because men were neither made commissars for their leadership ability, nor were they trained in military leadership techniques. Commissars had to fall back on their innate leadership abilities if they had any at all. Given this situation, it is no wonder that the Red Army during the entire period 1917–21 remained uniformly undisciplined. Not only was this manifested in chronic desertion and battlefield panic, but also in their refusal to fulfill orders that ran counter to their desires.

Babel's diary entry of 3 June [July] 1920, "Zhitomir pogrom, organized by the Poles, continued, of course, by the Cossacks," speaks volumes. It says more than that the soldiers were anti-semitic, it reveals that the officers and commissars allowed it to happen. Either they also hated Jews or they feared that to challenge the pogromists would hurt their authority. Certainly pogroms undermined order and discipline in the units.

The poor supply situation always aggravated the discipline problem. Thus, Babel, while regretting the soldiers' rough treatment of civilians, found himself doing the same when he got hungry enough:

We ride into Koniuszkow, we steal some barley, they tell me to look around and take what I can . . . women in hysterics, five minutes after our arrival the looting starts, women struggling, weeping and wailing, it's unbearable. I feel unbearably sad, I pinch a mug of milk from the regimental commander, snatch a flatcake out of the hands of a peasant woman's little boy.[19]

The supply situation must have been extremely bad for Babel, one of the few with a high moral code, to stoop to acting like a depraved Russian soldier.

Another area where the enforcement of discipline fell short was in the efforts to prevent the murder of prisoners of war. Babel made at least five entries describing the murder of Polish prisoners of war, both during the advance, and the retreat; the scale of killing increased during the retreat. On 19 August 1920 he recorded what was for him a shattering experience:

A bloody battle. The military commissar and I ride along the line begging the men not to massacre prisoners. Apanasenko [the division commander] washes his hands of it. I couldn't look at their faces, they bayoneted some, shot others, bodies covered by corpses, they strip one man while they're shooting another, groans, screams, death rattles, the attack was carried out by our squadron, Apanasenko remained aloof. It's hell. Our way of bringing freedom – horrible. They search the farm, drag people out, Apanasenko – don't waste cartridges, stick them. That's what Apanasenko always says – stick the nurse, stick the Poles.[20]

This was the second massacre of prisoners by the Konarmiia in two days. Such atrocities occurred on all fronts, not just in Poland. Some units would not take officers prisoners and boasted of it. Others would interrogate them first and then kill them. No less than three times in 1919 did Trotsky issue orders against the murder of prisoners. In May 1919 he specifically ordered units on the Eastern Front not to shoot prisoners or those who deserted Kolchak's forces to the Red side. Of course the Whites and Greens made it a habit to murder commissars, Bolsheviks and any Soviet officials that fell into their hands, and not just to reciprocate, but as a matter of principle. The difference is that the Soviet high command forbade the practice, but the leadership at the front did little to enforce it.

The several volumes of Trotsky's work on the Civil War reveal his general prescription for a successful military unit: politically reliable, trained, resolute, and honest commanders led it; politically reliable and knowledgeable, resolute, and honest commissars motivated it; workers and communists who knew what they were fighting for manned it. The unit was well-supplied, and received good political education. The men's families were taken care of by soviet agencies. The unit was continually purged of officers, commissars and communists who proved unworthy. It had strict, merciless discipline. Objective conditions in Russia during these years dictated that in reality a minuscule number of regiments met this criteria, and then only on a temporary basis.

The Civil War

The scope of this work does not allow for a digression into either the political origins of the Civil War or the Allied intervention. Rather, we delve into the military conduct of the Civil War and war with Poland with a brief overview of the war and a detailed treatment of only two campaigns, the Bolsheviks second campaign in the Ukraine in 1918–19 and the 1920 war with Poland, but only to illustrate some major features of the Red Army's birth and initial development.

The Red Army had two fundamental missions in the Civil War: the first was to preserve the one-party dictatorship of the Bolsheviks, and the second to restore the boundaries of the Russian Empire. The challenges to the Bolsheviks' grip on power came from several quarters: from the left, in the form of the Socialist Revolutionaries, who formed the government of the Committee of the Constituent Assembly (KOMUCH) in Samara on the Volga River in early 1918, under the temporary protection of the Czechoslovak Legion; from the rural Greens, represented by armed peasant anarchist bands; and from urban anarchists who waged a campaign of terror against Bolshevik officialdom. On the right, the opposition consisted of the White movement of former tsarist officers and their bourgeois and aristo-cratic supporters along with the inconsistent and halfhearted assistance of the Western Allies.

The nationalities also represented a threat to the Bolsheviks in that by seceding, or attempting to secede, from the old empire, they denied the Bolsheviks' right to rule over them. The various nationalities that took active steps to secede from the empire and resisted Bolshevik attempts to reincor-porate them included Finland and the Baltic provinces, which succeeded in defeating the Bolsheviks and securing independence, the Ukraine, Armenia, Georgia, Azerbaidzhan, the Basmachi tribes of Turkestan, Dagestan, and the Don cossacks, all of whom failed to achieve independence. The cossacks had reluctantly joined the White movement as part of their separatist quest, while the movements of the other regions remained aloof from the reactionary Whites. The recreation of the Polish state by the Treaty of Versailles led to a territorial challenge for the western Ukraine, which many Poles coveted.

By far the most serious military threat to Bolshevik power was the White movement, geographically divided into three distinct entities. First, the Volunteer Army, in south Russia, organized in November 1917 by General Alekseev and led by General Denikin. Soon the Volunteer Army allied with the separatist Don cossacks, who formed their own Don Army under cossack

General Krasnov. The second anti-Bolshevik force, under Admiral Kolchak, in Siberia, got its start by crushing the KOMUCH government in a coup in November 1918 and establishing its own government in Omsk. A third White movement under General Iudenich, operating out of Estonia, proved in the end to be of minor consequence.

The White armies remained smaller than the Bolsheviks' throughout the entire war and relied mainly on former officers and conscript peasants for manpower. Denikin never had more than 150,000 men and often less. There seemed always to be a surfeit of officers and dearth of privates, but by far the greatest handicap of the Whites was their reactionary ideology, which prevented them from attracting volunteers. Their program seemed tailor made to alienate the largest number of people possible: it called for restoration of land to the aristocratic and bourgeois landowners, return of factories to their owners, reaffirmation of the class-based structure of Russian society and maintenance of the empire under Great Russian political and cultural hegemony. Such a reactionary stance also inhibited Allied support for the Whites. Not until February 1919 did Britain reluctantly deliver supplies to Denikin. Nevertheless, despite great numerical odds at times, the Whites hung on through a combination of their own military skill and determination, and Red mistakes and disorganization.

In 1918 the Reds conducted two major campaigns, one in the east against the Czechoslovak Legion-supported KOMUCH army, and one in south Russia against the Don Army and the Volunteer Army. The campaign against KOMUCH started out badly for the Reds. In July the Red Army's first commander-in-chief, the Left SR Muravev, turned against the Bolsheviks in a wild episode in which he intended to rally the troops to reopen the war against Germany in unity with the Czechoslovak Legion. On only the second day of his revolt he was gunned down by the Bolshevik Party Committee of Simbirsk when he foolishly reported to the Simbirsk soviet in response to their invitation to explain his actions. Thus ended his revolt. However, the disarray it caused led to the collapse of the front and opened the way to Kazan for KOMUCH and the Czechs.

When the Czech Legion went into action against the Reds in May 1918 the disorganization of the Red Army became suddenly apparent. Trotsky's reorganization of the army had not yet reached eastern Russia where the basic unit was still the *otriad* (detachment) of 700 to 1,000 men under an inexperienced, elected commander. The fighting in the east saw the falling away of soldiers' committees, elected commanders and self-appointed commanders. On 27 June 1918, Mikhail Tukhachevskii arrived on the Eastern Front and took charge of the 1st Army and on Trotsky's orders began making it into a recognizable army. Combining detachments and various and sundry formations he assembled three divisions. He stiffened the desertion depleted ranks with both communists and mobilized military specialists and proceeded to hammer out a fighting Red Army.[22]

Not until the loss and desperate recapture of Kazan by the Red Army in September did the Eastern Front stabilize. The Reds then had a temporary advantage after Kolchak's coup in November 1918 led to the disintegration of the KOMUCH army and the refusal of the Czech Legion to support Kolchak. In south Russia the Bolsheviks squandered their advantages of numbers and popular support and failed to crush the Volunteer Army when it was very well able to. In a crucial battle in mid-June, Red forces under Kalnin (commander of Red forces in the North Caucasus) needed reinforcements but one Sorokin, commander of the needed reinforcements, refused to come to Kalnin's aid out of spite for not having been chosen commander of the North Caucasus. This led to the Bolshevik forces being divided into two enabling Denikin to fight them one at a time. First he defeated Kalnin who then resigned his command. Then the Volunteer Army attacked Sorokin, now commander of the North Caucasus, and defeated him too, completely annihilating the Red Forces in the North Caucasus by the end of January 1919. Oddly enough, one might consider the defeat of Sorokin's 11th Army a moral victory for Trotsky. The 11th Army had had no *voenspetsy* and a vigorous spirit of *partizanshchina*.[23]

Along the Volga, the cossack Don Army pushed the Reds back to Tsaritsyn which they put under siege. Only through a numerical superiority of 130,000 to 50,000 was the Red Army, by December 1918, able to push the Don Army back from Tsaritsyn. That the Don Army had as many men as it did was in part due to the Bolsheviks' undisciplined grain requisitioning and victimization of the civilian cossack population during spring and summer.

While Denikin destroyed Sorokin's 11th Army in the North Caucasus and Voroshilov broke the encirclement of Tsaritsyn, Lenin looked west with plans to reconquer the Ukraine, which was about to be evacuated by the German Army. On 12 November 1918, the Sovnarkom ordered Trotsky to recall Ukrainian Bolshevik Vladimir Antonov-Ovseenko from the Urals Front and place him in charge of the invasion force. The Sovnarkom set a firm but completely unrealistic timetable of ten days for Antonov-Ovseenko and his newly established Ukrainian Revolutionary Military Soviet (URVS) to create an army from scratch and invade. Additionally, the URVS was to found a Bolshevik government for the newly acquired Ukraine in the midst of great chaos before reactionary Ukrainians could rally around their government, the Directory.[24]

Unfortunately for all involved, neither the Sovnarkom nor the RVSR established clear delineation of command between the URVS and its forces, and the adjacent Southern Front which opposed Krasnov's Don Army in the southern Ukraine, a failure we can attribute to Bolshevik military and bureaucratic inexperience. As they prepared for their attack into the Ukraine the URVS considered itself an independent force. This became a problem because Commander-in-Chief Vatsetis, who was applying all his energies to the fight with Krasnov, did not consider it so, yet each assumed the other thought on their terms. Vatsetis, in the days after the creation of the URVS, acted as though he commanded Antonov-Ovseenko and his resources and he gave him assignments in support of the Southern Front's attack on Krasnov. Antonov-Ovseenko ignored Vatsetis and prepared to assault the city of Kharkov.[25]

Typical of all Red Army armies organized in 1918 and early 1919, Antonov-Ovseenko's had slim resources to begin with. The first division assigned to him, the 9th Division, was woefully under manned and ill-equipped – typical of many Red divisions. This division was raised in the Ukraine and consisted of soldiers who had mutinied or deserted from Tsarist units on the Western Front during 1917 and fleshed out with partisans and peasants. Its 6th Regiment consisted of 1,127 soldiers, fifty artillerymen with no field pieces, and about 158 cavalrymen with 130 horses, but no saddles. For weaponry the regiment had eleven machine guns, 2,000 rifles, 1,400 hand grenades, and 650,000 cartridges. There were no uniforms or boots, only 400 coats. The 9th Regiment was a regiment in name only, possessing a mere 828 infantrymen of which only 250 had rifles, fifty cavalrymen, two machine guns, and no uniforms. The 7th Regiment reported 1,288 soldiers, eight machine guns, and three cannon with no details on clothing. The URVS noted that the next division assigned to it, the 4th Orel Division, was in an even sorrier state. Antonov-Ovseenko regularly went over Vatsetis's head to the RVSR asking for more men and supplies. Consistently, however, the Southern Front took priority at his expense.[26]

The obstacles in manpower and equipment that Antonov-Ovseenko and his URVS faced at times seemed overwhelming, but were in fact not unique. Antonov-Ovseenko's problems exemplified the difficulties the whole Red Army faced as it formed itself in the midst of a Civil War. On all the fronts, the difficulties inherent in the work of recruiting, organizing, training and supplying new armies were complicated by the requirement of circumstances to simultaneously conduct combat operations. At the same time, the various fronts gathered in every able-bodied male they could get their hands on. Each front begged Moscow for more officers, rifles, uniforms, political agitators, ammunition, horses, food, all of which were in short supply. Moscow never had enough to give, yet Lenin and Trotsky refused to lower their expectations and consistently piled more demands on the struggling commanders. Consequently, and because of their own inexperience, front commanders, their staffs and subordinates had to make Herculean efforts to get anything accomplished. The powers that be in the party, government, and army hierarchies did their level if inefficient best to meet the needs of the war but often had to settle for getting men, supplies, and equipment to the most important fronts; leaving the others to fend for themselves. Most commanders lacked an appreciation of the big picture of the war and viewed their sector of the war as the most important and resented as slights any lack of support.

Illustrative of the way things were done in the realm of high command in the new Red Army is the way Antonov-Ovseenko worked to secure independence for his army and promote his strategy over Vatsetis's. Jumping his chain of command, Antonov-Ovseenko requested and won, after much persistence, an audience with Lenin. Antonov-Ovseenko began with factual reporting but then launched a barrage of complaints against Vatsetis which piqued Lenin's ire. Antonov-Ovseenko whined:

> There are no supplies. We have knocked together something resembling a staff. No planned work is possible. The decree of the government about an immediate attack in the Ukraine has been sabotaged. Vatsetis has ordered the commander of the Reserve Army not to be drawn into my adventure, but to form and train in the *raion* of Kursk. Thus deprived . . . it will be two or three months before our group can do anything.[27]

Antonov-Ovseenko then went on to disparage Vatsetis's handling of the Southern Front. Lenin, thoroughly angry by now, asked Antonov-Ovseenko what he thought should be done. Antonov-Ovseenko replied with a brief sketch of an alternate plan but then lapsed, once again, into an attack on Vatsetis: "Meanwhile, the commander-in-chief throws forces directly into the [Southern] Front, into certain destruction. This is either panicky stupidity, a trick of the military specialists, or – I don't even want to think this – it is treason." In a rage Lenin leaped from his chair yelling: "Where is your discipline? I shall have to arrest you. Learn to subordinate yourself once an order is given!" Concluding that, "From the failure to do this comes all our disorganization."[28] Throughout the war voluntary subordination proved difficult for Bolsheviks, particularly Politburo and Central Committee members on military assignment.

This was not the first time Lenin had had to deal with upstart, self-styled generals, as Trotsky termed them, who thought they had all the answers and that they could single-handedly win the war if only the higher ups would give them adequate resources and free reign. Such encounters tended to infuriate Lenin who wished his party stalwarts were as good at taking orders as the loathsome *voenspetsy*. Yet, such behavior is entirely in character coming from members of a party driven by debate and, prior to October 1917, not hierarchically organized.

In a spirit of independence driven by necessity Antonov-Ovseenko resorted to "front mobilization" of needed resources, particularly manpower. He renamed the 4th and 9th divisions the 1st and 2nd Ukrainian Divisions and set about organizing a third division. Antonov-Ovseenko sent emissaries to scour the Ukraine for volunteers, conscripts, partisan detachments and any miscellaneous army units they might come upon. Sure enough, his people managed to corral numerous small partisan bands (which proved to be desertion prone) along with a cavalry regiment sitting tight, quartered in some villages unsure of who it answered to, the URVS or the Southern Front. Equipment for his units consisted of whatever tsarist supplies left over from the First World War could be found.[29]

As the Soviet Army of the Ukraine finalized plans to attack Kharkov, held by self-proclaimed Ukrainian hetman, Petliura, Vatsetis nearly upset the apple cart by attempting to completely subordinate Antonov-Ovseenko's troops to the Southern Front thus canceling the attack on Kharkov. The Ukrainians resisted both formally and informally. Antonov-Ovseenko denied Vatsetis's authority to command the URVS and sent emissaries in his place when summoned by Vatsetis to a meeting. In the meantime, Antonov-Ovseenko did not turn his soldiers over to the Southern Front.

Finally, the Soviet Army of the Ukraine went into action and on 3 January 1919, Antonov's semi-organized army took Kharkov. This victory had profound effects on Moscow's attitude toward operations in the Ukraine, which it had not supported materially at all. Now the Council of Defense, on 5 January 1919, ordered the formal organization of a Ukrainian Front commanded by Antonov-Ovseenko and delineated its area of operations from that of the Southern Front under Vatsetis. Additionally, the disputed Reserve Army was transferred to reinforce the Ukrainian Front. Here we have an example of the periphery forcing Moscow's hands by successful field operations. Lenin was unable to argue with success. One month later, Antonov-Ovseenko's forces occupied Kiev on 5 February without a fight.

Just when things looked best for Antonov-Ovseenko and his credit rose in Moscow, the effects of his hasty and haphazard front mobilization began to show. The multitude of small Ukrainian partisan bands he had absorbed stubbornly refused to act as regular soldiers no matter how many of their leaders were replaced, arrested, or executed. Meanwhile, Vatsetis began taking troops away from Antonov-Ovseenko to reinforce the Southern Front even though the Soviet Army of the Ukraine still had to capture Odessa, now occupied by French troops.

At this time Ukrainian partisan leader Grigorev offered his services to Antonov-Ovseenko who was in no position to turn him down. As the Ukrainian Reds began to falter Grigorev saved the day, leading his men on a campaign that successfully cleared the right bank of the Dnepr of anti-Bolshevik forces. Grigorev and his forces were the first into Odessa in the wake of the French evacuation. Such success made Grigorev harder if not impossible to control, especially as he had no intention of being controlled by the Bolsheviks. Antonov-Ovseenko had to delay plans to rein in Grigorev in March because of Grigorev's success and Red Army failure.

Things became more complicated for Antonov-Ovseenko in spring 1919. The Bolsheviks' enforcement of domestic policy on collective farms and requisitioning caused the Ukrainian peasantry to begin rising up against Bolshevik power. This kept Antonov-Ovseenko's forces busy protecting requisitioning parties and suppressing peasant revolt. These repressive activities then led some of his locally raised units to mutiny. The ability of the Red Army to recruit locally became correspondingly more difficult.

There came a point in April 1919 where Antonov-Ovseenko refused to send any more of his troops to the Southern Front, even when ordered by Moscow. At the time Vatsetis's forces were being hammered by Krasnov and Denikin. Lenin personally ordered Antonov-Ovseenko to at least send supplies to Vatsetis and added new demands: open a front against Denikin, prepare to invade Northern Bukovina in support of Hungarian Communist Bela Kun, defend against Polish incursions, and reassert control over a rebelling Ukraine. Antonov-Ovseenko knew he did not have the forces to accomplish this multitude of tasks.

In May things got worse for the Soviet Army of the Ukraine; Grigorev turned against the Reds and Denikin launched his most ambitious offensive with the aim of capturing Moscow. The path of the offensive led right through the Ukraine. The suppression of Grigorev's revolt took only a matter of days but it completely disrupted Antonov-Ovseenko's preparations to support Vatsetis and led to rioting and pogroms by his cossack regiment and several former partisan units. The army in the Ukraine needed rest and extensive resupply, neither of which were forthcoming. Lenin prodded Antonov-Ovseenko to get moving in support of the hard-pressed Southern Front as though oblivious to the months of strain the men had been through.

The Red Army reeled backward under the onslaught of the Volunteer Army and on 6 June 1919 the RVSR relieved Antonov-Ovseenko of command of the Ukrainian Front which was subsequently done away with. The Ukrainian Army was renamed the 14th Army and placed under Voroshilov's command. Vatsetis fared no better. On 3 July 1919, Lenin relieved him of command of the Southern Front and of his duties as commander-in-chief of the army. He was replaced by *voenspets* Colonel S. S. Kamenev with Stalin's backing. The debacle in south Russia and the Ukraine had repercussions at the highest levels of the army. The Central Committee replaced Trotsky's people on the RVSR with two of Kamenev's associates, Smilga and Gusev. Trotsky tried to resign but the Central Committee forbade him. Kamenev then devised a plan to attack Denikin from the northeast and drive through the Donbas. Trotsky argued against this plan and in favor of an attack from the western Ukraine which Lenin rejected. Kamenev's plan called for a drive through the heart of Don cossack territory, which caused Krasnov's cossacks to fight with renewed determination and gained them the support of average cossacks defending their homes against the Reds. The offensive failed and Denikin swept north as far as Orel. He may have gotten farther if Makhno had not launched an offensive against the White rear.

The very real threat of White victory under Denikin, combined with Trotsky's amnesties, sparked the return of hundreds of thousands of deserters to the colors in July–September 1919. Peasants feared White victory more than Bolshevik social and economic policies. Red propaganda played to this fear portraying the Bolsheviks as the only bulwark between the Whites and peasants' land. The return of deserters gave the Bolsheviks the numerical edge they needed to launch their autumn counteroffensive and defeat, but not destroy, Denikin in fall–winter 1919.[30]

Although at the start of the offensive the Whites did have some advantages over the Reds, namely professional leadership, cavalry, and plentiful supplies, the weaknesses of the Red Army are perhaps most responsible for Denikin's temporary success. The chaos in the Ukraine left the door open for Denikin. Antonov-Ovseenko had a legion of problems. Grigorev's uprising sapped men from the Southern Front and elsewhere in Ukraine. Vatsetis had taken away too many troops earlier. The Ukrainian Front had suffered from a poor supply situation. There were not enough resources locally to make up for Moscow's neglect. Because of the plethora of tasks Lenin assigned him Antonov-Ovseenko had been unable to focus his energies on a single mission. He had been plagued with subordinates who were as independent and insubordinate to him as he was to the high command. The Communist Party and government had not established effective and durable control of the Ukraine in support of the war effort. The army's rear areas were never secure because the rebelliousness of the Ukraine remained, represented by small, local bands ready to rise up to resist procurement and conscription. Clearly, Bolshevik military methods in the Ukrainian offensive of 1918–19 constituted a recipe for disaster.

Arthur Adams holds that the Red Army did not stop the White offensive, it just ran out of steam. The Whites had become overextended on a major gamble that they could not sustain. Between October and December 1919 the Whites suffered from internal problems in the Ukraine similar to those of the Bolsheviks (civilian reaction to requisitioning, conscription and pogroms) making them vulnerable to counterattack, and they too collapsed from within, retreating into the Crimea in March 1920. Denikin resigned and turned command over to General Wrangel.[31]

In early March 1919, Admiral Kolchak, now self-proclaimed Supreme Ruler, launched his main attack out of Siberia and eastern Russia known as the "Ufa Offensive." The ultimate goal was to capture Moscow and unite with Denikin and subsequently eradicate Bolshevism from the face of the earth. In only eight weeks Kolchak's forces advanced 250 miles westward. They captured Ufa on 14 March and in another month occupied the Urals mountain range, and reached their farthest penetration into Red-held territory only 75 miles from the Volga. Kamenev, commander of the Eastern Front, appealed to the RVSR for reinforcements. In turn, Trotsky called for a special mobilization of communists to save the situation.

Finally, at the end of April, the Reds began their counterattack. In the meantime Kolchak began to have problems in the newly occupied territory. Ordinary peasants had no desire for Kolchak's military dictatorship the potential evils of which were magnified by Bolshevik propaganda. A partisan movement sprang up to offer active resistance as the Red Army retreated. In contrast to the partisan detachments in the Ukraine and southern Russia, the partisan movement in Siberia was firmly under Bolshevik control and directly served the goals of the Eastern Front command. Siberian and Urals partisan detachments maintained contact with the RVSes of the Eastern Front's 5th, 2nd, and 3rd Armies and under their orders blew up Kolchak's supplies, disrupted communications, and provided intelligence on White unit strength, movement and dispositions. When a partisan detachment's territory was liberated by the Red Army the entire unit would then join the nearest army unit en masse as regular soldiers.[32]

Aided by the disruption in the White rear, the Red Army advanced with a few temporary setbacks and the usual supply and desertion problems and captured Omsk, Kolchak's "capital" in mid-November 1919. Kolchak's forces then began to disintegrate and he was himself turned over to the Bolsheviks by remnants of the Czech Legion on 15 January 1920. The Bolsheviks executed him several weeks later. The Western allies then washed their hands of what remained of the White movement in Siberia with the exception of the Japanese who continued to supply diehards for another two years. Not until October 1922, with the fall of Vladivostok, did the Red Army gain complete mastery of far east Russia. The threat to Soviet power, however, had ceased much earlier with Kolchak's death.

The war with Poland

The war with Poland in 1920 shows the Red Army at the height of its capability after a full two and a half years in existence and extensive combat experience, although by mid-1920, when there was little danger of a White victory with the Volunteer Army bottled up in the Crimea, the Red Army at over four million strong was unable to defeat a smaller, ill-equipped and uncertain Polish army. A close look at the Red Army in this war shows not only how far it had come, but also how far it still had to go to become a competent, unified fighting force.

The simultaneous collapse of the German, Austro-Hungarian and Russian empires led to the resurrection of independent Poland and the Polish romantic and emotional attachment to the historic (pre-1795) eastern borderlands. These borderlands consisted primarily of the western Ukraine. Hence the Polish motivation to secure as much Ukrainian territory as possible before the victorious Allies began redrawing the map of Europe at Versailles and before the Red Army could defeat the Whites and turn all its attentions to the disputed region. The Bolsheviks naturally wanted to preserve as much former imperial territory as possible but also saw the borderlands as the land link to a Europe they needed to flare up in revolution. When the Germans withdrew from Poland and the Ukraine the borderlands acted as a magnet pulling both Polish and Soviet forces into it.[33]

The Polish Army made the first move attacking a small Soviet detachment on 14 February 1919. The "war" lapsed into a lull until the Poles went on the offensive in April with the aim of capturing or "liberating" Vilno, Lvov and Minsk, which they accomplished by the end of August 1919. At that point Josef Pilsudski, leader of Poland, was willing to negotiate with the Soviets who refused. The front remained static for another nine months.

Pilsudski ordered the resumption of hostilities and attacked on 25 April 1920. The Red Army had two armies facing the Poles, the 12th and 14th armies both outnumbered at the outset. More pressing problems than the numerical superiority of the Poles were the mutinies of two brigades made up of Galicians, one of which went over to the Poles in its entirety, and the attacks of Makhno's bands on the Soviet rear area destroying supplies and bridges and disrupting transportation and communication.

The Red Army fell back in fairly good order after some fierce engagements, giving up Kiev on 7 May without a fight. To meet the emergency, the RVSR reinforced both armies and transferred the Konarmiia from the Kuban to the Polish front. The Konarmiia rode its horses rather than trains. It covered roughly 750 miles in thirty days at a pace that crippled or killed fifty horses per day – rather a lot of wear and tear on a unit expected to be thrown into the fray on arrival.

Trotsky and the Commander-in-Chief of the Red Army, S. S. Kamenev reorganized the enlarged forces into two fronts, the Western (in the north) and the Southwestern (to the south – on the left – of the Western Front). Mikhail Tukhachevskii was assigned to command the Western Front RVS and its four armies, the 15th Army, 3rd Army, 16th Army and 4th Army, all of which were commanded by former tsarist colonels. Tukhachevskii created his own version of the Konarmiia by combining two cavalry divisions and a rifle brigade into III Cavalry Corps (Kavkor). The RVS of Aleksandr I. Egorov, a *voenspets*, Stalin and Voroshilov commanded the Southwestern Front. It consisted of the 12th Army, the 14th Army and the Konarmiia.

The Red offensive to regain the Ukraine, and possibly more, began on 26 May with the Southwestern Front's attack followed by the Western Front on 4 July. From the start, Egorov intended that the Konarmiia, headed by Budenny and Voroshilov, with its mobility and shock power, would be the key to success. After ten days of fighting the Konarmiia finally broke through the Polish lines and began to advance uninterrupted for ten weeks. The Polish army abandoned Kiev and by 10 July 1920 were back at the lines they had held in August 1919. The key to the advance turned out to be the Konarmiia's ability to continually find the Polish weak spots and penetrate quickly into their rear or to turn the Polish flank in the flat wide open country. Budenny defeated Polish counterattacks by holding in the middle and sending horsemen around the flanks of the attackers. Nothing the Poles did seemed to work, nothing the Reds did seemed to fail.

By mid-August the Southwestern Front had penetrated deep into eastern Poland but Egorov's three armies had spread out from each other. The 12th Army on the right faced west alongside the Western Front but had been bogged down in marshy terrain; the Konarmiia was moving in a south-westerly direction having been ordered to take Lvov, and the 14th Army was oriented more to the south expecting to be ordered to invade Romania. All three armies had lost their momentum, suffered significant losses, and the front was beginning to lose its cohesion.

Tukhachevskii opened the Western Front's offensive on 4 July after extensive material and ideological preparation. Tukhachevskii went to great lengths to convince the soldiers of the significance of the forthcoming offensive. For example, the 33rd Division, over a period of three weeks, was subjected to a course of political education consisting of eleven meetings, one hundred reading sessions, one thousand discussions, twenty-five lectures, 104 cell meetings, thirty-seven general meetings, and twenty "spectacles".[34]

The Kavkor spearheaded the Western Front's offensive. The first main objective was Vilno. The offensive had great success at first, breaking the first Polish defense line in a matter of days. Vilno fell on 14 July. At the end of July, after very heavy fighting, Tukhachevskii's forces took Grodno. Yet, Tukhachevskii's attack on Poland failed to smash and surround the Polish forces as planned because they fought stubbornly and counterattacked consistently which took some of the fight out of the Russians. The Poles then retreated to avoid encirclement unhindered by Tukhachevskii's forces, eventually falling back to a line on the Bug and Narew rivers, roughly the recently pronounced Curzon line (established by Lloyd George of Great Britain on 11 July in consultation with the Polish Government as a pre-condition for opening peace talks with the Russians).

The Curzon line lay just beyond Grodno. To cross it and invade Poland would be to challenge Britain and France. Sensing total victory and perhaps a march on Berlin, the Soviet government rejected the appeal for peace talks. Tukhachevskii ordered his forces to cross the Curzon line and take Warsaw no later than 12 August 1920. The Kavkor reached the Vistula in the second week of August. Of his four armies, however, Tukhachevskii had only one rather weakened army in position to attack Warsaw, the others he optimis-tically oriented in the direction of East Prussia.

In the days preceding the Battle of Warsaw the Red Army had been victorious everywhere: it had armies poised to finish off Poland, invade Romania, and liberate Germany from capitalism, yet in only a week the fortunes of war would be completely reversed. Even as Tukhachevskii's forces marshalled for the assault on Warsaw proper, Pilsudski personally drew up a plan, not merely for a counterattack, but for a complete and crushing counteroffensive. In the first week of August 1920, stubborn Polish rearguard actions and energetic counterattacks held up Tukhachevskii's armies for six days, giving the battered Polish army just enough breathing space to regroup.

The battle opened on 12 August as the lead Soviet division attacked Warsaw's eastern defenses head on. In savage fighting that day the Soviet attacks were finally beaten off. By the end of the day, because of Polish attacks, counterattacks, raids and successful defense of the eastern approaches to Warsaw, Polish morale and hope had been completely restored. The initiative passed to the Poles, spelling doom for the Red Army. One Soviet division commander later wrote: "The moment had come when not only individual units but the whole mass of the army suddenly lost faith in the possibility of success against the enemy. It was as though the cord which we had been tightening since the Bug had suddenly snapped."[35] That same day, in a cavalry raid into 4th Army's rear, the Poles captured much of the 4th Army's staff and only radio transmitter. The loss of the transmitter left the Kavkor and 4th Army out of contact with Tukhachevskii for days. They did almost nothing in the way of restoring communication, but just followed their old orders. Because of this break in communications, for several days afterward, Tukhachevskii, in Minsk in his special train, remained unaware that morale was at the breaking point and his plans for restoring the situation unviable.

Pilsudski's plan was to attack Tukhachevskii's forces in the left flank from the south through a huge gap between the Western and Southwestern Fronts. It worked to perfection taking Tukhachevskii completely by surprise. Three of Tukhachevskii's armies, the 3rd, 15th, and 16th beat a hasty retreat suffering heavy casualties. By 22 August, Tukhachevskii's forces had been utterly routed. The Western Front had lost some 5,000 killed, over 50,000 prisoners, and more than 200 artillery pieces. To avoid capture or annihilation, the Kavkor and the entire 4th Army except two regiments and its commander and some of the staff sought internment in East Prussia. The Poles succeeded in annihilating two Soviet rifle divisions. Tens of thousands more men deserted completing the collapse of the Western Front.

Prior to 13 August 1920, when Pilsudski unleashed his counteroffensive, the Red Army had been at its zenith. It was no longer the ragtag bunch of novices of early 1918, but a seasoned, practiced army. After the Battle of Warsaw and subsequent second surge by the Polish Army, the Red Army would not recover its confidence until after several years of peace and reform. Through a near fatal act of hubris Tukhachevskii had thrown away an army, one of the best prepared and trained armies the Red Army had managed to produce to that date. He had lost over 100,000 men. Of the twenty-one divisions he had started with only seven were fit for service when he retreated across the Niemen.

How the Red Army was denied its victory and crushed by a seemingly beaten army became the source of some controversy within and without the

Red Army after the war. In truth, no one person can be held responsible for the debacle that overtook the Red Army; as an organization the army suffered from a number of problems at the time, especially regarding decision-making. The Konarmiia and 12th Army were supposed to have been transferred from the Southwestern Front to the Western Front, but Kamenev took two weeks from the time he explored the idea to make up his mind and give the appropriate orders, which were delayed in transmission and were then discussed between himself, Tukhachevskii and Stalin, and then between Tukhachevskii and Stalin. The high command appears to have been overwhelmed by the task of coordinating two fronts simultaneously and was distracted by Wrangel's breakout from the Crimea. The renewed White threat necessitated a transfer of troops from the Polish operation to the Don. Another problem was that the fronts were rather wide apart which would have involved much travel time for the 12th Army and Konarmiia to make a difference in conditions on the Western Front. Both the Konarmiia and 12th Army were engaged in the advance on Lvov, making it somewhat difficult to disengage, and thus further delaying their transfer to the Western Front. Another problem was that some of Tukhachevskii's orders to the RVS of the Southwestern Front were senseless and provoked discussion.[36] The absence of a master plan for the whole Polish operation further complicated the work of the high command.

Having stopped and dug in on the Niemen, Tukhachevskii regrouped, absorbing some reinforcements and supplies in preparation for a hoped for return to the offensive. In two weeks he had recouped his losses numerically with the addition of new units and thousands of individual replacements. He even created a new 4th Army. Pilsudski struck first in great strength in what became the Battle of the Niemen which lasted from 20 to 28 September.

The Poles turned Tukhachevskii's right flank at Grodno and the Lithuanian border after a few days of intense fighting. At first the Red 3rd Army fought well at Grodno against fairly even numbers, but after a few days its units could not keep up the fight and retreated. The retreat went badly but stopped temporarily at the old First World War Russian trenches. The Poles breached these on 2 October 1920 on their first try. The renewed retreat turned into a rout with the front for the most part falling apart.

The new 4th Army disintegrated with two infantry divisions in full flight and a cavalry division defected to the Poles. A third infantry division surrendered *in toto*. The 3rd Army became encircled and collapsed as an organized entity. The 14th, and 15th armies also retreated. The Battle of the Niemen led to a general advance by the Polish army all along the front.

The Southwestern Front also came in for a pounding in the Polish counteroffensive. From 30 August to 2 September 1920 the Konarmiia was surrounded after having been separated from the 12th Army which was supposed to cover its right flank. There was a major "pure" cavalry battle on

31 August between two brigades of Polish cavalry and elements of the Konarmiia's 6th and 11th Cavalry Divisions. Both sides took heavy casualties. In its fighting retreat the 11th Cavalry Division lost 2,400 men and 3,000 horses, the 6th Cavalry Division lost sixteen of twenty squadron commanders; the 4th and 14th Cavalry Divisions fared about the same. The Konarmiia, despite its casualties and fatigue, broke out of the encirclement to fall back to the east with the 12th Army.

By the end of September, the Red Army had been pushed entirely off of Polish territory and was losing ground in the Ukraine. On 15 October the Poles took Minsk and advanced to within 90 miles of Kiev. According to historian Norman Davies, the severity of the punishment meted out by the Poles in the pursuit of the Red Army out of Poland, combined with the mutiny in the Konarmiia, desertions and food shortages in Soviet-controlled western Ukraine, caused Trotsky and Kamenev to give up their ideas of forming a new task force to go back into Poland. Total Red Army casualties in the war amounted to some 17,500 combat deaths, 17,400 noncombat deaths, 130,000 prisoners lost to the Poles, 40–50,000 men interned in Germany, and 102,000 seriously wounded and debilitated. On 18 October 1920 an armistice, sought by Pilsudski who had no illusions about retaking Kiev, went into effect. Peace terms, which granted Poland substantial areas of western Ukraine, were formally agreed to in early November 1920.[37]

Wrangel and the last of the White forces bottled up in the Crimea were duly dealt with and dispatched into exile under the protection of the French fleet in November 1920. The Civil War was not yet complete, however. The sailors, workers, and garrison at Kronstadt rose in revolt against Bolshevik power in March 1921. Their demand that the Bolsheviks share power with other socialist parties could not be entertained nor let out to the public. Trotsky took charge of the extermination of the revolt which severely tested the loyalty of many units involved. Numerous regular Red Army regiments had to be withdrawn from the action because of their sympathy for and reluctance to fight the rebels. In addition, various revolts by Green movements remained to be crushed before Bolshevik power could be considered secure. The largest of these movements, and the most costly to suppress in terms of lives of Red Army men, were Makhno's army, related above, and the Tambov peasant revolt. In summer 1921 the Tambov revolt, and hence the Civil War, for the most part came to an end.

One cannot help but marvel at the institution that was the Red Army in 1921. It had been created by a political party that did not believe in standing, centralized armies, by ideologues who by training and temperament were unsuited to hierarchy and subordination, with the coerced aid of military experts whose interest was not in serving the cause of the masters who loathed them, and manned by men who were for the most part indifferent if not hostile to the goals the army fought for. Under the circumstances the

Red Army had served the Bolshevik Party reasonably well. The party retained power. All organized opposition on the left and right had been bloodily eliminated. Most of pre-war Russia had been preserved in the new Soviet state. The cost had been high, close to half a million Red Army men died.[38] The number of deaths of civilians and anti-communists are unknown, but certainly exceeded one million and could easily be twice that.

The war and military service had a profound effect on the party and individual party members, though how this affected their subsequent work is a matter of some debate. Overwhelmingly, however, party members left the army for civilian employment. PUR, too, lost dramatic numbers of party activists. Few saw service in the military as the way to the top. Even Trotsky no longer had a serious interest in military affairs by the end of 1922. Building socialism meant reconstructing and expanding industry, not serving in God-forsaken garrisons out of touch with political and economic development.

3

THE RED ARMY BETWEEN
THE WARS, 1922–39

The period between the wars can be characterized for the Red Army para-
doxically as one of growth and decline. The army grew in virtually every
material aspect except size in which it experienced *regrowth* after demobilization from five million in 1922 to near half a million men and then expanded
back to its former size on the eve of the Second World War. The military,
political, and civilian leadership all gradually matured in their appreciation of
the practical (as opposed to theoretical) demands of a national military establishment. The military education level of the officer corps grew through
schooling. Through economic recovery and investment the quantity, quality,
and technological level of armament increased. Internal stability increased as
the army assumed a more manageable size. Training slowly began to become
routine and standardized. Even popular attitudes toward military service
seemed to improve as the regime sought to change the historically negative
image of the soldiers' lot in Russia. These positive trends, however, began to
reverse in 1928. The army's effectiveness began to decline as the regime,
now under Stalin's sway, sought to manipulate the army in its socialist reconstruction of society, and simultaneously make rapid leaps, rather than gradual
steps, forward in the size of the armed forces. The re-growth of the army
soon outpaced the ability of civilian society to provide volunteer officer
candidates, and arms and equipment. By mid-1939 because of the political
manipulation of officer cadres, purges, and expansion the Red Army was
short tens of thousands of officers; the recent entrants to the officer corps
were not trained well and often lacked motivation. Because of expansion
many units lacked necessary arms and equipment. The social fallout from the
violence of collectivization and pace of industrialization led a great many
soldiers, most of whom were peasants, to harbor ill-concealed contempt for
the regime. They acted out their contempt in ways detrimental to order and
stability in the ranks. This chapter illustrates and explains the basis and results
of the growth and decline of the RKKA on the eve of what was to be the
greatest war it would ever fight.

At the end of the Civil War the Bolshevik leadership had to come to terms
with the question of what type of army to have in peacetime. Should it

retain its standing army or create the ideologically correct citizens' militia army? The issue had been under discussion since 1919 with proponents for each view. Finally, in March 1921, the party, at the Tenth Party Congress, decided to compromise; the regime would create a mixed military system comprised of two parts: a small standing regular army of just over half a million men, and a large territorial army of conscripted citizen–soldiers serving part time led by cadres of regular army personnel.[1] A citizens' militia remained the long-term goal but its creation depended on two conditions: that there be no immediate threat to the security of the Soviet Republic, and the peasantry adopt a pro-Bolshevik outlook. Everyone, including the proponents of the all citizens' militia such as Podvoiskii, understood the practical reality of this decision and agreed for the time being to give up the cherished notion that the world's first socialist state could do without a standing army. That the stipulated conditions for a militia would not be met anytime in the near future encouraged those in favor of a regular army.

Assured of continued employment the Red Army high command sought to define the ideas it would use to direct its steps in developing the armed forces, both practically and theoretically. Two viewpoints emerged in the debate over how to develop the armed forces. Mikhail Frunze, an old Bolshevik who decided to make his career in the military and had by this time attained membership in the Central Committee, put forth the idea he called the "unified military doctrine." What he meant by "unified military doctrine" was simply a comprehensive set of ideas and principles that would govern the outlook and actions of the army as it prepared for future war. Frunze's doctrine had two parts, the technical and political. The technical aspect involved the organizational development, training, and methods of carrying out combat missions. The political aspect was the subordination of military tasks to the political leadership and its will regarding what it wanted the military to do and how the political leadership organized society and its productive capacity (human and material) to support its military objectives.[2]

The basic principles of the unified doctrine reaffirmed much of the Red Army's basic assumptions, such as: the Communist Party would continue to have the leading role in military affairs; as an army of a "new type" the people and the army would be one; and that the army should represent and defend an international proletariat. The doctrine established that the army would be led by a cadre of regular (career) leaders rather than elected leaders and would continue to have centralized authority not local as had the Red Guards or partisans. It sought to end the dual command of officers and commissars and replace it with the one-man command (*edinonachalie*) of officers. Frunze called for iron military discipline and high political consciousness. Finally, the army was to be in a state of constant readiness.

Leon Trotsky opposed the "unified military doctrine" on principle because he considered it dangerous to impose a binding set of ideas on the leadership that could restrict free thinking regarding the army's status and future. He proposed that the army really needed to pay attention to the fundamental task of training peasants to be soldiers, Red Army men (*krasno-armeitsy*), and that all the theory in the world could not replace the benefits of a well-trained army. In particular, Trotsky argued against those who wanted to focus, or even limit, the energy of the General Staff to issues of strategic theory. Trotsky advocated giving the platoon central importance saying, "There can be no better school for a commander of a regiment, or a brigade, or a division than the work of educating the platoon commander," because "this cannot be done without clarifying more and more in one's mind all the questions of Red Army organization and tactics without a single exception."[3] The generals objected, favoring academies and courses of higher learning for their self-improvement.

Sergei Gusev, head of PUR from 1921 to 1924, took the middle ground on the issue of the unified military doctrine, citing the unity of effort an army-wide doctrine would bring which he thought would enhance the ability of the army to train its soldiers for modern war.[4] The "unified doctrine" was adopted and, as it turned out, Trotsky's fears that the high command would neglect its role in training the soldiers proved well founded.

To adequately train and structure the army the high command had to decide what kind of war awaited Russia. Frunze and A. A. Svechin of the General Staff Academy dominated the discussion and decided to include in Red Army doctrine that for the Soviet Union future war would be one of life or death against the capitalist powers. Their preferred strategy was one of defensive attrition, letting the enemy attack and Russia, lacking a substantial industrial base, fall back on its reserves of manpower. Stalin, too, believed that at the time this was the most realistic course, and was prepared to base economic expansion in Russia's deep interior on the basis of the USSR's military weakness.[5] Mikhail Tukhachevskii unsuccessfully opposed this defensiveness with his rather confident "strategy of destruction" which hinged on maneuver and the offensive. The resulting *Field Regulations of 1925* (PU-25), which stayed in force until 1929, relied on infantry and cavalry forces to bear the brunt of any enemy invasion.

With the beginning of the first five-year plan (1928–32) to expand the USSR's industrial base, and the experience of nearly eight years of secret military cooperation with the German Army, Soviet strategy changed to follow Tukhachevskii's offensive strategy. In 1929, the General Staff concluded that because the military had sufficiently – but not completely – rearmed and the economy recovered from the 1914–21 devastation, it should henceforth avoid defensive positional warfare and restore maneuver to the battlefield. To materially support this changed outlook the high command decided that the RKKA should attempt to achieve superiority in tanks, aircraft, and artillery relative to its potential foes. The ideas of the offensive-based "Deep Battle," with its call for combined arms forces, were enshrined in *Provisional Field Regulations of the RKKA for 1936* (PU-36).[6]

The switch to an offensive strategy saw the Red Army begin experimentation with large mechanized forces. In 1932 the army formed what it called mechanized corps (actually groupings of tank and motorized infantry brigades). In only a few years, the strides the army made in the practice and theory of armored warfare were called into question as a result of the Red Army's experience in the Spanish Civil War 1936–39. The Soviet Union, in support of the Spanish Republic against Franco's fascist nationalist army, sent some 600 military advisors, 772 pilots, 351 tankmen as well as around 2,300 ordinary volunteers, men and women. The RKKA supplied enough armored vehicles and artillery pieces to equip four Soviet rifle divisions and more than enough rifles and machine guns to arm thirty more. The purpose of the aid was as much to strike a blow against fascism as to gain practical experience in modern warfare.[7] Dmitri Pavlov, head advisor on armor to the Republic, reached the conclusion that large armored formations were not feasible for modern combat, but smaller, battalion-sized units could serve to bolster the offensive strength of infantry divisions. On his recommendation, in early 1939, the mechanized corps were disbanded and the tanks sent to rifle divisions, although the offensive spirit of PU–36 was still the order of the day.

Organization after the Frunze reforms

Once the regime decided on the mixed system and attendant doctrine, the Red Army sought to establish routines and methods for preparing an armed force to defend the USSR. This was no easy task. The Red Army had to start virtually from scratch in setting up the conscription and preconscription training systems that for the most part had disintegrated with the end of the Civil War. Of course peacetime training routines also had to be established. Simultaneously, the army reorganized unit structures as it reduced its size to adjust to the postwar economic, social and political situation. The economic situation in the early 1920s was marked by dismally low industrial output, which meant that industry had to concentrate first on recovery before it could make a serious effort to rearm the Red Army. The educational level of the population was characterized by continued mass illiteracy, which hindered the army's development of technical units. The political situation was complicated by the fact that the organs of soviet power had still not extended completely throughout the USSR. In establishing its routines and methods, then, the Red Army had to adapt to less than ideal conditions.

In 1924, Mikhail Frunze succeeded Leon Trotsky as Chief of the RVS USSR and Peoples' Commissar of Military and Naval Affairs – and had become a candidate member of the Politburo as well – to make an invaluable contribution to the Red Army in 1924–25 by establishing the framework that gave the military what little order and regularity it achieved before its transition from the mixed system to an all regular army in 1935. Under Frunze – who died an untimely death on the operating table in 1925 – the framework of the army hierarchy was rationalized. The process was aided by the demise of the oversight formerly exercised by the VTsIK, the abolition of its Council of Defense, and the elimination of the Supreme Military Council, the All-Russian Supreme Staff, the post of Commander-in-Chief, and the Field Staff. Hereafter the Commissariat of Military and Naval Affairs (renamed Commissariat of Defense in 1934), the RVSR and the General Staff constituted the high command. Frunze established military districts, reorganized conscription, began rearmament, and standardized the organization of regiments and divisions. The army likewise overhauled its recruiting of officers and the military education system.

Frunze was not content to merely adapt the army to the conditions reigning in the country, he also sought to modernize the armed forces. His efforts were constrained by the national budget; however, by 1928 they yielded some seven thousand new artillery pieces and several score tanks. Though Stalin appreciated the importance of defense production, once the military was deemed able to present a credible defense, he supported maintaining its share of the national budget at a relatively static 2 percent. At the onset of the First Five-Year Plan in 1928, the high command unsuccessfully pushed for a larger share of the budget and to increase production for the military and defense industries. At the Sixteenth Party Congress in 1930, the military made another effort to get resources diverted from the civilian sector to the military, but Stalin remained unconvinced of any pressing need. Through the end of the First Five-Year Plan civilian industry took precedent over defense industry, though military needs were by no means neglected.

Because the Red Army was a conscript army, the organization and efficiency of the conscription organs were vital to the life of the army. The annual draft officially began on the first of September and lasted until mid-November. Responsibility for organizing conscription lay with military district administrations which supervised subordinate regional military commissariats in their districts. Regional party organs kept track of men aged 21 through 30 who had military obligations and reported this to the army. The military district then used this information to formulate orders to subordinate conscription organs each year. The orders specified the number of young men needed and where they were to be sent once conscripted. The military districts passed down this information to the regional military commissariats, which then established quotas for town and village soviets to fulfill. In contrast to European armies, where the military handled conscription and recruiting, conscription in the USSR was a joint effort by the army, government, the Communist Party, trade unions, and the Komsomol. The most important of these was the party.

The actual social composition of the regular army in the 1920s did not mirror the social composition of the draft cohorts nor did the army want it to. Conscription commissions put as many workers into the regular forces as possible. Workers and those categorized as "other" (among them white collar workers and government employees) were overrepresented, although peasants constituted the largest social group. Peasants were more likely to be assigned to the territorial forces. Conscription commissions checked the social background of conscripts – often not thoroughly – to weed out wealthy peasants, former noblemen and bourgeoisie who were neither conscripted nor allowed to volunteer for the military.

The Red Army sought to achieve two goals by its recruiting policy. The first was to get the most educated men into the regular army, which meant recruiting workers because they were more likely to be literate. The second was to enlist as many poor and landless peasants as possible, because the regime wanted not only to ally itself with the rural poor against the rural "rich" but also to prepare those men for leadership in the countryside. The army, despite its desire for a minimum percentage of proletarians in each unit, made no attempt to distribute workers and peasants between units to obtain uniformity.[8]

When conscripts appeared at assembly points for service in the regular forces, they were given a physical examination before being shipped off to their regiments. The men were inspected for vermin and fleas, and tested for contagious diseases. In the words of one conscript, "Our military training began with a steam bath, the disinfection of all our clothes, a haircut that left our scalps as smooth as our faces, and a political lecture."[9] After that, they were supposed to be fed a good meal and issued new uniforms, thus undergoing a full transformation, in appearance at least, from civilian to soldier. Processing recruits did not always go like clockwork and disturbances sometimes broke out among the draftees at assembly areas. Absolute mayhem in the form of drunken brawls was not unusual as the result of ambivalence to military service combined with alcohol abuse.[10]

As the army grew throughout the 1930s, the People's Commissariat of Defense (NKO) sought ways to expand the manpower pool. Initially, conscription commissions granted fewer exemptions. Then, in 1936, the government lowered the draft age from twenty-one to nineteen; however, the RKKA did not immediately draft all the men in the eligible age groups, but worked its way down to the nineteen year olds over a period of three years. The 1936 "Stalin Constitution" did away with class and nationality restrictions for all purposes, including military service. Those previously identified as hated wealthy peasants (kulaks) or children of kulaks became subject to military service. The army ended exemptions for religious believers and conscientious objectors in August 1939.

Because the length of service for soldiers was a comparatively short two years the army desired that conscripts acquire basic military knowledge and skills before they entered the service, so prior to induction all young men were supposed to undergo more than 200 hours of preconscription military instruction over the course of two years. The training consisted of the rudiments of drill, marksmanship, and individual and squad tactics. The preconscripts became familiar with the organization of the military, barracks life, etc.

From 1924, the regular army, the territorial forces, and the Communist Party shared responsibility for preconscription training. The military provided instructors, and the party organized the conscripts. Although the high command placed much emphasis on this training it was often conducted in a haphazard fashion. The army did not support it well with necessary weapons and equipment. Occasionally, local authorities simply ignored their responsibility to organize training and conducted none. For many years, almost right up to the German invasion, the party and army simply did not have the material and human resources to supervise or conduct training everywhere in the USSR. The preconscription training system was weakened in 1935 when supervision was taken out of the army's hands and left up to a myriad of loosely monitored and controlled party and civilian organizations, primarily the Society for the Advancement of Aviation and Chemistry (Osoaviakhim). The party and Osoaviakhim worked inconsistently and in general let the army down. Units remained at a low level of proficiency due to the many men that arrived untrained. The army did not have basic training units so every battalion set aside several months to conduct such training.

With the Frunze reforms, the Red Army settled down to peacetime training, but, because it was a new army it could not fall back on well established patterns and routines. Rather, it had to work out many things from scratch. Leon Trotsky, in 1922, understanding the army's inadequate proficiency, emphasized that the RKKA would have to concentrate on matters mundane to an established army but new to it and learn how:

> To supply sections properly with food; not to permit products to rot; to cook good cabbage soup; to teach how to destroy body vermin and to keep clean; to correctly conduct training exercises, . . . to prepare political discussions intelligently and concretely; to keep good records; to teach how to oil rifles and grease boots; to teach how to shoot; to help the commanding personnel thoroughly assimilate the statute regulations concerning maintaining communications, gathering intelligence, making reports, maintaining guards; to learn and to teach how to adapt oneself to various localities; to wrap one's feet correctly in pieces of cloth to keep them from getting rubbed raw.[11]

As obvious as these tasks may seem many officers who joined the army after the Revolution were unfamiliar with such concepts.

The training year was divided into two parts, winter and summer. From 15 September to 15 November the army discharged the second-year men and conscripted the new draft cohort. In the winter training cycle units trained as much as possible indoors. New recruits learned the necessity of discipline for the efficient functioning of the army, but that revolutionary discipline was different from the discipline of bourgeois armies. In bourgeois armies, discipline was based on class exploitation. The Red Army had socialist discipline. To have socialist discipline, a soldier needed to be functionally literate, politically literate, and had to work for the goals of Soviet power. According to a soldiers' manual, "These three requirements . . . are no less important than the study . . . of the rifle."[12] Socialist discipline, however, did not go so far as to rule out unquestioning obedience. Soldiers were instructed to obey orders even if they did not understand them – just as in the old army – but were repeatedly assured that they would not be exploited. On the contrary, there was supposed to be a strong comradeship, a brotherly relationship between commanders and Red Army men. Ideally, officers associated with their men in an easy and informal manner that would have been unthinkable in the Imperial Army. Soldiers could walk into their commander's office at will to bring matters to his attention.

In addition to teaching military subjects and Soviet patriotism, the army tackled some basic tasks, such as personal hygiene. Cleanliness was supposed to be a high priority in the barracks. Unit doctors periodically checked the cleanliness of barracks and camps to ensure soldiers followed the rules of proper sanitation. Doctors encouraged the men to brush their teeth and bathe frequently – new habits to many peasant conscripts. In addition to promoting health and cleanliness, the Red Army also tackled the long-standing vice of alcoholism. Regulations forbade alcohol in the barracks, and soldiers were discouraged from drinking in the local villages during off duty hours.

As had been the case with the Imperial Army, the annual spring/summer camp was the most important training period of the year for both the regular and the territorial forces. During the summer the army trained mostly outdoors and focused on unit tactical skills and large-scale maneuvers. Units packed up and moved out of their garrisons and went to training areas where they were free to maneuver across the countryside.

Training at camp was supposed to be at a more advanced level than that done in garrisons in the fall and winter. Yet, due to poor organization and commanders' lack of attention to their duties, many soldiers arrived at their first summer camp without the basic skills necessary to begin advanced training. Consequently, the first weeks of camp had to be dedicated to teaching skills that should already have been mastered. A great number of commanders held the attitude that time in garrison was for administrative tasks. What training they did not get done could be made up in the summer.

Regiment commanders trained their units according to their own whims and standards, with corps or division commanders setting broad training guidance. Little uniformity existed in large unit tactics and training methods. Not until 1933, in an effort to reduce the inconsistencies throughout the army, did the RKKA's Administration for Military Training publish a training manual for the infantry, *MTPP-33*. The manual covered training of the individual soldier, squads, platoons, companies and battalions. It spelled out duties and responsibilities for the individual soldier, squad leader and others on up through the battalion commander and his staff. The second part covered tasks for specialized units, such as chemical, sapper and mounted reconnaissance detachments found in infantry regiments.[13]

Through *MTPP-33* the army attempted to create a uniform training system for rifle battalions. It provided thorough and exact instructions on what was to be accomplished, yet it left room for initiative on how those tasks could be accomplished. It also served as a resource document with reference to other manuals and regulations. It is evident that sincere men with clear minds struggled to improve the army's training. Constant problems in organizing and conducting training, often because of officer ineptitude, however, made futile the efforts of higher military authorities to achieve consistency and quality.

One serious obstacle the Red Army eventually failed to overcome in its quest to thoroughly train its men was the many internal and external distractions from military training. Internal distractions can be understood as fatigue details and administrative tasks assigned by commanders or commissars that took soldiers away from scheduled military training. External distractions consisted of the re-assignment of entire units from military training to non-military tasks in support of state objectives, most specifically industrial and agricultural work. Regiments and divisions spent considerable amounts of potential training time building quarters, and this must also be considered a distraction. Political instruction was not a distraction because it was considered by the army part of the soldier's required training.

Beginning with the First Five-Year Plan, the regime frequently used army units as a labor reserve for constructing industrial sites. The party used Red Army regiments and divisions, both territorial and regular, to help build Dneproges, the Kharkov tractor works, the Magnitogorsk metallurgical complex, the Gomel' agricultural machinery factory, and many other industrial plants. The work lasted for months at a time. Assigning territorial units to industrial work was particularly detrimental to training because most soldiers only assembled for a month. Consequently, if they spent their month on a construction project, they received no unit training that year. The state also stole Red Army training time to have it support agriculture. In time of great need (usually the harvest or sowing) the party sent whole regiments or divisions to the fields for days on end. From the late 1920s to the mid-1930s, the military appears to have been the servant of domestic policy. As such, it was treated more as a labor army than as a fighting force.

With war clouds looming in the late 1930s, the army put more emphasis on training than ever before, yet, because of rapid growth and poor preparation of its leaders, the military each year became less able than the year before to provide quality training to massive numbers of new recruits. The harder the General Staff tried to think of new and better training methods the more glaring was the failure of the line units to fulfill training requirements. New field regulations published in 1936 (PU–36) were intended to affect training down to the lowest level. The high command intended that new techniques be taught at the first summer camp after the new regulations were introduced. It turned out to be somewhat difficult, however, to break people of their old habits. For several years thereafter many units continued to just do the same old thing every summer with little or no reference to PU–36. Beginning in 1935 the high command gave large unit training more attention than in the recent past, with military districts holding corps and army size maneuvers at the end of each summer camp. The actual quality of the training, however, was probably not as high as it could have been. There was little combined-arms work and not much lee-way for initiative on the part of lower and middle-ranking officers.

Noncommissioned officers

In Western professional and conscript armies, officers and NCOs formed the backbone of the armed forces. In contrast, the Soviet military did not have a professional noncommissioned officer corps to provide stability and continuity. The Red Army's NCOs were conscripts, not professionals, and normally only served for the duration of their conscription. Some in the army recognized this fact and tried unsuccessfully to convince the officer corps of the need to train noncommissioned officers more thoroughly and retain as many as possible as career soldiers.

In place of the traditional long-serving NCO, each regiment selected and trained some conscripts from its allotment of the annual draft to serve as noncommissioned officers for the duration of their conscription. These NCOs served in the same capacity as those in Western armies but without the experience and corporate esprit of their Western counterparts, if for no other reason than the fact that they did not have to work their way up through the ranks. Not only did most NCOs not stay in the service longer than their obligatory two years, but while they served they often were not used to their full potential. After their training in the regimental school, platoon and company commanders frequently seem to have had no interest in training them further. By and large unit commanders made no conscientious effort to improve noncommissioned officers' leadership and military skills and would even pull them out of their leadership training to perform menial fatigues. The slipshod training and use of sergeants to perform fatigue duties undermined their status as leaders in the eyes of both their superiors and subordinates. Consequently, Red Army officers did much of the rudimentary training of the draftees, making them an essential link in the lower levels of training. This detracted from the officers' ability to develop the skills appropriate to their position and to conduct the supervisory and administrative duties related to unit combat readiness.

61

The territorial forces

For all practical purposes, the Soviet territorial forces, always the step-child of the regular army, was a reserve army, much like the United States' National Guard, based on local recruitment and administration. For most of its existence, the territorial force was larger than the regular army in number of units and men, yet received less than its share of equipment and funding. The territorial force suffered numerous problems throughout its existence. Due to its novelty everyone supposed to make it work was unfamiliar with the system, and it depended very much on the voluntary cooperation of the average village peasant and factory worker, which was not always forthcoming. The degree of support from the army leadership for the territorial system is hard to gauge, but after Frunze's death it was never very enthusiastic. Many in the high command never fully accepted the mixed system as desirable or necessary.

The men in each area liable for service filled the local territorial unit upon conscription, unless designated for the regular forces. Unlike *krasnoarmeitsy*, territorial soldiers (*terrarmeitsy*) served a five-year stint. Soldiers received eight months of training over the course of the five years: three months the first year of service; two months in the second; and one month in each of the last three years. During their tenure soldiers also had to report for periodic assemblies of a few days every month or so. At the conclusion of their service, territorials' names went on registration lists for recall in wartime. Men drafted into the territorial forces kept their civilian jobs and returned to them after their periods of training.

For most of the year, territorial formations existed as skeleton units with only a cadre of regular army personnel who served as leaders, instructors and custodians of the equipment. The cadre consisted of unit commanders, their staffs, medical, veterinary, administrative and political personnel. The cadre was responsible for military and political training, and the administration of the units. A contingent of NCOs and regular enlisted men supported the regimental school, provided guard details, and did the menial labor necessary to maintain the units between assemblies. Company commanders and above were nearly always regular officers, but all platoon commanders were territorial personnel. Like their men, they had a five-year service obligation.[14]

In the 1920s, the territorial forces experienced the bulk of the Red Army's growth. In the spring of 1923, barely a year after its inception, the territorial forces consisted of ten divisions. By the end of 1925, the RKKA had forty-six territorial rifle divisions. Six months later the army's infantry strength stood at sixty territorial and thirty-seven regular rifle divisions. This shows how potentially significant a role the territorial forces played in training men for the national defense. At its peak, in 1935, the territorial force comprised 74 percent of the army's divisions and well over one million men. The sheer size of the territorial forces suggests its importance as a mechanism for the government to make its presence felt among the population as well as bolster the national defense.

Territorial units arranged the training year along the same lines as active units, with winter and summer training cycles. The territorials emphasized summer training camp even more so than the regular units, yet attempted to conduct training year-round. Cadre who conscientiously sought to fulfill their duties were extremely hard pressed to do so. Because their personnel were spread throughout the towns and villages of a region training was a complex undertaking. For example, the following tasks were laid on the cadre of the territorial divisions annually: in each region train groups of sixteen- to eighteen-year-old preconscript youths in a 210-hour program; conduct a three-month assembly for newly conscripted young men; conduct month-long assemblies for the other four year groups of territorial soldiers; train territorial officers and political staff for one month; work with *terrarmeitsy* in the periods between assemblies.[15] At the company level the only two cadre members, the company commander and the *politruk*, bore the entire burden of training. The training consisted mainly of basic military skills, shooting and political instruction. Due to limited resources the cadre generally delivered only sketchy training. For example, a detachment commander of the 2nd Ul'ianov Cavalry Regiment had fifteen pairs of skis, two small bore rifles, 2,000 rounds of ammunition, two gas masks, some military literature, and no horses to train 100 men at a collective farm. Because the commanders did not normally live in the vicinity of their men (they were quartered in the town where the battalion headquarters was located) they had to work through the local party committees to notify the transitory personnel and arrange dates for training.[16] Often their work went uninspected and unsupervised so flaws and lapses went uncorrected.

Just as with regular units numerous hitches hampered training. In some cases units lacked the material necessities for training. Some units received supplies late, and soldiers did not get their uniforms and equipment until well into the assembly. Like the regular forces, territorial units suffered distractions from training. During the First Five-Year Plan many units spent most or all of their summer assembly assigned as labor to industrial sites.

PUR required company *politruki* to spend between ten and fifteen days a month working with the *terrarmeitsy* in their local areas. Battalion and higher level political people were supposed to spend at least seven to ten days per month with the troops during the time between assemblies. Both *politruki* and commissars tended to minimize trips to the countryside, however, preferring to spend their time in town or garrison.[17]

The agreement to have a mixed system was made before Stalin came to power, and his consolidation of power saw the beginning of the demise of the mixed system. In 1931, several territorial formations converted into regular army units. The Politburo authorized the remaining territorial divisions to begin the transition into regular divisions in 1935. The party justified this change with the threat posed to the USSR by fascist Germany and Japan's territorial ambitions in the Far East. The change was also made possible by the economic advances of the five-year plans. It is not clear, however, that the stimulus for change originated in the Politburo. There were those in the military – most notably Tukhachevskii – who had lobbied for an all regular army for some years. By 1939 all major territorial units had been converted into regular units.

As events proved, eliminating the territorial system actually detracted from Soviet preparedness. By depriving the RKKA of a well-established, union-wide mobilization tool the army became less able to fight a total war on short notice. The territorial system had been the second echelon of defense. By transferring those units to the first line of defense, the RKKA deprived itself of an organized reserve. If the object was to have a larger regular army, it does not follow that the territorial system needed to be abolished. In 1935, untapped manpower abounded, and allocations for defense spending began to grow. By eliminating the territorial forces, the General Staff gambled that it could successfully fight a war solely with regular forces.

Here the General Staff committed a grave error in choosing its method of expansion. It created more partially manned divisions rather than filling its existing divisions, or creating new fully manned divisions. The creation of vast numbers of new divisions exacerbated an already critical shortage of officers. Partial manning created an overwhelming need for field and general grade officers. Had the RKKA brought its existing units to full strength, which it easily could have, it would have then created fewer divisions and eliminated the need for so many new commanders and staffs. As it was, the situation became common in the late 1930s where a battalion's highest ranking officer was a senior lieutenant rather than a major.

Since the end of the Civil War, the Red Army's regular rifle and cavalry divisions had purposely been only partially manned with from 6,000 to 8,000 men – between 40 percent and 60 percent of the authorized strength – at Frunze's instigation. Frunze's reasoning was linked to mobilization and the lack of a proven organized reserve system in 1923. The idea was that the army would have the structure for more divisions this way and in time of war the men on their three-years furlough could be called back to the regular forces to fill up the divisions. This plan presupposed ample time for reservists to travel to their units, and it ignored all considerations of unit cohesion and the need for refresher training. With 5,000–6,000 men joining a division overnight, existing cohesion in the regiments would be thrown into disarray; unit commanders would know the personalities and capabilities of only half of their men. This manning policy, which violated Frunze's own precept of constant readiness of the unified doctrine, may have been a reasonable alter-native for a small infantry army with a defensive doctrine in the early 1920s, but was not at all appropriate for an increasingly mechanized army with an offensive doctrine in the late 1930s.

From beginning to end, the plan was flawed, as history had already proven. The tsarist army had used partial manning as its mobilization method, with disastrous results under conditions of rapid mobilization. What is especially condemning about the army's mobilization plan is that many of the Red Army's General Staff officers in charge of mobilization had experienced the failure in 1914 in the tsar's army. Aleksandr Svechin, in his book *Strategiia*, published in 1927, prophetically warned against repeating the mistakes of August 1914 and trying to set records for mobilization speed.[18] Tukhachevskii, in particular, as a participant of the First World War and colleague of Svechin's at the academy, should have known better. In many ways, June 1941 would be a repeat of August 1914.

Daily life, conditions of service and discipline

Just as training did not live up to the high command's expectation, daily life in the army did not live up to the soldiers' expectations, thereby contributing to poor morale and sometimes discipline problems. Poor housing turned out to be a major disappointment for many soldiers. From the first days of Soviet power, housing had been a problem for the armed forces as well as for all urban society. In a speech to the Fourth All Union Congress of Soviets on 25 April 1927, Kliment Voroshilov discussed the state of military housing, admitting that accommodations for the military were bad, even, in some instances, worse than they had been under the tsar.[19] Five years after Voroshilov's speech, the Red Army was still trying to overcome its housing shortage and, like the civilian sector, came up short. Newly constructed barracks were a step up from living in tents, which many soldiers and officers had had to endure for months on end, but they were not as big an improvement as many had hoped. Many lacked indoor plumbing and electric lighting. After their completion, many of the barracks were found to be of extremely low quality. Many finishing touches went uncompleted, making the dwellings uncomfortable and unappealing. Additionally, paltry army budgets made maintenance and upkeep difficult. Besides poor construction, the RKKA had to contend with the fact that after 1928 its numbers steadily grew. The increase in manpower always exceeded the rate at which the army built barracks.

Abrupt and unplanned relocation of units contributed to housing problems. In his memoirs Georgi Zhukov noted that in 1932 the entire cavalry corps in which he served relocated to another military district and had to spend eighteen months building its own quarters from scratch, "degenerating, as a result, into an inefficient labor force. This disastrously affected morale and combat worthiness. Discipline grew lax . . ."[20] For all practical purposes, the divisions suspended combat training and political instruction while they built an entire military post. One can imagine the negative impact of this experience on the soldiers. The men spent most of their time building barracks and stables instead of learning cavalry skills. The men who joined the division during this time would have spent more of their service as laborers than as soldiers. At the same time, while living in tents and uncompleted barracks they were subject to the effects of the weather. In the early 1930s, as new units were formed, they went through the same housing ordeals as units that had been relocated. Units continued to relocate throughout the 1930s with virtually no improvement in planning.

Quality of life was greatly affected by the facilities the soldiers had at their disposal. For instance, although the Red Army promoted cleanliness, in practice soldiers did not bathe as often as the army stipulated if for no other reason than the necessary facilities did not exist. In the main, infrequent bathing was a consequence of the army's growth beyond the economic capacity of the USSR. Construction could not keep up with demand, meaning bathhouses were few and far between.

Food was another factor that could negatively affect morale of the *krasnoarmeets*. Every regiment had traditional mess halls. Larger garrisons also had dining facilities and department-like stores, to provide amenities like tea and extra food, and services ranging from barbershops to canteens run by military cooperatives. Soldiers ate free at the military mess halls but had to pay to join cooperatives.

Famine struck the Soviet Union in 1932–33 and soldiers, like civilians, did with less food. The army's central supply sources cut rations by 30 percent, except in the privileged Moscow Military District. However much the quantity and quality of food dropped in the military, it was still superior to that available to the general populace, which in many areas suffered starvation. For example, an artillery battalion commander reported that when the draftees of 1933 reported for duty they were all suffering from malnutrition. It took a month on special rations to get them ready for organized activity.[21]

Unfortunately unit commanders sometimes did not care how well fed their men were. They acted indifferently to the problem of food supply, preparation and distribution. In some units, the people in the chain of command responsible for such matters neither inspected nor supervised mess operations. Officers could afford to hold such attitudes if their unit had separate officers' messes. In some units, officers purchased all or nearly all of their rations from the military cooperatives, so they had no need to make the military supply system work. In those units where the leadership did not take an active role in ensuring good and adequate food for their men trouble often erupted. The men might collectively refuse to eat and call for an investigation which could lead to the arrest of individuals responsible for the food problems.[22] The difference between an officer's lot and a soldier's is illustrated by two letters, one from an officer serving in Kronstadt who wrote, "We are living well, like with Christ in heaven: there is always something to eat and to drink, every day we eat only white bread, herring, and beef, and a bottle of wine costs only 2 rubles 50 kopecks." The other, from a soldier in Leningrad who wrote: "The service is hard, and on top of this the grub is sh__ . . . I want to become a shirker, I still need to join the party – after that life will become easier."[23]

In response to the famine, the RVS ordered all units to create supplementary farms to bolster their rations. Regimental supply officers used appropriated monies to buy food for the soldiers' mess from both unit farms and cooperatives, thus putting unit farms in direct competition with the cooperatives. Sometimes, however, greed overtook the operators of unit farms, causing them to sell primarily to local civilians instead of their units, thus defeating the purpose of the farms. Some units had already created farms on their own initiative, and those units that had not quickly acted once the order was promulgated. By late summer 1932, one regiment already had more than 200 hogs, sixty cows, more than 100 rabbits, and forty beehives. The RVS's standard was for every division to have 400 cows, 3,200 pigs, and 20,000 rabbits, and to sow a thousand hectares with a combination of rye, wheat and fruits. One can only guess at how much time was spent by the men gardening instead of training. The emphasis placed on unit farming programs is illustrated by the example of the then assistant commander of the 87th Rifle Regiment who was so closely involved in the unit's farming operations that he knew each of the regiment's thirty-eight cows by name.[24] Eventually unit farms became institutionalized as part of the normal activity of major units and lasted up to the collapse of the communist regime.

During the entire prewar period the army's supply organs operated with regular inefficiency partly due to internal mismanagement and partly because of its reliance on civilian industry. Not until 1928 did the army receive, for the first time, 100 percent of the clothes, boots, mattresses, blankets and linen it ordered. Woolen clothes and warm winter clothing were still in short supply, however, and quality left much to be desired. Because of its own shortcomings the military made heavy demands on the system of military cooperatives, not just for food but for everyday needs as well. This was mostly in response to the needs of many units posted in remote locations, possessed of few amenities and whose needs the army supply organs could not meet.

No matter what was available in the military cooperatives, a soldier could not expect to buy much because of the miniscule amount he was paid for his service. In 1925 a Red Army man was paid one ruble forty kopecks per month. This gradually increased to eight rubles monthly in 1937. A first-term NCO's pay rose in the same time from one ruble ninety kopecks to twenty-four rubles a month.

When one considers the poor housing, low pay, the food situation, the often haphazard training, and the sometimes inattentiveness toward the men's welfare shown by officers, it is not surprising that discipline could at times become very weak in the units. In August 1932, *Krasnaia zvezda* reported on discipline problems in the RKKA. From an investigation of a railway regiment in the Moscow Military District came the following findings:

> Sometimes the cause [of indiscipline] lies in the poor organization of the daily routine. Tents are dirty, boots are uncleaned owing to the lack of brushes and blacking, clothes are torn owing to the lack of needles, thread and repairing material. There is an inadequate quantity of crockery in the mess halls and the supervision over the preparation of food is insufficient.[25]

One cannot help but notice that the findings of the investigation point out that conditions of life in the Red Army – shortcomings in supply, poor leadership and lack of attention to the details Trotsky had warned about – contributed to discipline problems much as they had during the Civil War.

One of the keys to understanding the often poor behavior of Soviet soldiers in the interwar years lies in their complaints. The RKKA promised soldiers a quality life, not only for themselves, but also for their families. The army guaranteed them adequate food, shelter, and rest, but these were not regularly provided. In addition to their personal woes, soldiers in overwhelming numbers complained about the plights of their families as they became subject to the Bolshevik social revolution, as well as about the state's failure to keep promises to their families regarding tax exemptions, housing, jobs, loans, schooling, and so on. The Soviet government, considering the soldier and his family crucial to the socialist reconstruction of the countryside, recognized the importance of addressing soldiers' grievances and established the Bureau of Red Army Men's Letters to handle them.

Just because a soldier sent his complaint to an official agency did not guarantee its resolution. In many instances local organs of the party and government failed to provide the guaranteed privileges and services to the families of serving Red Army men. Problems in fulfilling soldiers' rights and privileges stemmed not so much from a breakdown in the system at all, rather they were the result of the physical underdevelopment of the national infrastructure, and the lack of development of the party and government structure at local levels, all of which made incredibly difficult the communication of decisions, policies and procedures in a fashion understandable to the rather poorly educated people manning the party apparatus and government bureaucracy. Another part of the problem in addressing these problems lay with the Bureaus of Red Army Men's Letters in the regiments, the first stop for letters of complaint. A 1933 inspection of twenty such bureaus in the Leningrad Military District revealed that many bureau secretaries had not been informed of the appropriate statutes and codes governing actions concerning complaints. In the majority of cases, the bureaus did not even have the appropriate legal publications and codes on hand for reference. Many of the bureaus took no action but simply forwarded the inquiries to other agencies with requests for "compliance on the basis of existing resolutions of the party and government."[26] As a result, most letters went unanswered. Such inept handling of soldiers' problems must surely have contributed to discipline problems.

Lack of cohesion, in addition to the often poor conditions of life and slip-shod leadership, also contributed to discipline problems. Units experienced a high turnover of personnel because of the various terms of service. Every year, the army experienced roughly a 50 percent turnover. There was also natural turnover of nearly 8 percent annually for such reasons as medical discharges, death, desertion, bad conduct and imprisonment. Therefore, personal relationships and loyalties were harder to form than in volunteer armies with longer enlistment terms, such as the British army, which had a three-year enlistment, and the German army, which, in the Weimar period, had twelve-year enlistments.

When one notes the poor housing, low pay, the food situation, the often haphazard training, and the lack of attention toward the men's welfare shown by officers it is not surprising that discipline could at times become tenuous in the units. For example, in 1928, the army averaged eight mis-demeanors for every 100 servicemen per month. Of these, 21 percent had a direct derogatory effect on the military capacity of the units and 15 percent resulted in arrest.[27] The number of serious crimes was also quite high, if we can believe the Soviet military press. In 1929, not a week went by when at least one, if not a dozen, serious crimes by officers and men was reported in *Krasnaia zvezda*. The crime most often tried by military tribunal (court-martial) was theft of money or selling supplies to civilians. Besides thievery, the press reported breaches of discipline, desertion, and cases of criminal negligence. All attempts by the army to bolster discipline failed, and on the eve of the purge, between 1 January and 31 May 1937, the army recorded 400,000 disciplinary infractions.[28] "Police" work, i.e. keeping track of offenders, arranging hearings and punishments distracted officers from train-ing their units.

As early as 1926, Voroshilov had noted that peasants made up the majority of the army and called for raising the number of Komsomols in the RKKA to 300,000 to provide an example of self-discipline for the non-party men. What Voroshilov suggested, but did not say directly, was that non-party peasants were undisciplined (or anti-Soviet by nature) and their influence needed to be diluted by communists. His faith in Komsomols as examples of discipline was not especially well founded. Several years earlier Frunze had chastised a conference of Komsomols for their own lax discipline, which did not improve over the years.[29] Party membership did not guarantee any better behavior. In periodic discipline campaigns, PUR held up Communist Party members as examples for the rest of the army. Communist soldiers were reminded that as party members they were the "advance guard of disci-pline" and were to see to it that the commander's orders were carried out.

In some cases the work of party cells was applauded as strengthening unit discipline. At other times, the press upbraided them for failing to be the models the party intended. In 1932, PUR roundly chastised several units for the conduct of their party cells. In one unit, fully half of the party members had been convicted of disciplinary infractions. The army never ceased harping on this point indicating that Komsomols and party members continually fell short of the mark.

The army did not have a separate military police arm of service and relied on Special Sections of the secret police to act as the military police force of the RKKA. Special Sections investigated all crimes in the army from murders and suicides to theft of government property and desertion. Under authority of the military district procurator's office they arrested and incarcerated suspects pending trial by military tribunal. The Special Section had to secure permission from the Commissariat of Defense to arrest an officer. In cases where tribunals imposed the death penalty Special Sections organized firing squads to carry out the sentence. These sections (one detachment per division) also watched over all soldiers, officers, and political workers to insure political reliability. They created networks of informers to report on their fellow soldiers.

Ever mindful of the need to enforce obedience, the RKKA, as part of the Frunze reforms, published a new set of discipline regulations in 1925 to update those first written during the Civil War. These regulations, updated almost every year afterwards, addressed the powers of platoon, company, and battalion commanders, to reward and punish their men without recourse to military tribunals. The regulations provided administrative punishments such as extra fatigues and confinement in the guardhouse for several days. They were intended as tools for unit commanders to maintain order within the unit and were normally used only for minor infractions of discipline. Regulations forbade corporal punishment. Serious crimes were subject to trial by military tribunals. Divisions, corps and separate brigades were empowered to convene tribunals and could impose penalties of from three months' confinement to death with confiscation of property. Regulations stipulated that in combat situations, unit commanders could shoot on the spot soldiers who defied orders.[30]

In many ways the Red Army had become a regular army during the years of peace, mostly as practical matters of organization and discipline forced the dropping of revolutionary idealism. And, try as it might, the regime failed to make the army an appealing and rewarding experience for most of its conscripts.

4

PUR AND THE ARMY:
THE POLITICAL SIDE OF
MILITARY SERVICE

The Red Army man experienced far more than just military training during his service, and that was exactly what the Communist Party intended. From the beginning the party saw the Red Army as a vehicle for molding the young peasant and worker into the "New Soviet Man." According to PUR doctrine, "Instilling in each Red Army man the discipline of a citizen-soldier and selfless devotion to our party, this is the basic task of all political work in the Red Army."[1] This was to be done through political indoctrination, anti-religious instruction, and basic literacy and elementary education.

Like the army, PUR also underwent reform in the 1920s – after surviving an attempt to abolish it and the institution of commissar – becoming more firmly structured but also less powerful. Now army and civilian party bodies were to work together, taking part in each other's special projects on an equal basis. This meant the end of the Civil War practice of a PUR coming into an area and forcing the local party organs to submit to the needs of the military. Political leaders were automatically made members of corresponding civilian party organs, however, they no longer had voting rights. Therefore, civilians had the upper hand and could in theory more easily influence party life in the units than the other way around.[2]

The real political work in the army was done in the regiments, under the supervision of the regimental commissar. The regimental political apparatus consisted of: the commissar; the regimental bureau of the party, headed by a secretary; a Komsomol organization; battalion commissars; company *politruki*; and the regiment's assorted clubs and libraries. The regimental party bureau admitted soldiers to party membership. Of all the political personnel, the company *politruk* interacted most closely with the soldiers organizing the company's political discussions. He was most active in identifying potential new party members. The *politruk* was responsible for establishing a party cell in his unit, though a secretary, who was not a PUR functionary but just a member of the unit, headed it. PUR had the goal of having a party cell in every company. It did not succeed. The tasks of a regiment's political leaders were to "firmly and clearly lead the bolshevik line in all party work" and give a correct Leninist education to all party members, candidates and Komsomols, and promote the activity and initiative of cells. Regimental organs were to establish a close association with non-party soldiers, "taking the opportunity to discover and act on their feelings, needs, and questions." Finally, PUR sought to pay maximum attention to the problems of military life and instruction, and to reinforce discipline.[3]

The Communist Party had responsibility for manning PUR and training its members. Given its limited educational facilities and rapid turnover of personnel formal training of political workers was almost nonexistent. In peacetime PUR followed its Civil War practice of assigning novitiate party members or candidates to political duties with no special instruction. PUR expected commissars to learn through practical experience and self-instruction from Marxist classics. From these inauspicious beginnings, men rose through the political administration hierarchy. By the mid-1920s, the more politically knowledgeable and ambitious people seem to have moved on and were replaced by men for whom political work was just a job and not a calling.

PUR had significant problems with manning throughout the 1920s and 1930s. Recruiting and retention both proved to be difficult. Replacing losses in sufficient quantity proved impossible as the army expanded. At the beginning of 1931, PUR was short more than 1,600 men, by the end of the year it lacked nearly 2,500, due both to discharges and increased requirements. As the army grew during the 1930s PUR's shortages increased, spreading thinner and thinner its representation and consequently degrading its influence in the units. By 1934, 15,000 political personnel had responsibility for educating some two million regular and territorial soldiers. One-third of them had joined PUR after 1930 as a result of party mobilizations with little or no training.[4]

Generally, as a result of poor preparation, political instructors could not always provide the most sophisticated instruction. Many were unsophisticated and semi-educated, and poorly understood what they taught. Consequently, political training was usually very poor, and efforts of political leaders varied widely. Social origins also at times inhibited indoctrination, in that most *politruki* were from the working class, but most soldiers were peasants. Ian Gamarnik, head of PUR 1929–37, lamented in 1932 that because of the insufficient preparation of *politruki*, little successful ideological work had been done in the army in the preceding few years.[5] For the rest of the decade, political training, like military training, received emphasis from the top but was haphazardly administered at the bottom.

In the opinion of Mikhail Soloviev, a Red Army correspondent in the 1930s, the lower grades of *politruki* were just talking machines. Their instruction in Marxism–Leninism and its application to interpretation of current events was well beyond the comprehension of most communists and "what is left is not knowledge itself, but a stereotyped version of the particular subject in question."[6] The quality of instructors and instruction declined as the army expanded and the level of experience plummeted in the political organs. The question remains open of how much influence PUR actually had over the men especially because so many *politruki* and commissars were equally as transient as soldiers. They tended to stay in the service only as long as required.

In the late 1920s, the purpose of political instruction was not to explain Marxism–Leninism to illiterate peasants, but to emphasize the benefits of Soviet power and to convince them of the need to obey the Soviet regime. According to one high-ranking PUR leader in 1928, "The real backbone of the worker and peasant army is the young peasant, who comes into the ranks of the Red Army with all the prejudices which exist in the countryside, who receives letters from the countryside fostering these prejudices."[7] Such was the rationale for two of the primary concepts conveyed to the soldiers: Soviet patriotism and proletarian internationalism, which were intended to loosen the peasant's ties to the village and give him broader national and international outlooks.

Political instruction was always haphazard and conducted inconsistently from unit to unit. Occasionally commanders ran roughshod over their *politruki* and their duties. In the mid-1930s an artillery regiment reported that the battery *politruk* was conducting political instruction with young soldiers when, during the first ten minutes of instruction, five men left to do a fatigue detail on the orders of the battery commander. Several minutes later a new order came for the release of six more soldiers. Nine men remained in the group. Not yet halfway through the hour of instruction, a third order came from the commander to release another two men for fatigues. This was considered normal in the regiment. Such practices made a mockery of Voroshilov's statement, "The Red Army is a first-class school of military-political and cultural education of men."[8] Complaints by *politruki* generally went unheeded.

An essential part of turning conscripts into new Soviet men was teaching them to read and write. For the most part, this task fell to the political workers and military officers in the units. Initially, this was a huge task, considering that an overwhelming percentage of soldiers were peasants – the least educated segment of Soviet society. Because the increasing technological sophistication of the armed forces required basic literacy and elementary mathematics, the Red Army could not treat the literacy campaign as an inconvenience or distraction from training, indeed it took the task quite seriously. In 1934, the stress on literacy instruction shifted from the army to the preconscription organs although literacy classes continued to be held in the units for several more years.

The army had special expectations of Communist soldiers. In the 1920s, the party expected them to help in grain requisitioning on weekends. In the 1930s they were the first to be enlisted to "help" the peasants collectivize.

Communists were supposed to watch their fellow soldiers and report any anti-Soviet attitudes. Those Communists who actually fulfilled these expectations were often not well regarded by their non-party peers.

To keep the cells in order the party called meetings for self-criticism (*samokritika*). At these meetings, the faults of everyone were supposed to be aired so corrective measures could be taken. One did not actually offer serious criticism of oneself; rather, one criticized those in his unit. All ranks were supposedly open for criticism, but, according to one private, "It was very risky and dangerous for a man to criticize his superior at an open meeting."[9] Not all enlisted men were intimidated, however, and officers sometimes complained that at party cell meetings privates often acted as though they had the right to give orders. Not only officers, but even enlisted party leaders tried to squash criticism of their actions or at least keep knowledge of their shortcomings from getting outside the cell.

The security of a communist's membership in the party could not be taken for granted as the Red Army, like civilian party organizations, was subjected to membership purges called *chistki*, designed to expel undeserving and politically unreliable people from the party. The party announced these purges months in advance in the military press and in memoranda to the military's party organs. To facilitate the work of certification commissions, the regimental party bureaus were told to prepare their records, and company cells were instructed to engage in self-criticism to identify the unfit beforehand. Explicit guidelines were periodically published on preparation and conduct of *chistki*.

Reasons for being purged included: holding Menshevik or Trotskyite ideas; associating with capitalists; failure to adhere to the party line; party passivity; isolation from the party masses; having no value to the political apparatus; sexual depravity; associating with kulaks or other enemies of the people; as well as being militarily undisciplined or incompetent. The effect was that *chistki* served as a means of reinforcing both military and political discipline among party members. Until 1937 officers and men expelled from the party were usually not ousted from the military. When soldiers were discharged as a result of *chistki* it was usually for a combination of political and moral factors.[10]

Under Stalin the Soviet regime was intent on changing the existing system of private capitalist agriculture to socialized agriculture through collectivization. The party intended to collectivize all peasants, so it made sense to organize peasants serving in the army. PUR took on the task of organizing everything in the army associated with collectivization. The movement to involve soldiers in collectivization included having peasant soldiers establish collective farms on land given them by the state after they were discharged, encouraging soldiers who owned independent farms to join their village collectives upon their discharge, and using soldiers still in the army to persuade civilians to join collectives. The movement called for training peasant soldiers in various trades associated with agriculture so they could work on collective farms, machine tractor stations or in rural administration upon their discharge.

PUR experienced a great failure in its efforts to lead soldiers in the socialist reconstruction of the countryside. Not only did PUR fail to win over a sizeable number of peasant soldiers to the idea of collectivization or dekulakization (ridding villages of kulaks) in the manner envisioned by the state, but it aggravated an already tense discipline and morale situation to the point that the loyalty of the rank and file and some officers became unreliable.[11] Most peasants conscripted into the army in 1929–30, when coercive grain procurement methods were in use and massive collectivization and dekulakization were begun, did not favor the goals of the regime or the means employed to achieve them. Being forced to choose between joining collectives and maintaining their individual holdings created conflict within and between individuals, families and whole villages and, consequently, between those entities and the Soviet state – not unlike the choices men had had to make during the Civil War. Considering the turmoil that developed in the countryside in the years 1929–32, unrest in the army should not have come as a surprise. Peasants resisted coercive grain requisitioning and forced collectivization in all parts of the USSR. The scale of opposition amounted to a virtual civil war.

The effort to get soldiers to form or join collective farms was especially intense among the territorial forces, and for good reason. There were more peasants in the territorial forces, and PUR presumed, greater results could be obtained more quickly. Therefore, the political administration made a major effort between 1929 and 1931 to draw peasant *terrarmeitsy* into the collectivization movement. First PUR encouraged landless peasants to found collectives on government land. Next came a campaign to enlist middle peasants in local collective farms (kolkhozes). By and large territorial soldiers proved very reluctant to collectivize.

In the summer of 1930, PUR ordered *politruki* of territorial units to intensify their work among the soldiers during both the assembly and periods between assemblies with the goal of having them found kolkhozes in their villages. The Political Administration of the Leningrad Military District soon reported: "There is active resistance by Red Army men, especially among those who have family with a kulak sentiment. Parallel with this observation is the well-known spreading of kulak sentiments, which is most highly developed in the territorial units and only a little less so in regular divisions."[12] When *politruki* fully explained collectivization policy soldiers sometimes reacted in the extreme, as exemplified by one soldier's exclamation, "I would sooner shoot myself than join a kolkhoz."[13] As the mass collectivization drive grew in intensity families wrote more and more frequently to their soldier relatives of the difficulties in the countryside. In sympathy with their families, many soldiers wrote home swearing they would never join a kolkhoz and went so far as to agitate against collectivization

75

among their peers. One soldier told his friends, "The party is worse than the kulaks in its exploitation of the peasants."[14] In many units the political organs and unit leaders proved reluctant to push collectivization after meeting resistance from their men. In some cases they could not even get their own cell members to agree to join kolkhozes on discharge.

A coincidental campaign by the regime to "eliminate the kulaks as a class", created even more serious problems. The question of what to do with kulaks, which translated into anyone excluded from the collective farms, tore party cells apart and caused confusion in PUR's ranks. The fundamental problem was that the average soldier, whether peasant or worker, party or non-party, enlisted or officer, thought if kulaks were to be eliminated as a class through confiscation of their wealth, they ought not be persecuted by the state. They felt that former kulaks should be allowed to join kolkhozes, but state policy was to arrest and exile them to Siberia. A large number of soldiers objected immediately and openly, and challenged their *politruki* and commissars with some insightful logic as they questioned party policy. One soldier, at a meeting of his party cell, asked, "If we can keep old officers who were former class enemies, in our army, then just why is it impossible for kulaks to enter kolkhozes?" Such opinions were roundly condemned to no avail by higher officials in PUR during fall and winter 1929–30. Because dekulakization caused such discord in the ranks – to the point of violence – Voroshilov, in February 1930, forbade further use of military personnel, even on a volunteer basis, in the campaign.[15]

In an effort to eliminate opposition to the party's rural policies, the army discharged nearly 10,000 recalcitrant soldiers and officers from the regular and territorial forces in 1929–30. Simultaneously, the party conducted a *chistka* with the aim of cleaning out kulaks and those sympathetic to them, and restoring party discipline. Not many were expelled from the party, however, and *politruki* reported a reluctance among soldiers to recommend people for expulsion. Others quit the party or Komsomol out of moral conviction.[16]

In the end, neither the Communist Party nor PUR were able to quash the anti-collectivization sentiments of many soldiers. What finally brought the crisis to a close was Stalin's "Dizzy with Success" speech of March 1930. With this speech Stalin called for a relaxation of the tempo of collectivization, leading the peasantry to think it would in the future be voluntary. The immediate effect of the speech in the army was for thousands of soldiers, who had signed up to join collectives, to cross their names off those lists. Similarly, thousands of kolkhozes broke up as civilian peasants left them in droves. The collectivization campaign in the army quietly picked up again in 1931, but by and large the regime concentrated on civilians.

Beginning in the mid-1920s PUR began a program to train men for work in agriculture after their discharge. The party trained men to operate tractors and other heavy agricultural equipment, to drive trucks and operate technical machinery, and expected that when they were discharged their skills would give collective agriculture a boost. Soldiers who volunteered for this training received instruction from PUR personnel or local party organs, beginning six to eight months before their discharge. The courses usually consisted of between 150 and 200 hours of instruction. PUR assigned each military district quotas of men to train and the particular skills to teach. In 1930, PUR set itself the goal of training 100,000 soldiers. PUR expected all peasant Komsomols, party members, and noncommissioned officers to participate in the program. The bulk of these men were trained for working on farms – which the party hoped would already be collectivized by the time demobilized soldiers got there. Training for work in the countryside continued through to 1935, although in 1931 this effort subsided greatly, mainly as a result of the soldiers' dissatisfaction with the pace and violence of collectivization and the high command's concern about the time it took away from military training.

Because of the political work and literacy, anti-religious, and agricultural skills instruction, the Red Army man's military experience was truly unique in comparison with that of his tsarist predecessor or counterpart in any other army. This is not to say that his experiences made him a better soldier. The regime attacked the soldier's lifestyle and values from all sides, which may have caused disorientation and aversion both to the military and to political authorities. Lives were changed by the newly acquired ability to read and write; the economic and social lives of peasants was altered by collectivization. One of PUR's goals was to inspire "Soviet patriotism," yet in the process it created the conditions for backlash, not only with the programs mentioned earlier but also with the promises, often unkept, of privileges for soldiers and their families. The Red Army man was supposed to be a "new Soviet man" by the time he was discharged. Most probably were, but not necessarily in the way expected by the party.

The Red Army officer corps

The Soviet military, in the years between the Civil War and the Second World War, failed to create a competent, well-trained, self-confident, cohesive, and motivated, professional officer corps. The lack of competent leadership contributed greatly to the army's and USSR's suffering in the early years of the Second World War. The primary causes of this failure were: the inability to recruit sufficient numbers of officers; insufficient training; and the recruitment of low quality and undereducated men. What resulted was an officer corps with little cohesion, talent, and ability, unprepared to fight a major war. The problem stemmed from a regime that created an army larger than its society could man with volunteer officers.

During the 1920s and 1930s the army acceded to the party's wishes in attempting to recruit its officer candidates primarily from the youth of the working class and poor peasantry. The army focused its search for officer candidates on its enlisted ranks. This recruiting policy clearly indicates that the very rational desire for political reliability came before efficiency.

Ideally, the army sought to train officers in a three-tiered military education system. The first level consisted of military schools, the second of short courses of specialized instruction for officers of several years experience. The highest tier was the academy level where officers were sent to get several years of instruction in technical or tactical matters. All three levels provided not just opportunities for training but also for instilling or reinforcing military values and breaking down barriers between party-recruited and army-recruited officer candidates.

Each branch of the armed services had its own military schools. For the infantry and cavalry the course of study lasted three years. For other branches, training spanned four years, although, after 1928 the curriculum was usually condensed sometimes to as few as eighteen months. The curriculum consisted of military and general education subjects. To qualify for a military school, applicants had to be from seventeen to twenty-five years of age, be recommended by two people of authority, preferably Communist Party members, be physically fit, and have a general education of at least seven years. Any of these requirements could be waived, and the army, until the late 1930s, was forced to settle mostly for young men with approximately four years' education – provided they could pass the entrance examination.

The advanced courses that comprised the second level of officer education trained officers on new equipment. After completing the courses, officers returned to their regiments to pass on what they had learned. Other courses attempted to upgrade military performance primarily of the higher ranking officers who had had little or no military education but had achieved their rank during the Civil War. After 1929, academies also became sources of commission. There the student officers received technical schooling in such fields as medicine, electrical engineering, veterinary medicine, armored warfare, artillery, engineering, aviation, and chemistry, to name the most prominent. The Frunze Academy, the only academy to provide advanced instruction on tactics and staff skills, never became a source of commission.

The acquisition of higher military instruction by the officers was very uneven in the Red Army's initial years, but grew year by year. The most revealing statistic on military education and expertise is that in 1935 half of the corps and division commanders possessed some higher military education, though regiment commanders lagged behind at only 15 percent.[17] The Red Army exhibited justified pride in this level of military training, considering it virtually started from scratch in a generally uneducated population. Nonetheless, it is far from impressive in comparison to Western armies, which normally had all their higher officers trained in advanced military schools, and this after a complete secondary education and often university training or its equivalent.

To extend its influence over and ensure the creation of a class–conscious and loyal army the party manipulated the social composition of the officer corps. In doing so, the Central Committee decreed, in March 1928, that 50 percent of students in military schools were to be from the working class. In February 1929, it increased the requirement to 60 percent. This was to be done by drawing in young workers, party members and Komsomols, and classifying poor peasants as workers. The army succeeded in increasing the number of students of working class origins in military schools to the decreed 60 percent or more, but it failed to increase the representation of workers in the officer corps to a similar level because the RKKA consistently com-missioned officers by means other than military schools. Commissioning officers outside the military school system invariably produced a large peasant contingent. For example, in 1933, workers represented 63.1 percent of all students in military school, but only 43.5 percent of all army officers. The number of workers rose slightly to 44.2 percent in 1936.[18]

The party sought to increase its membership among officers as another way to extend control over the army. In 1926 fewer than half of all officers were party members. Subsequently, the percentage of communist officers rose steadily. The party accomplished this primarily by recruiting officers into the party. The party also did intensive work among the several thousand *voenspetsy* who had been allowed to stay on, and by 1930 over half of those still in the army had joined the party.[19]

Beginning in 1925, trusted unit commanders were allowed the privilege of *edinonachalie* and by the early 1930s all commanders had *edinonachalie*. Even after all unit commanders had sole command commissars remained, but only to oversee political affairs. Commanders and their commissars occasionally became close friends. Sometimes commissars proved to be irritating to unit commanders, especially when they overstepped their political duties and pre-sumed to involve themselves in military activities, yet they had a vested interest in the performance of the unit. If something went wrong, serious enough for the commander to be punished, the commissar often got the axe as well. As Timothy Colton has pointed out, the system was set up to foster mutual dependence and cooperation, yet the possibility for friction existed if the leaders' personalities clashed.[20]

The occasional differences between commissars and officers did not seem to negatively affect the outlook of officers toward the party. Indeed, party membership among officers grew at a steady rate throughout the 1920s and 1930s. Some officers joined out of belief in the party and the Revolution, others as an opportunistic move to further their careers. The higher the military rank, the greater the frequency of membership in the party proved to be. Party membership did not necessarily come before promotion, but because a commissar also had to sign promotion orders, the potential to use party membership as an incentive existed. Some men perceived that swift and high promotion came only with party membership. Whether a party member used his membership for personal gain depended on personality, yet the very existence of alternate avenues of success available only to a few created in-group out-group situations. Back-stabbing and petty quarrels could occur with more serious consequences than in apolitical bureaucratic organizations.[21]

The Red Army officer corps, despite the meritorious service rendered by thousands, suffered four major problems from 1928 to 1941 that would negatively affect its performance in battle: a crippling shortage of officers; an inability to retain many of the officers it did recruit; poor discipline among officers; and an inability to raise the level of competence of the officer corps as a whole. Time after time training and even combat operations, were bungled because the same things went wrong, suggesting that a great many Soviet officers did not become experts at their jobs and were neither externally nor internally motivated to become so.

In 1926, the RVS discharged 16,000 officers and PUR personnel. This, the last of the massive post-Civil War dismissals of officers and political personnel, heralded the beginning of the Red Army's continual shortage of leaders. In 1928, the army had 45,867 regular officers in the line units. That same year, in a speech to the Sixteenth Party Conference, Voroshilov spoke of recruiting more leaders and asked the party to make manning military schools a top priority.[22] The next year found Voroshilov pushing for still more officers.

The Central Committee agreed that there were not enough officers to provide adequate leadership and ordered the number of military education facilities to be increased. In 1930, the army put together a report showing its current strength in officers, its needs through 1933, and a plan for meeting those needs. The report identified a current shortage of 3,103 officers and projected that, if no changes were made in recruiting, the army would be short 8,600 officers in 1931, and 11,300 in 1932, but, if its plan were followed, the ground forces would have a surplus of some 1,100 officers in 1933. This was a very ambitious plan, because in the preceding three years the army had only managed to grow by about 3,000 officers each year.[23]

The basis of the shortage, as stated in the report, was the creation of new units. To meet these needs the RKKA counted on the military schools to graduate 6,850 new platoon commanders in 1931, over 10,000 in 1932 and more than 15,000 in 1933. In addition several thousand reservists would be called to active duty and several hundred NCOs assigned to serve in officer posts. All this was predicated on the assumption that no new units would be created after 1932.[24] The Commissariat of Defense then launched a campaign to increase the recruitment of officer candidates to military schools to quadruple the number it had as of 1930. This proved to be an impossible task.

The essential difficulty in recruiting was that the Soviet peasant/worker society did not readily provide willing career officers. There was no tradition of professional, long-term, voluntary military service among the masses because before the Revolution careers as military officers were accessible only to a small segment of the population. Service as an enlisted man was old hat and unpopular, but the broad peasant and worker masses had no frame of reference for service as an officer. Consequently, recruiting volunteers to the officer corps proved to be very difficult. The Soviet high command did not understand the depth of this problem, causing it to miscalculate its ability to recruit officer candidates. Consequently, not once during the 1930s did the RKKA meet its goals in recruiting to military schools, and in 1931, abandoned its plans and, under pressure of circumstances, proceeded to deviate greatly from its ideal process of officer training.

In response to the army's request for help in increasing the number of officers, the Central Committee, also in 1931, ordered that party organizations make a special effort to recruit communists into the ranks of the officer corps. "Special mobilizations," reminiscent of the party's handling of Civil War personnel crises, thereafter became regular occurrences in the 1930s. The party sent many young communists and Komsomols directly to military schools and academies as part of their obligation to the party. Between 1931 and 1935 approximately 27,000 specially mobilized party members and Komsomols became students in the military school system. In the process of absorbing the party members curricula were shortened from three years to eighteen months. This resulted in a lower quality of training and cohesion. In 1933 Voroshilov admitted, "In general the training of the commanding personnel is not as good as it ought to be."[25] Simultaneously, the army renewed its efforts to recruit leaders from within its enlisted and non-commissioned officer ranks for military schools. The majority of those who stepped forward were party members or Komsomols. For its part, in the course of 1931 and 1932, PUR transferred 1,244 political workers into the military. In a move that completely contradicted its manning needs, the army transferred 2,500 officers and 500 NCOs to PUR to serve as political leaders, negating PUR's transfers to the military.[26]

Unfortunately, the army's and party's efforts failed. The four years after 1933 represent the worst years for recruiting officer candidates – the military schools produced only 23,217 officers. The many men who left the service further aggravated the officer shortage. Between 1928 and 1938, the army lost 62,000 officers either because of death, injury, judicial action, or simply quitting the service for civilian life. The army transferred another 5,670 officers from the ground forces to the air force. Nearly 200 more men left the ground forces than were produced by the military schools in the same years.[27]

Although many outstanding officers mastered their responsibilities or even showed brilliance in tactical or strategic command of troops they were the exception. The larger the army grew the further the level of basic military skill declined, until, by the outbreak of war, the truly capable leaders and thinkers had been so thinly spread among the fighting divisions and regiments that they could in most cases make only a temporary and local contribution to the national defense. More prevalent was a deep-seated lack of concern for raising standards and self-improvement on the part of officers. Their lack of responsibility affected all areas of military life, but nowhere was it more harmful than in training, and the health and welfare of the men. For example, in 1927, officer irresponsibility reached such proportions at one summer camp that a general order was issued to address it. The camp commander noted that only small numbers of soldiers attended training, and that many of the officers and political personnel were absent, having sneaked into a nearby town to consort with whores. His general order required commanders to keep track of their personnel and supervise their units. Finally, he forbade officers to go to town without permission and promised dire consequences for infringements.[28] That officers had to be ordered to be at their posts and to know what their men were up to is appalling. Such behavior continued throughout the 1930s.

Besides incompetence, criminal activity among officers manifested itself at an astoundingly high rate. The most frequently reported crime committed by an officer was the embezzlement of pay and unit funds. The military press published only a few select crimes each week, but between 1925 and 1929, a week seldom passed in which military tribunals did not sentence to either death or imprisonment at least one officer.[29] The most frequently abused position in these years was that of supply company commander. The item most often stolen for sale was fodder, but even weapons and ammunition were illegally sold to civilians. Economic crimes began to taper off to be replaced primarily by crimes committed under the influence of alcohol. The party cited drunkenness and drunken debauchery as reasons for arrest or expulsion for a large number of officers in the early 1930s. The occasional, but never ending, murders of or by officers, suicides, AWOLs, and desertions kept the Special Sections busy. Misdemeanors and crimes by officers often numbered in the hundreds at the corps level on an annual basis.

It was bad enough that officers conducted themselves unprofessionally on military bases, but it did not stop there. Officers often acted irresponsibly off duty. Their behavior reflected the low social origins of the new breed of Red commanders. By far the most pervasive problem of the officer corps to negatively affect the performance of its members and taint the public impression of Red Army officers was alcohol abuse. Public drunkenness of officers of all ranks in and out of garrison, alone or in groups, and even in the company of enlisted men was a never ending plague on the officer corps. The army regularly cashiered incurable or unrepentant alcoholics. The negative effects this behavior had on soldiers' morale is incalculable.

Part of the responsibility for such aberrant behavior must lie in the recruitment of officers. Because the army was short of officers, it was not choosey about recruits – not that military commissions let in known criminals. One advantage of the military school system was its ability to weed out ne'er-do-wells. Unfortunately quite a number of men did not go through this system, therefore the army could not closely scrutinize the characters of candidates until after commissioning.

When one considers how Red Army officers lived, their pay, and their treatment in relation to leaders in other sectors of society, it becomes clearer why the military had trouble attracting and keeping leaders. In December 1926, in a speech to the senior officers of the Moscow Military District, Voroshilov admitted that officers did endure substandard living conditions and hinted that they would not get much better in the near future. Not surprisingly, many men chose to leave the army of their own will to seek better employment. The voluntary request of officers to be released from active duty because of some disaffection with the army constituted the single greatest cause for discharge before the purge. The RKKA lost a good number of trained and educated men every year – men who thought they could do better elsewhere, or because they proved to be unsuitable physically or morally – all told between 1925 and 1936, 47,000 officers voluntarily and by compulsion left the army.[30]

Low pay may have been a cause for some to leave. Pay differed for the various branches of the RKKA; artillery and engineer officers and air force pilots received higher pay than infantry officers. Not until 1934 did an infantry platoon commander make more than a blue-collar worker. Thus, it is not surprising that the factory floor may have looked more appealing to young men than a hard military life. Factory foremen and supervisory personnel earned slightly more money than officers in the 1920s and early 1930s. During the First Five-Year Plan wages for supervisory personnel and technicians rose dramatically. In 1934, factory foremen could make from 250 to 350 rubles a month – equivalent to the pay of a rifle battalion commander – and supervisors could make from 450 to 650 rubles a month, the wages of division and corps commanders. Industrial wages went up again in 1935 keeping them ahead of military pay raises.[31] Service-related expenses further diminished officers' pay. Unlike enlisted men, they had to provide their own uniforms and food, as well as furnish their quarters. Some uniform items, such as boots, could cost as much as 400 rubles. Clearly, for many years the Soviet state put more stock in industry and in its workers than it put in the military and its leadership. Unfortunately for the military, potential officers understood the state's priorities all too well.

Poor housing for officers also hurt the image of the Red Army and may have hindered its ability to recruit and retain good men. In 1931, for example, the RKKA could not provide nearly 5,000 of its officers with military quarters. In the Leningrad Military District some officers lived in their offices because there simply were not enough quarters, and civilian housing was also hard to get. Officers with families expressed considerable anger and anguish over the plight of their wives and children. The married officers of the Ukrainian Military District complained that two families had to share a two- or three-room apartment. They also claimed the facilities for their children, such as day-care, kindergartens and playgrounds, were inadequate. In 1931, the Moscow garrison could not provide 1,730 officers and their families with quarters and another 529 had what the army classified as "bad" quarters.[32] That officers and their wives complained so bitterly indicates that they expected to live better. They were not appeased by the knowledge that civilians often lived under identical conditions.

What housing existed was often in a pitiful state. In some garrisons even the living quarters for senior officers were overcrowded and dilapidated. Throughout the entire interwar period officers complained bitterly about substandard accommodations. A 1932 *Krasnaia zvezda* article described officers' housing of an aviation brigade thus: "The officers' apartment house is in a dilapidated state; the plaster is coming down, and the doors and windows do not shut properly; and no sink is provided for a block of three buildings."[33] This was typical of officers' housing. In a letter to the military press, an officer complained that the officers' quarters in his garrison had no running water. The previous winter, officers, their families, and enlisted men had crammed into the soldiers' barracks together, because officers had no separate quarters. Overcrowding required that even classrooms be used for sleeping spaces. It was not unusual for housing to have insufficient heat or even none at all, which in a Russian winter was a real health hazard.[34] Because the overall quality of life for the officer corps was often lower than that of the equivalent sector in civilian society, it is not surprising that people were reluctant to take the responsibility of defending a society that would not provide them even basic comforts.

Housing conditions may have affected the composition of the officer corps in that they influenced who stayed on for a career. Opportunities for upward mobility abounded for educated men during the interwar period causing many to leave the army for other work and better conditions while others, not educated enough for civilian work, became officers – no matter what the conditions – to get educations, which, ironically, they hoped would enable them to improve their lives. The poor peasants and young workers recruited to the officer corps were more likely to be forgiving of bad conditions rather than mobilized urban party workers or students who had greater opportunities out of the service.

In a belated acknowledgement of its personnel problem the RKKA made a concerted effort to enhance the social status of its leaders. The army, in 1935, raised officers' pay, came out with dress uniforms, allowed officers the privilege of being tried by military courts for civil infractions, and brought into use many tsarist titles of rank. The reason for the changes was simple; the regime needed to make a career in the armed forces more appealing in order to recruit more officers. This is not to suggest that all the changes were merely a recruiting ploy. There had long been a movement within the military stressing the acquisition of the trappings of a professional military, it just took a crisis in manning for this movement finally to bear fruit.

The introduction of personal titles of rank meant that an officer kept his rank until promoted to the next higher rank. In the previous system duty positions had titles, which were a form of rank. Not only did positions have titles, but they also had insignia to identify them. When an officer received a new duty position, he took the title and insignia of that position. With the introduction of ranks, an officer kept his rank until promoted, no matter his position, which was the practice in European armies and had been the practice in the Imperial Army. Henceforth, an officer could only be deprived of his rank by court-martial, confirmed by the Commissar of Defense. The length of service before promotion was now formally regulated and the rules for retirement clarified. Like their aristocratic predecessors, some Red Army officers began to see themselves as a caste separate from society at large – just as the military opposition had feared in 1918.

The leadership catastrophe on the eve of the Second World War: purge and expansion

In June 1937, Stalin, with the consent of the Politburo and People's Commissar of Defense, ordered the arrest of eight high-ranking army officers (Mikhail Tukhachevskii, Iona Iakir, Ian Gamarnik, Ieronim Uborevich, Avgust Kork, Sangurskii, Boris Fel'dman, and Robert Eideman (two others, Vitaly Primakov and Vitovt Putna, had been under arrest since February 1937) on charges of treason. The charges may have been based on falsified documents leaked to Soviet intelligence by the Nazis, or perhaps were due to other fears of Stalin's of a military plot against him. The full story is still unknown. In the ten days after the trials and subsequent execution of these men (except Gamarnik who committed suicide) 980 more officers and political workers were arrested.[35] Three of five marshals were executed, as were fifteen of sixteen army commanders first and second rank, sixty of sixty-seven corps commanders, and 136 of 199 division commanders. All seventeen army commissars first and second rank were killed as were twenty-five of twenty-nine corps commissars, representing without a doubt, a serious loss of talent, expertise, and experience. All told, by May 1940, 22,705 army, air force and PUR leaders remained discharged after either arrest or expulsion from the party. The number of enlisted men arrested and discharged is still unknown.[36]

Even as the terror purge, known as the *Ezhovshchina* after Nikolai Ezhov who at the time headed the Peoples' Commissariat of Internal Affairs (NKVD, originally *Cheka*), unfolded, myth and misunderstanding about its scope and impact were in the making. Until recently it had been accepted that the purge may have swept up to half of the officer corps into the camps or the grave and that the army was subsequently unable to physically or psychologically recover before the German invasion of 1941. The Soviet Army, in particular, pushed this interpretation thereby casting responsibility for its disastrous early performance in the Second World War onto Stalin's shoulders and escaping scrutiny and blame for its role in the greatest calamity in the history of the USSR. The true casualties of the *Ezhovshchina* are not the old estimate of 35,000 officers out of 70,000, but 22,705 army, air force and PUR personnel out of 206,000.[37] Numerically the armed forces made up its purge losses before the purge ended. The depth of the psychological suffering may not have been as great as supposed either, given that the officers and men, the military procuracy, and the high command of the RKKA willingly, and most probably with clean consciences, participated in a process of personal and institutional conformity and adaptation that predated the terror which resulted in the denunciations necessary for the *Ezhovshchina* to have taken on the scale it did.

Not only are the numbers of officers and political leaders lost during the *Ezhovshchina* lower than originally thought, but there were also far fewer arrests. Previously all officers repressed in 1937 and 1938 were thought to have been arrested by the Special Sections. Now, archival evidence suggests that the NKVD arrested 9,506 officers and PUR men, or less than half of all those repressed: 6,300 on its initiative, and 3,177 officers, commissars, and *politruki* at the army's instigation. Of the nearly 3,200 arrests ordered by the army 1,713 were for politically related crimes, and 1,464 for other crimes relating to military service and just plain criminal behavior such as drunkenness, hooliganism, abuse of power, murder and other assorted crimes commonly associated with the officer corps.[38] We do not know how many officers were executed, but certainly not all those arrested were killed – several thousand were released and rehabilitated after May 1940. The remaining 13,000 victims of the *Ezhovshchina* were discharged from the service in disgrace for having been expelled from the party. Some of these men may subsequently have been arrested – how many is unknown.

The majority of the victims of the purge were repressed as a result of the actions of their fellow officers and soldiers in primary party organizations who, in orgies of denunciations well beyond Moscow's control, independently expelled thousands of officers for their associations with "enemies of the people" and foreigners. The army almost always subsequently discharged expelled officers. The processes of arrest, expulsion, and discharge became interrelated, making the *Ezhovshchina* seem more pervasive and bloody than it was. And yet it was not completely out of control. All told, 34,300 military and political officers had been discharged between 1937 and 1939, but 11,596 had been reinstated to their posts and the party after successfully appealing their dismissals. In fact appeals commissions were set up in the military districts at the time they were purged.

Because the Red Army stepped up officer procurement during the *Ezhovshchina* at a rate that outpaced discharges, the ground forces actually had more officers at the end of the purge – 179,00 at the end of 1938 – than at the beginning – 162,000 in June 1937. The same situation holds true for the Red Air Force and PUR. The air force had approximately 13,000 officers in 1937, lost 4,724 in the purge, and numbered about 60,000 officers in 1940. PUR began 1937 with about 31,000 personnel, lost 5,000 in the terror, and grew to 34,000 in 1939.[39]

The actual process of the *Ezhovshchina* points to a less terrifying experience than has so far come down historically. Orders to the military districts to clean the army of enemies were preceded by a letter from Voroshilov to be read to all servicemen and units, and an article in *Krasnaia zvezda* on 14 June 1937. In his letter Voroshilov denounced Gamarnik, Tukhachevskii, *et al.* saying, "The enemy was able by means of bribery, blackmail, provocation, and fraud to entangle in its criminal nets these morally-lapsed putrescent people who forgot their duty and transformed themselves into outright agents of German-Japanese fascism." He implied that there could be others when next he wrote, "And we can also not be certain that they have given up all their confederates and accomplices."[40] The article in *Krasnaia zvezda* called on all army party organs to assist the NKVD in "exposing enemies of the people." Therefore, denouncing enemies in one's unit became a patriotic and honorable deed and presumably if a man turned out to be innocent he would be reinstated. Officially, the RKKA claimed it was bolstered by the purge of fascist-Trotskyite traitors, which enabled it to promote young, loyal, and deserving communist and non-party officers.

What happened during the *Ezhovshchina* was that the process of cleaning the army of "enemies of the people" turned into an informal but deadly party membership purge or *chistka*. Party cells now looked for enemies of the people in addition to politically errant, morally corrupt, or incompetent individuals and therefore, Communist Party members suffered the most. People of high rank and responsibility (overwhelmingly party members) bore the brunt of the purge. When associations with such people became grounds for expulsion and discharge, their associates, other party members and ranking officers, became vulnerable to terror and expulsion. Prior to June 1937, servicemen expelled from the party as a rule only lost their party cards, but, during the *Ezhovshchina*, they were most often discharged from the military becoming potential candidates for arrest.

Belief in the veracity of the charges leveled against people emanated from the highest levels. Aleksandr I. Egorov, commander – along with Voroshilov and Stalin – of the Southwest Front RVS in the war with Poland, and in 1937 deputy Commissar of Defense and candidate member of the Central Committee, seems to have sincerely believed in the guilt of the ten men he authorized Stalin to have arrested in December 1937. In the name of the Politburo, Stalin sent a top secret memorandum to Egorov asking for authorization to arrest ten Central Committee members, including Andrei Bubnov (head of PUR from 1924 to 1929) on charges of being German spies. The accused had supposedly confessed their crimes, though Stalin presented Egorov with no evidence. In the left margin of the note Egorov wrote, "All these reprobates . . . are to be wiped off the face of the earth as the lowest possible scum and disgusting filth."[41] Egorov continued blithely along at his job until Stalin purged him too.

Whence the credulity? Historian Robert Thurston cites the existence of genuine Trotskyite circles in the USSR and a general fear and insecurity in the Bolshevik leadership. In the army, the average soldier and party member had the blessing and encouragement of the Commissar of Defense and the great Stalin himself. Politburo member Nikita Khrushchev, PUR Chief Lev Mekhlis, and other top officials personally supervised the purge of military districts. Who were their underlings, common soldiers, and officers to question them? But most important, the *Ezhovshchina* was not out of character for the army and party which had been purging communists and non-communists in large numbers for years.

On the one hand there is no doubt that the NKVD illegally circumvented the military judicial system and then proceeded to act arbitrarily in administratively arresting without proper authorization, and then torturing, killing, and imprisoning thousands of officers, but on the other hand the army prepared the way for this. From the beginning the army not only acknowledged the supremacy of the Communist Party, but embraced it and the political and social order it was creating – the army was the party's child. The army itself, in conformity with the growing Stalinization of society, in 1931 established the precedent of discharging soldiers and officers for political deviance. In that year the military procuracy discharged 883 officers for political considerations. None, however, were arrested.[42]

In the party purge of 1933–34 the party deprived 3,328 officers and men of their party cards. Of them, 555 were Trotskyites and of those 555 the army discharged 400. Another 244 former Trotskyites and former Zinov'evites also lost their party cards. Between 1934 and 1937 army party organs expelled another seven hundred former Trotskyites, former Zinov'evites and other "rightists." In February 1937, Voroshilov reported to the Central Committee that between 1934 and 1936 the RKKA had discharged 22,000 men, of whom 5,000 were oppositionists of all sorts – equivalent to the number of men discharged during the *Ezhovshchina* – though no one has ever made a fuss of this.[43] The army, then, had tacitly agreed years before the purge that politically unsuitable officers should be expelled and either arrested or discharged, and that it would lend a hand, even take a leading role, in the process. The RKKA gradually but surely fell into line with the trend in civil society to hunt for wreckers, diversionists, spies, Trotskyites and so on.

During 1937, 10,341 military party members were expelled from the Communist Party, yet at the same time 23,599 officers and men gained admittance to the party. The party admitted over 100,000 soldiers and officers in 1938; more than 10,000 joined the party in the first month of 1939.[44] A great many people appear to have retained faith in the party as a positive force, or at least as a means for personal advancement. Thus the *Ezhovshchina* did not alienate the army from the party and suggests a lower level of psychological trauma than heretofore believed.

In August 1937, concurrent with the onset of the *Ezhovshchina*, the Commissariat of Defense reinstituted dual command at regiment level and higher. Now, just as during the Civil War, all military orders had to be countersigned by a commissar. In early 1938, the NKO re-established collegial leadership at army and corps level by creating military soviets of the commander, chief of staff and a commissar (the same membership of the RVSes of the Civil War). Along with dual command and military soviets, PUR created two new political positions: deputy political instructor (*zamestitel' politruk*), to assist the platoon commander; and assistant political instructor (*pomeshchnik politruk*), to assist the company *politruk*. These measures were designed to enable PUR to do more political training, bolster discipline at the company level, and to safeguard the army from treason from within.

The Soviet military, in the post-Stalin years, claimed that the reimposition of dual command hamstrung the army and put it under the control of the political organs, but, as Timothy Colton has shown, this suggestion does not hold up well to close scrutiny. The terms of dual command officially were, "The military commissar answers together with the commander for all spheres of the military, political, and economic life of the unit."[45] Therefore, if anything went wrong, the commissar stood to be included in any punishment. Before dual command the commissar could not be blamed for a unit's shortcomings in strictly military matters. Dual command, then, gave the commissar added authority, but it also made him responsible for results and vulnerable for failure. That commissars had been executed during the Civil War for a unit's failure was well known to the commissars of the 1930s. It behooved them to support the unit commander as best they could and it seems most did. In many cases commissars just signed whatever the unit commander asked of them, trusting the commander not to get them both in trouble. One commissar justified the rubber stamping of his commander's orders saying, "Why should the commissar worry about the plans for combat training? This is the unit commander's business. The commissar has enough work without it."[46]

Whether the army returned to "normal" or not after 1938 is an open question. The scars on the psyche of the army remained at least as long as Stalin was alive. Some officers retained physical and emotional scars from their interrogations and imprisonment despite their rehabilitation, and no doubt a certain inhibition characterized their actions thereafter.[47] But neither did the army stop in its tracks, and its failure to overcome the dysfunctions of the pre-purge years does not permit the assumption that those problems would have been cured had there been no purge.

Transition from the mixed system to an all standing army, combined with further expansion and the purge in 1938, created a new crisis in officer manning – a crisis that could be resolved by neither normal nor extra-ordinary recruiting methods. For at least a year before the onslaught of the *Ezhovshchina* many officers held positions normally reserved for men at least one or often two ranks higher. Many majors instead of colonels commanded regiments, numerous captains rather than majors commanded battalions, and lieutenants and senior lieutenants commanded companies, batteries and squadrons in place of captains. In maneuvers held in September 1936, only four of eighteen brigade- and larger-sized units had commanders of the appropriate rank. All the others were commanded by officers with ranks at least one level below the authorized rank.[48] The creation of scores of new divisions and separate brigades created thousands of posts to which officers had to be reassigned from their current posts. The increase of new assign-ments over four years contributed to upward and lateral mobility, as well as overall instability in officer assignments in units. In 1936, nearly 38,000 officers were reassigned due to promotion or first duty assignment. In 1938 it leapt to 143,000, and in 1939 to over 198,000.[49] The large number of new assignments and reassignments illustrate that the instability in officer assignments was not due solely to the purge. Not including reinstatement of purged officers, at most 23,500 officers would have had to have been reassigned to cover the losses of the *Ezhovshchina*. The army's creation of new units and the termination of the territorial system contributed most to this phenomenon.

Despite its creative use of *ad hoc* commissioning processes the army never achieved its full complement of officers before the war because it continued to expand and officers continued to leave the army at a steady rate. By 1937, to lead adequately the 1.3 million men in the regular army, the RKKA needed at least 117,000 combat arms officers, but the army had only 107,000 officers for the line units. At the end of 1938 the army was short 93,000 officers. One-quarter of the shortfall was due to the purge, the rest was caused by the increased requirement for officers resulting from the creation of new units during the year.[50]

To address the shortfall the Commissariat of Defense, in August 1937, when the purge began picking up steam, ordered each military district and separate army to set up special short courses for training noncommissioned officers to become junior lieutenants (*mladshie leitenanty*). The courses were to last from 15 September 1937 to 15 January 1938. What Voroshilov had intended as a one-time event soon became institutionalized for the simple reason that the army's continued growth outpaced the output of military schools. Well after January 1938, these short courses continued to turn out *mladshie leitenanty* every three to six months. Other NCOs became junior lieutenants simply by examination and were offered no extra training. In exceptional cases, as the pace of expansion quickened, noncommissioned officers were given company commands. As a result of expansion, intensive recruitment of NCOs for the officer corps, and the army's failure to re-enlist large numbers of noncommissioned officers, the army also created for itself a shortage of NCOs and resorted to allowing second-year privates to lead squads. True to form, the regiments gave these men no special training in preparation for their duties.[51]

In March 1938, the NKO officially shortened the course of instruction in military schools for training officer candidates from three to two years. This merely acknowledged a practice that had been in effect for several years. Simultaneously, the RKKA raised entrance requirements. The shortened duration of schooling from three to two years, or even more commonly to eighteen months, reduced the quality and quantity of instruction. This is especially important considering that the army intended military schools to be institutions of higher education, not simply courses in particular military skills. To assist in filling these schools, the party conducted another "special mobilization" in 1937, which netted thousands more non-volunteer communist and Komsomol officers. In 1938–39 the army asked for 210,000 new officers, of them the NKO wanted 85,455 to be school-trained officers.[52] As it turns out, military schools produced only about 63,000 officers in stark contrast to the 1930 plan to produce an officer corps trained and commissioned entirely through the military school system.

Part of the problem with quality was the magnitude of the task given to the military schools. In the ten years, 1928–37, the entire military school system had commissioned 67,487 officers for the ground forces. In the following two years, 1938–39, they commissioned an astounding 62,800 officers. This was done partly by increasing class sizes, which reduced the effectiveness of instruction, and by creating new schools, which invariably had difficulty establishing themselves due to shortages of instructors, weapons, billets, office and classroom buildings and prepared training areas.[53]

Despite efforts to raise competence through schooling, military proficiency continued to suffer partly because of the increasingly short time officers spent in assignments. In the 1920s and early 1930s, a unit commander might have held his position for anywhere between four and eight years. But, during expansion, commanders were rapidly promoted to higher commands with less time at each level. By mid-1938 the average regiment commander was between the ages of twenty-nine and thirty-three. Before expansion, this had been the average age for battalion commanders. The youth and inexperience of the commanders surely affected their ability to train and lead their subordinates.

Even as the Red Army began to engage in armed conflict in the opening rounds of the Second World War against the Japanese at Khalkin-Gol, eastern Poland, and Finland, the high command's one response to the

USSR's defense needs and territorial ambitions was to make the armed forces larger, not recognizing that the previous ten years of expansion was the source of so many of its problems. The ensuing measures to increase the quality of the armed forces all failed. Already by the summer of 1939 the RKKA had grown too large to be effectively managed, led, trained, and equipped at the prescribed pace with the resources available.

5

THE RED ARMY AND THE
SECOND WORLD WAR, 1939–45

By 1939, Stalin was acutely aware of the German threat – he took the oath
of the Red Army soldier in February showing his solidarity with the troops.
Distrusting the western democracies after the appeasement at Munich, Stalin
sought to buy time to prepare for the expected clash of arms by signing the
Nazi–Soviet Nonaggression Pact in August. Stalin seriously believed he
could both avoid war with Hitler and completely rearm and man the Red
Army to war strength by the end of 1942. Beginning in 1939, Stalin threw
as much of the Soviet economy into arms production as he dared. Between
1 January 1939 and 22 June 1941 the army created 111 infantry divisions and
scores of tank divisions and increased its manpower by three million men for
a total of 198 infantry divisions, sixty-one tank divisions and thirteen cavalry
divisions. This vast growth coincided with the introduction of new equipment, making training and small unit leadership more important than ever.
The RKKA pursued expansion in 1939, and thereafter, at a frantic pace.
As it grew, the army inconsistently changed unit organization and reshuffled
its leaders, creating a great deal of confusion, instability and systemic incoher-
ence. In sum, the Red Army's last minute attempts to become a bigger fighting force in fact made it less capable of performing its missions.

The maladies the army experienced in the interwar period became magnified with the Red Army's entrance into the Second World War in 1939. By
mid-1939, the shortcomings had reached crisis proportions: officer procurement and training were in a terrible state; discipline in the ranks and among
officers worsened; the ability to provide housing deteriorated steadily; and
conducting individual and unit training became an ever greater challenge.
The increased pace and scale of expansion further complicated matters. With
its recent territorial expansion additional crises arose: the Red Army now had
new boundaries to defend; the experience of war and larger forces called for
a crash rearmament program; and the new armaments and territory forced
re-evaluations of doctrine that resulted in no consistent or definitive solu-
tions. These crises overlapped, creating a situation beyond the control not
only of the high command, but also of company and platoon commanders.

Nevertheless, the USSR won the war against Nazi Germany and became a military superpower in the process. In dealing with the experience of "The Great Patriotic War", which Stalin quickly labeled the fight with the Germans, this chapter is concerned primarily with the experience of war for the army as an organization and the individual participants rather than on strategy, tactics, weaponry, or great battles of which numerous volumes are available to the reader. Here we will see popular attitudes to the armed forces change for the better and a broad-based – though not universal – willingness on the part of the Soviet peoples to support the war effort.

May 1939–June 1941

Up to 1939 Tukhachevskii's PU-36 was the doctrine guiding Red Army organization and training. It emphasized offensive action by large mechanized forces maneuvering for advantage against the enemy. In support of this doctrine the army had consistently been adding tanks and artillery to its inventory. Subsequently, Stalin helped write (perhaps directed) *Draft Field Regulations of 1939* (PU-39) in which he stipulated three "regulations." The regulations were that: any enemy attack against the Union of Soviet Socialist Republics was to be met by a crushing blow of the entire strength of the Armed Forces; if the enemy forced the USSR into war, the Workers' and Peasants' Red Army would act more aggressively than any army that ever existed; the USSR would conduct an offensive war, carrying it into enemy territory.[1] PU-39 then, does not seem to have been a big change from the principles of PU-36, but to support the offensive doctrine the Red Army needed still more tanks, aircraft, and artillery.

The rate at which the state and army sought to create mechanized units and produce the necessary armored vehicles created serious problems as did the indecision over the priority of distribution of armor. Initially the army assigned individual tank battalions to infantry divisions, and disbanded the few mechanized corps in early 1939 in contradiction to PU-36. As a result of the fall of France in June 1940 and the impressive success of Germany's panzer forces the General Staff reversed its decision and for the first time authorized the formation of armored divisions. The army acted slowly on this decision, however, and did not begin to organize the majority of its armored forces until spring 1941, far too late for them to equip, train sufficiently, or develop unit cohesion before the German invasion. At the end of 1940, the Red Army was organizing eighteen tank divisions, by June 1941 it had sixty-one. At the beginning of the war the majority of the tank units were not yet at full strength in either men or vehicles. Likewise, equipping new artillery units with tractors in place of horses, especially those of mechanized and motorized divisions, proved to be impossible because the army created units faster than it could supply them.[2]

Expansion put strains not only on personnel but also on equipment requirements. By creating so many divisions, the army actually hampered its modernization program. The original idea had been to replace aged and obsolete equipment and weapons with modern weapons and equipment, but because there were so many new units, the old materiel could not be discarded. Instead it remained in use, often mixed with the new equipment, creating a host of logistical and training difficulties. Some units had special problems in 1940 as a result of their participation in the war with Finland. They were badly in need of all items of supply due to combat losses and exceptional wear and tear. Some divisions suffered severe shortages of ordinary gear such as boots and greatcoats for many weeks, which greatly impeded training and caused morale to plummet.[3]

To meet manpower requirements the army expanded conscription and continued to man most units at only half strength. The state passed a new military service law in 1940 increasing the length of conscripted service from two to three years. The army encouraged women to volunteer for non-combat units and by the end of 1940 one thousand had. Finally, the army recalled tens of thousands of reservists in August 1939. That same year Voroshilov ordered the 1.4 million army to take in another 1.6 million men but discharge only 600,000 by August 1940. The army exceeded this plan and had 3.4 million men under arms by July 1940 even though in May, Voroshilov and the new Commissar of Defense Marshal Semion K. Timoshenko had both recommended a reduction in the size of the armed forces. In May 1941, the army called up 800,000 reservists. Despite these huge additions of manpower many front-line divisions in western Russia remained at less than full strength in June 1941.

The calling up of reserves in an atmosphere of lingering resentment over collectivization and general abuse of the peasantry, resulted in widespread disobedience on the part of soldiers. Many of the reservists called to duty were in their thirties or forties, had established careers, and families. Being back in a private's uniform created tremendous resentment in many that resulted in breaches of discipline. Desertion was the most prevalent disciplinary infraction, but more serious were threats and attempts on the lives of officers. Both desertion and the desire to murder officers were linked to the soldiers' lack of confidence in their officers. The horrendous casualties suffered by the Red Army in Finland were common knowledge in the ranks and soldiers seem to have placed the blame for this on their officers. In late 1939 and early 1940, notification of a unit for transfer to the war in Finland would cause hundreds of soldiers and NCOs to desert overnight. The alert of the Kiev Special Military District to prepare to invade Bessarabia in June 1940 led to scores of threats to officers' lives and large-scale desertions. Several officers and NCOs were actually murdered by their men.[4]

To counteract a tidal wave of discipline problems the army enacted the Disciplinary Code of 1940. The rewritten definition of military discipline in

1940 made no mention of socialism or social-political duties. Instead, the army stressed unquestioning obedience to superiors and referred to Lenin's admonishment that, "Without discipline there is no army." The most important changes in the regulations made guardhouse confinement an unpleasant affair. Before the changes a stint in the guardhouse involved virtually no hardship: prisoners had bunks with sheets and mattresses and could sleep as much as they wanted. They frequently were allowed out on pass to go to movies and cultural events, could have friends visit, etc. Under the new guardhouse regulations, life in the guardhouse became harsh. Soldiers were allowed only six hours of sleep and had to sleep on the floor. Prisoners henceforth received only partial rations. The new disciplinary code also created penal labor battalions for men sentenced to two years or less for serious crimes and deprived soldiers of their long-standing right to file complaints against their commanders.[5]

In a campaign to bolster discipline military tribunals handed down stiffer sentences in 1939 and 1940. In 1939 the army executed 112 officers and men for their crimes and in 1940, 528. In 1940, 12,000 officers and soldiers were sentenced to serve in penal battalions. In 1939, military tribunals sentenced 2,283 servicemen to from three to five years in prison, and 17,000 in 1940. The number of men given more than five years in prison for their misdeeds also drastically increased in 1940 to 7,733 from only 812 in 1937.[6] It is not clear, however, whether the increased severity of punishment had the desired effect. The crisis in officer manning continued as the army expanded. The army kept creating more military schools, commissioning enlisted men as *mladshie leitenanty*, and calling up thousands of reserve officers, but the new units swallowed them up and begged for more. Simultaneously, the army lost more than 15,000 officers killed and missing in the conflicts in Mongolia, Poland, and Finland. At the beginning of 1940 the army had 60,000 officer positions vacant and went on to create scores of additional divisions. The leadership of the RKKA continued to be a very mixed lot. By 1941, most commanders of regiments and divisions had started their careers in the 1920s, were all volunteers, almost all were party members, and most of those who assumed division commands had a total of at least sixteen years' service. Many, but not all, were military school graduates, and had attended military academies. In comparison to European armies, most senior Soviet officers were promoted to high positions of responsibility at younger ages, with less experience and less military schooling.

A great many men who rose to positions higher than corps level before the war had revolutionary and political origins, as well as prior experience in the Imperial Army as soldiers or junior officers. Some spent many years in the military as commissars before becoming officers with little or no military training. It was the unusual general who had a well-rounded experience, with time in regiments, and staff experience at various levels. Despite the purge, the army had enough senior officers available to fill the top slots, although not all were prepared for their assignments. For example, in June 1941 all the military districts were commanded by generals who were veterans of the Civil War and had at least twenty years of military service.[7]

The most serious weakness in the Red Army officer corps was at the battalion and company levels where thorough tactical training and leadership skills were so vital in combat. These men were the least trained of the officer corps. The majority of new officers after 1936 were *mladshie leitenanty*, enlisted men plucked from the ranks and commissioned after a few months of instruction. By 1939, a significant number of company and even battalion commanders were senior lieutenants who had never commanded platoons. Never having been platoon commanders, the young company and battalion commanders of 1939–41 could not pass down lessons of experience to their platoon leaders, thus leaving a void in their training – a void Trotsky had prophetically warned against. When considering their sense of duty and professionalism one must take into account that in 1939 over half of all new officers began their careers as conscripts before going on to military schools or courses for noncommissioned officers. Add them to the thousands specially mobilized by the party and the Red Army ended up with most of its leaders serving by compulsion, that is to say it was a conscript officer corps at the rank of major and below. Many reserve officers avoided returning to service ignoring appeals from the Commissar of Defense. Compounding the problem of training, experience, and motivation was the frequent transfer of officers between established and newly formed divisions, which inhibited cohesion and stability.

Training did not improve to any great degree despite greater attention given to it by the high command. New field service regulations incorporating the lessons learned from the recent combat experiences of the Red Army were ordered drawn up, but somehow, through bureaucratism and institutional inertia, they never were. In 1940, the military districts on the USSR's western border each held large-scale maneuvers involving almost all their units yet the maneuvers lacked realism and there was little or no combined arms work. As usual, the generals gave the training of small units and individual soldiers low priority. After all was said and done, the RKKA was no better prepared for combat in June of 1941 than it had been when it invaded Poland in September 1939. Timoshenko himself admitted in 1940 that,

> We have spent a very long time in the classrooms, we have become accustomed to learning by verbal explanations, without bothering ourselves with the difficult conditions of a combat situation or difficult terrain conditions, in a word everything that rests on the shoulders of a fighter, commander and political worker during a war and in combat.[8]

Because of relocations westward, training was often cut short by the need to construct garrisons, training grounds, and defensive works.

In August 1940, dual command was once again abolished. Commissars reverted to their roles as head of unit political activities and no longer had to countersign orders of the unit commanders. *Edinonachalie* was completely restored making the commander fully in charge of all military and political affairs of his unit. The same order introduced the designation of deputy commander for political affairs (*zampolit*), which gradually replaced the term commissar. Military soviets, at corps level and higher, reinstituted in 1937, remained intact through the war.

Prior to the German invasion, the Red Army was able to test its mettle in combat during a battle with the Japanese at Khalkin-Gol in Mongolia from May to September 1939, in a two-week invasion of eastern Poland in September 1939, and in a winter war with Finland from 30 November 1939 to mid-March 1940. The RKKA prevailed in each of these clashes of arms but without particular distinction, and in the case of the war with Finland ended up being humiliated. By far the invasion of Poland was the most successful of the three operations. Alerted on short notice after the Germans had invaded western Poland on 1 September 1939, the General Staff mobilized the Belorussian and the Kiev Special military districts to attack on 17 September which they did, securing the eastern portion of Poland by the end of the month against light and disorganized resistance from the Polish Army. The invading forces suffered fewer than 2,000 deaths. That the RKKA experienced difficulties in coordination and cooperation between units and arms was to be expected considering the limited amount of time available for commanders and staffs to plan.

The Battle of Khalkin-Gol provided some examples of the Red Army's unpreparedness for war and also some remarkable resourcefulness. The battlefield was far from supply depots and supported by an inadequate distribution scheme. Three months of extraordinary effort by supply and transport personnel overcame these problems. The initially poor organization and maneuvering of the forces under General Georgi Zhukov led to confusion between units for much of the battle, yet, in the final offensive beginning on 20 August, Zhukov's imaginative use of armored forces proved to be the undoing of the Japanese. Initially, the morale of the men was atrocious. In several instances whole battalions broke and ran from the battlefield abandoning their rifles and equipment. Recently arrived reservists were more of a detriment than an asset. Throughout, the conflict was characterized by arbitrary punishment of commanders by Zhukov and an obvious willingness on Zhukov's part to take considerable casualties to insure victory – an astronomical 34 percent of all troops involved became casualties.[9]

By far the worst showing the Red Army made before the war with Germany was its attempt to invade Finland. Stalin and the high command expected a quick and easy victory. With an unsound strategy and poor coordination of units, the Red Army attacked into Finland on three separate axes of advance, only to be decimated by the outnumbered Finns, who fought from well-built and well-situated strong points and whose ski battalions, using daring small-unit tactics, isolated and annihilated the Soviets' large armor-supported infantry forces. Only when the RKKA concentrated its forces and attention in the south in January 1940 (abandoning thousands encircled in the north) and assembled a huge infantry and artillery "steamroller" did the Red Army manage to overwhelm the Finnish defense by sheer weight of men and materiel.

Red Army casualties amounted to some 126,875 dead and missing and 265,000 wounded (including 29,000 killed, wounded, and missing officers) and 2,500 tanks destroyed in this short war. During the war, the high command proved its own worst enemy, throwing thirteen of its newest divisions into the fight without time for the regiments and battalions to train together and develop the teamwork and cohesion necessary for success. All told, the RKKA used the equivalent of forty-six rifle divisions against twelve Finnish divisions. Another self-created handicap was the army's bringing its units to full strength with completely untrained recruits just days before sending them to the front. Half of all platoon commanders in the war were *mladshie leitenanty*.[10]

The war with Finland led to a major re-evaluation of military policy and some important personnel changes at higher levels. Marshal Voroshilov was replaced as Commissar of Defense by Marshal Timoshenko, who was then charged with putting the RKKA into condition for fighting a war against Nazi Germany. Before he left his post, Voroshilov compiled a lengthy report detailing the shortcomings of the RKKA. It was a sobering report that revealed inadequacies from the highest to the lowest levels, inadequacies of such dimensions that, unresolved, could potentially render the army useless against a prepared enemy. As of the date of the report, 8 May 1940, only two days before the awesomely successful German invasion of France began, the Red Army High Command had no operational plan for war either in the west or east although it expected to fight in both. In fact the General Staff had ordered the military districts in the west to come up with their own plans to defend their districts and submit them no later than 12 June 1941.[11] The army had no up-to-date mobilization plan, and its reserves consisted of over three million unorganized men. It had no plan to refresh their training in the event of war.

The army was still short of officers, especially the infantry, which had only 79 percent of its authorized officers. The military schools were inadequate to the task of putting out the necessary numbers of men, nor could they train them to the minimal standards deemed necessary. Voroshilov's report bluntly stated, "The quality of officer training is poor, especially in the platoons and companies . . ." Noncommissioned officers were especially poorly trained. In the field and in combat, the various arms were unskilled in working together.

Artillery did not know how to support tanks, and aviation did not know how to support the ground forces. The infantry was not resolute in pressing home attacks and did not know how to disengage from enemy contact when necessary. Neither did the infantry know how to attack fortified positions, construct or overcome obstacles, nor force rivers. The use of camouflage was amateurish. The armored forces had a serious problem with maintenance procedures and suffered a shortage of trained mechanics. The rear services were totally unprepared to support the army in combat. It had been over two years since there had been any planning for the rear services and the army's situation in 1940 called for an entirely new plan.[12]

Operation Barbarossa and the beginning of the Great Patriotic War

On the morning of 22 June 1941 Adolph Hitler reneged on his promise of non-aggression and set his armed forces against the most powerful Russian army ever assembled. The general scheme and goal of the first phase of the attack on the USSR – codenamed Operation Barbarossa – was to destroy the bulk of the Red Army in the Ukraine and Baltic region and prevent the withdrawal of intact units into the Russian interior. The next phase was to push the Soviet military so far into the Urals that it could not bomb Germany proper. Hitler's ultimate objective was to isolate the surviving remnants of Bolshevism behind the Volga and thence along a general line extending northward toward Archangel. The German armed forces very nearly achieved these goals besieging Leningrad in September, reaching the outskirts of Moscow by late October, though failing to take either. Going on the offensive again in spring 1942 the Germans pushed the Red Army all the way back to the Volga at Stalingrad by summer's end. Looking back at the state of the RKKA between 1922 and 1939 this turn of events is not surprising given the myriad internal weaknesses of the Red Army. What was surprising was that the Red Army survived at all and then completely turned the tables on the German war machine and, with the help of allies, eventually destroyed fascist Germany utterly.

With the German invasion, the party and government, just as in the Civil War, added new structures to coordinate and control the functions of the army and society. The major additional structure created by joint decree of the Supreme Soviet, the Communist Party, and the Sovnarkom on 30 June 1941 was a State Council of Defense (GKO) with Stalin as its chairman. Marshal Voroshilov was the only military representative. The decree invested the GKO with all power in the nation. All elements of state and party power had to obey its commands. The GKO's primary function was to coordinate and oversee the production of armaments in particular tanks, aircraft and artillery, and other war materials such as ammunition, rations, and gasoline. It did not, however, claim a role in military command, yet in the summer of

1941 Stalin did use his authority as chairman of the GKO to issue military orders.[13]

On the second day of the war with Germany, the Politburo created the Supreme Headquarters of the Main Command, commonly known as Stavka, to conduct military operations. Initially composed of Stalin – who took the title Supreme Commander – Molotov, Timoshenko, Budenny, Voroshilov, and Shaposhnikov; Zhukov (Chief of the General Staff) was added in August 1941 and later became Deputy Supreme Commander. Although Stalin assigned Stavka the responsibility of strategic planning of the war and major campaigns and gave it authority over the General Staff, it took him some time and disastrous results before he accepted the counsel of his generals and kept from meddling in ongoing operations.

The most infamous of his operational blunders came in summer 1941 in the battle of Kiev. After the fall of Smolensk in July, the Germans sought to trap another large group of Soviet armies in the Ukraine. As their plan unfolded Zhukov saw that the Soviet forces in the area would be unable to stop the two German pincers and recommended immediate withdrawal behind the Dnepr river. Stalin refused and sacked him as Chief of Staff. Even as Zhukov's prediction was coming true, Stalin's old friend from his days with the 1st Cavalry Army, Marshal Semion Budenny, commander of the Southwestern Front, asked for permission to retreat out of certain encirclement. As a result Budenny too was relieved of command and replaced by Marshal Timoshenko who took over just in time for the majority of the Southwest and Southern fronts to be captured by the Germans for a loss of some 665,000 men in mid-September. Still, it took until mid-1942 or so for Stalin to keep out of tactical details and concentrate on major questions of strategy in cooperation with the generals of Stavka.

Mobilization and manning

Official data enumerate military losses during the war at 11,444,100. One unofficial estimate puts the losses at over seventeen million. Unofficial sources put civilian deaths at between ten and twenty million. In any event it is clear that bringing the Red Army up to the size necessary to fight the Germans and then maintaining that level of manpower was a colossal and continuing task which, if not pursued successfully, could have cost the Soviet Union the war. As it turned out, the USSR quite successfully tapped human resources, yet, rather than follow the logical and straightforward process of manning the army by calling up reserves, and processing volunteers and conscripts through military commissariats of local soviets, the party, government, and army adopted a multitude of methods, some of them resurrected Civil War practices. Typically, lines of authority and responsibility became confused making training, supply and accountability a rather complex matter. Without a doubt, however, the flexibility inherent in their hodge-podge methods served the authorities well in critical moments, yet it also contributed to the high death toll of Soviet citizens.

The pattern of the military mobilization of society was established in the very first days of the war and was directly shaped by the scale of the initial defeats at the borders with their large losses of personnel. In 1935, the General Staff proposed that the army be manned at 6.8 million men for war with Germany. In fact the Red Army would fight the war with a strength of roughly seven million at any given time as losses were incurred and made up. This means that as the first shots were fired on 22 June 1941 the mobilization organs needed to produce two million men to bring the army to war footing. Subsequently, they had to make up for losses of some four or five million by the end of December, which is to say they had to completely replace the Red Army by 1.5 times in a span of six months. As it turned out, the USSR was able to mobilize nearly 5.3 million people by the end of February 1942. Ideally, the task involved training, organizing, and equipping the replacements, not just shoving live bodies in front of the Germans, although at times manning did degenerate to that level.

In the course of the war mobilized people, male and female, were brought to the front in three ways: as individual replacements in march companies, through front mobilizations, or in newly formed units. New units were formed throughout the war, but seldom in division size after 1943. One still unexplained practice was keeping units at nearly half strength the entire war while at the same time creating new divisions, brigades or regiments that thinly spread command and combat experience. Despite steady improvement in the tactical and technical performance of the army leadership units took heavy losses all the way through the war, not just in the beginning, continually taxing the ability of society and the mobilization organs to provide enough soldiers. In addition to the millions of combat losses hundreds of thousands were lost to disease, especially typhus and cholera, as well as to overburdened, inefficient, or inept medical treatment. In summer 1942, when most of European Russia was occupied by the Germans and therefore inaccessible for military recruitment, the number of casualties and the number of new recruits were almost even, and the possibility that the military might not have enough replacements to conduct further offensive operations became a real concern in mid-1943.[14]

The first act of the Soviet regime to address the immediate need to move to manning at wartime levels was, on 22 June, to order all reservists in non-essential industries to report to the local military committees of their districts and wait assignment. The second move was to resurrect the *opolchenie* (citizens militia army) of the 1812 Great Patriotic War in response to two phenomena: the need to create even more divisions, because scores of divisions had been annihilated and there was no territorial force to mobilize, and the mass voluntarism on the part of Soviet citizenry. On 28 and 29 June 1941, in preparation for the defense of Leningrad, General-lieutenant Popov, commander of the Leningrad Military District, and Andrei Zhdanov, head of the city party organization and Politburo member, ordered the Leningrad city military and party committees to raise 200,000 volunteers and form them into fifteen divisions of 12,000 men each. The volunteers were to be between the ages of eighteen and fifty, physically fit and politically reliable. All officers were to come from the reserves or ranks of volunteers. General Popov gave the staff of the military district three days to bring their plans together. Zhdanov gave the party organs of the city until 5 July to get volunteers lined up and units formed.[15]

The first unit actually began to assemble on 30 June and by the end of the year Leningrad had 135,000 volunteers organized into ten rifle divisions of 10,000 men and women each, and fourteen separate artillery battalions. Workers, communists, and Komsomols composed two-thirds of the personnel. Units were formed on a workplace basis as much as possible to promote morale and cohesion. Some volunteers had previously served in the military, but not many. Most of the volunteers had no elementary military knowledge.[16]

On 29 June, Stavka ordered the formation of volunteer *opolchenie* divisions in all urban areas. On 4 July, on orders from Stalin, the commander of the Moscow Military District, General-lieutenant Artem'ev, with the aid of the secretaries of all of the city party organizations as well as the Moscow soviet and trade unions, began to raise 200,000 volunteers from the city of Moscow and 70,000 more from the surrounding province. Stalin wanted twenty-five divisions to be formed, the first twelve by 7 July 1941. Like in Leningrad, to enhance patriotism and local identity the divisions would be manned on a city-district basis. Each district would also form a reserve regiment to gather replacements for those killed.[17]

Supplying the *opolchenie* with arms proved to be an understandably difficult task as the army mobilized and replaced combat losses. In August, four *opolchenie* divisions found out they were armed with foreign rifles (Polish) for which no ammunition could be found. Two divisions had French machine guns, artillery pieces and mortars. Both the Leningrad and Moscow divisions in general, when sent to the front, were short of rifles, cartridges, overcoats and vehicles. Some divisions had no heavy weapons, and no tanks. The *opolchentsy* had only molotov cocktails for anti-tank defense.[18]

The *opolchenie* divisions, in matters of personnel, resembled the "army of a new type" that Trotsky and Lenin had so fervently sought. At the end of August they were completely manned by workers in the rank and file and noncommissioned officer slots. The maximum age of men admitted turned out to be forty-five years old. The majority of the men appointed NCOs had prior military service; however, many were basically unprepared for their duties. Platoon and company commanders had no experience whatsoever in those positions.[19]

The Moscow *opolchenie* did not fill all their political slots, but those it did were held by party members from the Moscow party committee, lower level party workers, and members of the Moscow city soviet. Because of the shortage of political workers, political education work got off to a weak start. Overall, the political situation in the divisions was reported to be healthy at the start of September, but there were cases of people who wished to leave the units saying they were in the *opolchenie* against their will. It is likely that the Moscow party organs may have twisted the arms of some of their members to meet Stalin's goal of 200,000 people. As it turned out Moscow produced about 130,000 *opolchentsy*.[20] The army drafted tens of thousands of muscovites straight into the regular forces.

Once formed, the *opolchenie* did not begin intense training – odd considering there was a war on. Chief of the political section of the Main Administration of Forming and Manning the Red Army, Brigade Commissar Sviridov, in a report to Stavka on 3 September 1941, noted that for the past weeks the men had put in ten hours a day working on the defenses of Moscow, and only afterwards did military training for four to five hours. With the knowledge that the *opolchenie* would soon be committed to battle, Sviridov asked that the shortages of weapons and equipment soon be made up. He likewise requested that fifteen to twenty days be set aside for military training. As it turned out, training time was always short and in some cases nonexistent before *opolchentsy* were sent into the fray.

Falling under the rubric of *opolchenie* were "fighting" (*istrebitel'nyi*) battalions and volunteer communist battalions. Such battalions were formed in less densely populated areas where there was no possibility of raising divisions, or were designated as separate battalions for special or immediate tasks. Many communist battalions were organized as tank or anti-tank battalions – fighting against tanks being deemed a task requiring especially high motivation in 1941. The first *istrebitel'nyi* battalions were formed in the Ukraine and Belorussia, the areas closest to the fighting. The initial tasks allotted to these battalions were to secure the rear areas from parachutists and saboteurs and to round up deserters. Belorussia created seventy-eight *istrebitel'nyi* battalions with 13,000 members. In the first ten days of July, the city of Mogilev produced a unit with 8,000 members. It was committed to the defense of the city almost immediately. As the Red Army retreated through Belorussia these battalions were absorbed into active divisions or became partisan detachments. The city of Gomel' created a regiment of workers, army veterans, youths and young women with virtually no assistance from the army. It ended up being commanded by the chief of military instruction of the local Osoaviakhim council. Its commissar was the director of a drama theater. In the Ukraine the party, by early July, organized 657 fighting battalions of from 500 to 600 men and women each, but had only 319 machine guns and 34,000 rifles to arm them.[21]

That the *opolchenie* and *istrebitel'nyi* units were important to stemming the German onslaught is made clear by the example of Tula in October 1941. In late September, German units were driving on Moscow from north and south, the Red Army reeling before them. As the Germans approached Tula, to the south of Moscow, the Red Army sent Captain Andrei Gorshkov to Tula to organize a fighting battalion. Gorshkov began work the morning of 3 October 1941 and by the evening had 1,000 volunteers on the way to the front. By that time Tula was the front. The volunteers ranged from teenagers to pensioners, recruited mostly from the factories. Half were communists or Komsomols. The Tula unit defended a railroad station and a grain elevator just outside town. Suffering many casualties, they stayed in the line until ordered to return to Tula on 25 October. Between 25 and 28 October the battalion was disbanded and in the course of those three days a workers' volunteer regiment was formed in its place and sent to the front. It then became part of the regular army, Gorshkov its commander.[22] Without the Tula *opolchenie*, that part of the line would have either gone undefended or been defended by a depleted Red Army unit stretched dangerously thin and the Germans likely would have charged through on to Moscow.

In 1942, recruiting shifted to the east and south of Moscow. The term *opolchenie* was dropped in favor of the term "volunteer." For example, in the summer of 1942, the Altai krai party organs sought to recruit 2,400 men for a "Volunteer Stalin Brigade" and due to an enormous patriotic outpouring exceeded this goal; 6,800 men volunteered for the brigade, although not all turned out to be fit for service. In providing political workers, the Altai party leadership, it seems, was determined to match the patriotism shown by other party organizations that formed *opolchenie* units but was unable to do so on a volunteer basis. It then nominated numerous party members to join the brigade but several proved to be faint-hearted and refused to go. Such people were ordered expelled from the party. Simultaneously two full divisions were being formed in Altai and surrounding areas of Siberia, one on a volunteer basis, and one by conscription.[23]

One of the main differences between *opolchenie* and volunteer units, and *istrebitel'nyi* battalions was the time that elapsed between formation and being sent to fight. For the *opolchenie* and volunteers it was usually two or three months, the first Leningrad divisions were in combat in the second half of August, while most of the Moscow units were not put in the line until September or even October, but for *istrebitel'nyi* battalions it was a matter of days or even hours. In either case, because they were largely untrained, underequipped, and inadequately led, they tended to suffer horrendous casualties, sometimes to the point of complete annihilation. Those formations that survived were soon incorporated into the regular army and given regular numerical designations, for example the 1st Moscow *Opolchenie* Division became the 60th Rifle Division, the 2nd Leningrad *Opolchenie* Division became the 85th Rifle Division. They continued to be manned, however, by replacements from their place of origin, thus retaining their geographic identity. In the course of the war nearly four million people served in *opolchenie* and *istrebitel'nyi* units (over 700,000 in the critical months of summer and autumn 1941), providing the Red Army with sixty rifle and cavalry divisions and two hundred brigades, regiments and smaller units.

A third method of manning the armed forces, in addition to calling up reserves and relying on volunteer formations, was the regime's mass training of individuals for eventual use as replacements or to form new regular army units. This method was vitally necessary given that the army had no basic training units – in peacetime each regiment trained its own men, an impossible task when a unit was at the front – and that Osoaviakhim, which was supposed to provide military training to preconscripts had fallen far behind its duties. In 1939, 500,000 preconscripts failed to receive any preconscription training. In 1940 the number rose to 1,000,000. Thus, in order to supply trained personnel as replacements for active units the army reestablished Civil War-era Vsevobuch.[24]

On 17 September 1941, the GKO adopted a decree on universal compulsory training in part stating, "Each citizen of the USSR capable of bearing arms should be ready with weapons in hand to defend his motherland." The GKO then created, subordinate to the Commissariat of Defense, the Main Directorate for Universal Military Training which then organized sections of universal military training – Vsevobuch – in the military district, provincial, and subordinate military commissariats. By order of the Central Committee all local party, Komsomol, soviets, and Osoaviakhim organizations were to assist in establishing Vsevobuch and facilitating its work. It took until the second half of September 1941 to establish Vsevobuch detachments, assemble command and political personnel, and equip training centers.

In line with the new military obligation law, Vsevobuch provided military instruction for military age males as well as volunteer women. Sixty percent of the eligible people would receive their training through Vsevobuch, the others (mostly students) were to be taught at their schools, universities or institutes. Originally set at 100 hours of training, but later raised to 110 hours, the program included instruction in individual and squad tactics, use of weapons, combat engineering, drill, chemical warfare, first aid, physical training and military regulations. The first "class" of 1.15 million trainees finished their training in January 1942. The training took roughly four months because the participants remained civilians pursuing their normal activities, training only part time. Eventually Vsevobuch operated 15,000 training centers.

Poor training facilities and shortages of manuals, weapons, equipment, and training aids impeded training until late 1943. Conditions improved with every class; however, not until the fifth class did the majority of Vsevobuch centers have all the necessary training supplies and equipment. By the end of the war, Vsevobuch had produced seven classes of trainees with a total of

9.8 million graduates. Osoaviakhim's role was to take selected Vsevobuch graduates and train them as small units, or in advanced specialties such as machine gun use, sniping, anti-tank weapons, mortars, demolitions, driving, radio operation, and so on. Once a trainee graduated he or she was then assigned to a regiment.

For most of the nearly ten million men and women who passed through the Vsevobuch system their 110 hours proved to be the extent of their military training before being fed into the meatgrinder of the front. Millions of other soldiers received far less training and sometimes none at all before being thrust into combat. Men who were conscripted but had not gone through Vsevobuch were usually assigned to reserve regiments where they were supposed to undergo basic training for from six to eight weeks before being assigned to active units. Reserve regiments were not regiments held in reserve, they were not actually regiments at all in a tactical sense, rather they were simply replacement detachments. Men were delivered to them from a variety of sources, local military commissions, Vsevobuch, interior military districts and so on. The reserve regiment was then to train and equip the soldiers before organizing them into march companies of between one and two hundred men, which were not tactical units but just groups of replacements, and send them marching to a division for assignment to a regiment.

Frequently men marched straight from the reserve regiment into the firing line with no orientation to their new unit. Often the reserve regiment neither trained nor completely outfitted the recruits before sending them off. One reason was that they seldom had time to train them as the demand for men at the front never slackened, and another was a dearth of weapons and supplies that lasted the duration of the war. Gabriel Temkin, a Polish Jew who found himself in the Red Army in 1943, relates his experience as a replacement, "I stayed in that reserve regiment only a couple of days, just enough to be enlisted as private of the 4th *Marshevaia Rota* (marching company), go through a refreshing shower in a field *bania*, and receive a new military uniform, shoes, a knapsacklike bag, a spare pair of underwear, and a soft cap."[25] Temkin and the other men were not issued rifles as there were none. When someone asked the *politruk* about military training he told them, "Never mind, there you'll learn," meaning, of course, at the front. On 4 May 1943, Temkin's 4th Marching Company was sent straight into combat as replacements for the 458th Rifle Regiment, 78th Rifle Division, which at the time was defending a bridgehead across the Donets River. Of his initial experiences Temkin wrote:

> The *politruk* was right. There were plenty of rifles, ammunition, and hand grenades left by the dead and wounded in the field and trenches, and I was soon to "learn on the job" how to use them. I had not seen yet the first sunrise on the bridgehead when, before daybreak, and with no support from our artillery behind the river,

our company was rushed into an attack on enemy positions. We were led by a junior lieutenant . . . We were supposed to engage in a hand-to-hand fight and, as soon as we passed the barbed wire, everybody on our side began shooting wildly. I did likewise, not aiming at anybody or anything in particular, because visibility was poor, and even if it were excellent, I would not have performed any better, as I never practiced shooting from a real rifle to a target. Be that as it may, the Germans were not caught by surprise. Their heavy machine guns began to crackle and mowed down our soldiers.

Those two weeks included some ten days of savage fighting during which our regiment's cost per day in killed and wounded was about two hundred men. Almost every second day the reserve regiment would pump in another two hundred men of a marching company to replenish the losses at our bridgehead. It follows that, despite reinforcements, the total net loss incurred in those ten days was about one thousand men, which our 458th Rifle Regiment could hardly afford any longer.[26]

At the end of ten days the attacks halted having produced no territorial gains whatsoever. From this perspective one can appreciate that the war was made more costly for the Soviet Union by lack of training and preparation which made some attacks unsuccessful, even futile, or perhaps criminal.

Women comprised a reservoir of personnel that was far more thoroughly exploited by the Soviet Union for its war effort than those of any other belligerent. Legally, women could be mobilized for any aspect of the war effort, but the state used this power only to put millions of women into civilian defense work; service in the armed forces was left voluntary. Around 800,000 women served in the Soviet armed forces during the war, most of them in the army ground forces. By 1 October 1942 nearly 350,000 female volunteers had been trained by Vsevobuch, 12,000 as rifleman, 300,000 as nurses and medics, and 20,000 as radio operators, telegraph operators and telephone operators. In the army, the presence of women was especially telling in two areas, the medical services and sniping. Many medical battalions were staffed almost exclusively by females, not only as doctors and nurses, but also as orderlies, technicians and ambulance drivers. Tens of thousands of women served as front-line medics. In this capacity they often showed courage risking their lives to administer first aid and evacuate wounded under enemy fire. Consequently thousands lost their lives at the front.

In contrast to their female comrades who saved lives, female snipers caused the deaths of tens of thousands of German officers and men. Women began serving as snipers in 1941, but not until December 1942 did the army open that gender's own sniper training program. The course of instruction lasted six months; applicants had to be twenty-five years old or younger, have finished eight years of school and already know how to shoot. The average woman sniper was quite proud of her work and certainly not reluctant to write home about it. All kept a running tally of kills for which they received much coveted rewards.

Women did occasionally serve as riflemen, machine gunners or mortar crewmen in combat roles in mostly male units where they often set the example for courage, tenacity, and leadership, yet the army resisted forming any but a few all-female tactical units during the war. In November 1942, when losses of male soldiers were particularly high due in part to the ongoing battle for Stalingrad, the GKO ordered the Moscow Military District to begin forming a volunteer women's rifle brigade, to be completed no later than the first of February 1943. The GKO specified that certain crew-served weapons would need to be manned by more females than were ordinarily manned by males, for example, two men normally handled an anti-tank rifle but the women's brigade would assign three women, a five man 45 mm anti-tank gun would have eight women and so on. Trucks and all special vehicles would have two female drivers instead of the one male. The brigade's school battalion trained its own NCOs. All told, the brigade was authorized about seven thousand personnel, over a thousand more than a male brigade.[27] The combat record of this unit has not been made public so we are left unaware of the success of this endeavor.

The mixing of men and women in the army also had its negative aspects. Some men resented the presence of women in their midst. Zoya Medvedeva, a machine gunner, was not well received by everyone when she arrived at the front, the only woman of a 150 person march company. The receiving company *starshina*: "frowned, and in a quiet voice said bluntly and stubbornly: 'Broads only bring bad luck when they meddle in men's business.'"[28] According to Gabriel Temkin:

> In a regiment like ours the ratio of women to men was approximately one hundred to one. Sooner or later she would be in some relationship with a man (or men), either because she fell in love, or just to satisfy sexual desires, or to improve her lot, or because she expected to find a husband, or she wanted to get pregnant and as such be released and go home. Some became what was called derisively PPZh (*Pokhodno-Polevye Zheny*), "marching field wives." These were willing partners almost exclusively of officers, usually of higher ranks.[29]

Officers' sexual relations with servicewomen often caused resentment among the men toward their leaders, but worse were the casualties sustained when battalion and company commanders neglected their duties to entertain female soldiers.

A traditional method of increasing unit personnel strength borrowed from the Imperial Russian Army was the practice of adopting orphans, so-called "Sons of the Regiment." Because this practice was strictly informal the strength acquired was necessarily "off the books" so the true number of young orphans in the service can never be determined. One Russian researcher, with personal knowledge of 3,500, claims that at least 25,000 young people ranging in age from six to sixteen served in front-line units. A particular twist to the sons of the regiment tradition was that during the Second World War units also adopted females. The soldiers who looked after the children came to love them as their own. These children, however, were not mere mascots or charity cases; many actually fought as soldiers in the front-line toting submachine guns as big as themselves, earning medals for valor and service which they pinned to uniforms tailored to their small frames. Others served as medics, nurses, and radiomen.[30] In some way everyone was put to useful work.

Some daughters of the regiment actually began by masquerading as boys. In 1941, Mariia I. Makarova allowed a unit to adopt her, which was in the area when her village was destroyed and her family killed. When the commander asked her name and age she said Misha (Mikhail) and that she was fourteen, in reality she was thirteen. While in the unit she heroically fought in the defense of Moscow under the famous General Panfilov. When presenting her medal Panfilov asked her, "Hey lad, what's your name?" She replied honestly, "I'm not a lad, I'm a soldier."[31]

One of the least desirable ways a person could find himself at the front was through the process of front mobilization, a technique first used by the RKKA in the Civil War. More akin to impressment than conscription, front mobilization usually consisted of units at the front getting their hands on military aged civilian males and putting them in the ranks of a front-line or reserve regiment. One of the first and few authorized front mobilizations was in July 1941 when the Western Front command enlisted the aid of the Minsk military committee to mobilize 10,000 men and sent them immediately into the firing lines, without training, arms, or uniforms. Under such conditions even willing and brave men do not stand much of a chance to turn the tide of battle, let alone survive.

A General Staff report in spring 1942 criticized the continuing practice of front mobilization which brought untrained men into the ranks observing that:

> There is a great disproportion in combat qualities between soldiers tempered in battles and the novices, who are far from being experienced. The former are steadfast in a combat situation and fight well. The latter are less steadfast and at first are often subject to panic. As a result, the mixed units of seasoned soldiers and poorly trained

newcomers often do not carry out their combat missions and suffer heavy losses.[32]

This criticism went unheeded.

Another method of reinforcement was to send men from the Gulag to the front. Between August and December 1941, the prison camp system sent to the front 420,000 men whose crimes "did not pose a great public danger." In the subsequent three years another million inmates were released for duty at the front and in military industry.[33]

The army also managed to reinforce itself in 1943 and 1944 during its westward march by repeating the Civil War practice of incorporating liberated partisan bands into regular units at the front. Partisan bands were broken up and their members put into existing regiments. First of all, however, Red Army men turned partisans had to survive a background check by the Special Section to determine if they had deserted or otherwise willingly gone behind German lines rather than fight in 1941. Those that failed the check were still allowed to serve the Motherland, but as members of disciplinary combat battalions.

Until 1939, non-Russian minorities, with the exception of Ukrainians and Belorussians, had been sparingly used by the RKKA, but, with the army's expansion, the conscription organs purposefully began taking in large numbers of young men of the USSR's national minorities. For the most part minorities had been segregated into ethnically-based units. In 1939, the Commissariat of Defense ceased such manning and began integrating minorities into largely Russian divisions. For many minority conscripts this was a negative turn of events. For the first time they were thrust into a social environment that made them acutely aware of their minority status. They now had to live in unfamiliar climes and were fed Russian cuisine which most found unappealing. The language barrier complicated every aspect of their existence in the Red Army, the most important of which were training, combat orders, and social integration.[34] Few spoke Russian, and even fewer Russians spoke any of the minority languages. Most disturbing was the racism they often encountered. Many Slavs particularly disliked Georgians and Armenians.

An exact number of minorities who served in the army during the war years is not available, however, it is certain that at least hundreds of thousands served in the rank and file, and thousands served as officers. For example, on the Volkhov Front outside of Leningrad in 1944, one-fifth of the personnel were non-Russians primarily from Central Asian Republics. The tens of thousands of medals awarded for meritorious service and valor attest that non-Russian minorities served not only loyally, but also bravely despite their special obstacles.

The final significant method of providing manpower for the army was the mobilization of communists for the front, continuing the peacetime special mobilizations of party members. In 1941, the party easily procured tens of thousands of its members, male and female for the army. Communists and Komsomols flocked to join the regular army, *opolchenie* units, and *istrebitel'ny* battalions, especially those designated "Communist battalion" or "Komsomol battalion." The closer to the front, the more readily they came. The Communist Party of Belorussia mobilized most of its communists and over 100,000 Komsomols in the first weeks of the German invasion. In Leningrad in the first days of the war 29,000 party members and 17,500 Komsomols volunteered for the army. Most of the initial volunteers were young, idealistic, and convinced anti-fascists without positions in the party apparatus. Somewhat more difficult to get into uniform were party members in responsible positions. Some claimed their jobs were vital to the war effort or else held out for positions in PUR that would give them authority, status, and perhaps keep them out of the firing lines.

Motivation

Understanding the fighting capacity of the Red Army soldier once mobilized is essential to appreciate the eventual victory of the Soviet Union over Nazi Germany. Historian Amnon Sella postulates that obedience to the point of self-sacrifice is possible in two types of soldiers, "soldier–philosophers" who believe in the values represented by his side in a war and "soldier–victims" who are prepared to die because they do not know how to avoid it.[35] Clearly the Red Army was able to garner enough such soldiers to propel it to victory (one estimate puts the total to serve in uniform at thirty-one million), but it is less clear how soldiers became philosophers or victims. The first soldiers faced with the choices of philosopher or victim were those on active duty at the start of the war. The state had not prepared the soldiers to make that choice on the eve of the war in part because official adherence to the 1939 Nazi–Soviet Nonaggression Pact had brought about an end to anti-fascist propaganda. Stalin's unwillingness to believe that Hitler would break the pact led him to prevent significant preparations for war in the border areas. The Eleventh Army is a case in point. It was pervaded with the illusion of peace and unprepared to begin combat activities despite the abrupt beginning of the military propaganda organs, on 14 June, to talk about the possibility of war with Germany. Many units were still in their winter quarters, at one-quarter unit strength, pursuing normal peacetime training. On the evening of 21 June the men were issued ammunition, but were in a state of "political disorientation." They had a careless attitude and were unprepared for mobilization to a wartime footing.[36]

In the ensuing battles for the borders untold tens of thousands of Red Army men deserted or voluntarily gave themselves up for prisoners to the Germans, unable to become philosophers in support of Stalin's regime, nor willing to die in defense of it. The majority of the men opting out of the fight originated from the border regions, namely Ukrainians, Belorussians, Lithuanians, Latvians and Estonians. Some were nationalists who hoped to see sovereignty restored to their native lands, others were peasant farmers hoping the Germans would abolish collective farms. Others had been victimized by Stalin's terror and saw the potential defeat of the Bolshevik state as a blessing. Many had no motive other than to avoid being killed for a system to which they simply felt no loyalty. Subsequently, the German military was able to enlist the participation of thousands of these men in military and paramilitary groups primarily to fight partisans and murder Jews, but also to fight at the front against the Red and Allied armies.

Some peoples, acting on national patriotism rather than Soviet patriotism, saw the war as an opportunity to throw off the Russian–Bolshevik yoke. Armed anti-Soviet bands were active in the North Caucasus in 1942–43. And, despite the sometimes harsh treatment of civilians by the Germans, many Ukrainians did not welcome the Red Army as liberators in 1943 and 1944 and instead undertook organized armed action against Soviet forces.

Overwhelmingly, however, most Soviet citizens remained loyal and supported the regime against the invaders. For some soldiers, the basis of their motivation to fight willingly to the point of death was straightforward Russian patriotism. As he lay dying in a field hospital in December 1942, Lieutenant Gari Tarasenko, who had volunteered for a communist battalion on the second day of the war, wrote his last letter to his toddler son saying:

> I die deeply confident that you, my beloved son, will live in a free, prospering country – a socialist country. You will learn in soviet schools, and independently make your way in the world like I used to. You will know from history about the days of the Great Patriotic War and read stories of the selfless deaths of the heroes of the war. And you, my beloved son, do not blush for me, your father, but with unabashed pride say, "My father died in the struggle for future freedom, loyal to his oath, a patriot." I, in this hard struggle with the fascists, with my blood, won you the right to a free life.[37]

Some soldiers were anti-fascist by conviction and needed no convincing of its evil, but many needed first-hand experience before becoming soldier–philosophers. The often brutal and merciless treatment by the Germans of civilians and captured soldiers convinced many soldiers that fascism was truly worth fighting against to the death. Collective farmers who escaped German occupation told that the Germans confiscated wheat, cattle, etc. Virtually all edible foodstuffs were seized. Some collective farms were burned to the ground. Any resistance by the villagers to requisitioning meant being shot on the spot. One villager reported that the Germans acted like, "bandits and robbers," and that village officials were shot as a matter of course. PUR made sure to disseminate this type of information to the troops, and arranged to have peasants who had suffered at the hands of the Germans meet Red Army men to relate their tales.[38]

In a letter home in June 1942, Junior Sergeant Kokhman K. Fel'dman spoke for millions of soldiers saying: "I am able to say that now I have a proper hatred of fascism. I have seen bodies of dead and burned women and children. I have seen places that once were villages. It is horrible."[39] It took a year of war before Fel'dman came to hate fascism, but when he and others like him finally came to that conclusion it provided enduring motivation to risk their lives if for nothing else but to save their country from the Nazi scourge, and then take their revenge. Those soldiers, with families behind the German lines, had a special motivation to liberate their loved ones, especially when they were convinced that they were being oppressed. One soldier in this situation, Georgii N. Kidin, wrote to a friend:

> We know that our wives, children, fathers, our mothers, everyone, who by chance found themselves in the hands of the invaders are waiting for us. There, we know, is a sea of blood and tears, hunger, cold and slavery. We will soon bring to them freedom on our bayonets, and the lucky will have their lives back to build socialism once and for all.[40]

Some soldiers had family members who had become partisans and under those circumstances knew that they could not avoid doing their utmost to liberate them.

Initially many soldiers saw surrender as a means of escaping becoming victims of war but several days into the war rumors began to circulate that Germans were killing prisoners. Indeed, indiscriminate murder of POWs was not uncommon. Hitler's "Commissar Order" instructed German soldiers to kill all captured commissars and partisans, but many German soldiers tended to shoot all party members or Komsomols that fell into their hands and other soldiers on whim. With this information some Red Army men may have reconsidered surrendering. In the first week of the German attack some men, particularly officers and commissars, committed suicide rather than be captured.[41] Such immoral and counterproductive behavior on the part of the German Army continued to the very end of the war.

Although reasons for self-sacrifice abounded, the state still introduced an element of coercion to further ensure obedience and unwilling sacrifice if necessary. Courts-martial ordered men executed not only for cowardice, but also for failure in their military duties. But the most drastic punitive measures, on Stalin's orders, were the promulgation of Stavka Decree no. 270, in August 1941 and NKO Order no. 227, in July 1942. This order was never published, just read out to the soldiers. It provided for the families of officers and political workers to be arrested by the Special Sections if their men deserted – just like those of *voenspetsy* during the Civil War. The order mentioned that the military soviet of the Western Front, generals Pavlov, Klimovskii, and Grigorev had recently been shot. This led some soldiers to believe that the army was being betrayed by its leaders, thinking why else would Stalin issue such an order?

Order no. 227, issued during the retreats of summer 1942, called for "not one step backwards." To ensure this, regiments were ordered to create blocking units of their best troops. Blocking detachments of the NKVD already existed (as they had in the Civil War) to corral or shoot fleeing soldiers, but were deemed insufficient. Order no. 227 also created penal combat (*shtrafnyi*) battalions for cowards separate from the already existing penal labor battalions. Each front was to have three *shtrafnyi* battalions of officers convicted of cowardice or "instability," and an additional five to ten companies of enlisted men and NCOs.[42]

Order no. 227 was not well received by the front-line leadership. A military correspondent serving at the front wrote in his diary: "The division commander announced NKO 227. As he read people stood rigid. It made our skin crawl."[43] Some interpreted the order as an indictment of the army for cowardice and deeply resented it. Others took it fatalistically. Private Ivan A. Veselov wrote home: "On orders from our dear leader comrade Stalin – not a step backwards, only – forward! Our task is either to destroy the bloody monster or die ourselves . . ."[44] As it turned out, military commanders at the front did not obey the spirit of the order. Rather than creating blocking detachments of their best troops – a waste of manpower in their view – they either put their most useless soldiers in them and assigned them menial tasks, or used them as shock units to act as emergency reserves. Some commanders used them as bodyguard detachments to protect their headquarters. In October 1942, Order no. 227 was rescinded, though *shtrafnyi* battalions remained in service through to the end of the war.

For most members assignment to a *shtrafnyi* battalion was merely a delayed death sentence. Such battalions were put into the worst of the fighting at the most exposed or otherwise dangerous positions. Their casualties were always horrendous. A first-hand account of Lieutenant Zia Buniiatov, who was put into one as a convict in 1942 and then rose to commander, is illuminating on the use and dynamics of these units.

> I came to know about it [Order 227] at the village of Vesely outside of Rostov. Our retreat was barred by a special purpose detachment [of the NKVD]. A few hundred officers of retreating units were driven to a large farm. They were escorted one at a time, into a house. Three men sat at a table. They asked us about our rank and where our personnel were. The answers were generally stereotyped: "What's the use of asking it if everybody is fleeing. The Germans have broken through the front. What could have possibly a platoon leader or a company commander done in that situation?"

The trial was short. The sentence was passed then and there. The accused were led behind a pigsty and shot.

When my turn came, Marshal of the Soviet Union Semion Budenny suddenly appeared in the village. The execution was suspended. We were lined up. Budenny asked us "Who wants to fight?" Everybody made a step forward.[45]

Buniiatov attributed his survival in the battalion's subsequent engagements to providence. In the summer of 1944 Buniiatov had his record expunged and was offered and accepted the command of a *shtrafnyi* company. His company at times numbered as many as seven hundred men. After each major engagement it was usually reduced to a few dozen men. Recent estimates put the number of men who served in *shtrafnyi* battalions at a million and a half. No records were kept of the number killed.

Men who had been caught in German encirclements were prime candidates for *shtrafnyi* battalions. When they returned to Soviet lines they were put in the custody of the NKVD which then investigated the circumstances of their being behind German lines. Mostly they checked for deserters or men who had voluntarily gone into captivity. If a soldier was determined to have become separated from his unit or captured under suspicious circumstances he was assigned to a *shtrafnyi* unit.

Not everyone at the front became a soldier–philosopher and many tried to avoid becoming victims, some successfully, others not. That men tried to avoid becoming victims is attested to by the presence of twenty *shtrafnyi* battalions belonging to the First Belorussian Front alone in January 1945. In the years 1942–45 the NKVD detained or arrested 88,859 traitors, 125,956 deserters and 251,408 draft evaders, suggesting that patriotism was not all-pervasive. The number of deserters in 1941 will never be known because of poor record keeping under adverse field conditions and the flux of attack and retreat that easily masked desertion. The incidence of desertion, however, is generally accepted as being quite high. In addition, in 1942, the NKVD apprehended 509,666 servicemen away from their units without documents. Another 514,366 were taken into custody in 1943. In 1942, 50,274 servicemen and women, and in 1943, 144,401 were detained as stragglers from their units. Other less than patriotic behavior resulted in the arrest of 156,875 officers and men in 1942, and 616,704 in 1943. Men taken into custody for having been captured or encircled under suspicious circumstances numbered 9,291 in 1942 and 15,848 in 1943.[46] Figures for 1944 and 1945 for the above infractions are not available.

Those unwilling to desert but desperate to avoid death often resorted to self-mutilation. Most often they shot themselves in the hand or foot. Gabriel Temkin remembers that self-mutilations were not uncommon, especially during times when his regiment found itself in nightmarish conditions on river bridgeheads in May 1943, and May 1944. When officers suspected that wounds were self-inflicted they investigated and held trials. Convictions carried the death penalty. Soldiers held a very dim view of their comrades who sought this way out.[47]

By and large, however, soldiers who did not become philosophers but would not desert or inflict wounds upon themselves adopted fatalistic attitudes while doing their best to preserve their lives. Typical of this behavior was junior sergeant Mikhail F. Shvetsov who wrote home, "All I think about is how to stay alive." Timofei A. Gessal', a communist, told his wife: "Death is before my eyes each second. I just want to stay alive, nothing else." Vasilii I. Gusev, a veteran of the Civil War conscripted at age 45, wrote home from the front: "There are no people here, only wild animals. Frightful, merciless beasts who have to fight without pity."[48]

The best way to save oneself without risking severe consequences was shirking or loafing about the rear area. This problem plagued the leadership for the duration of the war. In September 1941, the Southwestern Front reported disturbing incidents of cowardice and hesitation in the face of the enemy, by "morally unsound" and undisciplined men as well as numerous instances of desertion by privates and sergeants. In the battle for Poznan in February 1945 some battalions could muster only 10 percent of their men for attacks, the rest were hiding out in cellars getting drunk with the locals.[49]

The motivation of the Red Army as a whole to defeat Germany and its allies never failed. The morale of the ordinary soldier and officer, however, tended to fluctuate with the course of events at the front, the availability of supplies, how well they were taken care of, and how confident they were in themselves and their leadership. Conditions at home also weighed heavily on the men's minds and could greatly affect their moods. The enticement of rewards also had a bearing on morale. The words of one soldier perfectly sum up the morale situation in the wartime Red Army, "One day life is good, the next bad, the next worse, and the day after that good again." Morale was important because it directly affected the daily behavior of the soldier in and out of combat.

In many cases low morale could be linked to conditions of wartime service. One would expect morale to be low in summer 1941, but an investigation revealed that more was at work than battlefield reverses. Training and supplies had much to do with the apparent indiscipline and poor behavior, just as it had in peacetime. Soldiers recently conscripted were only incompletely supplied with uniforms. Thousands had no boots and wore their civilian shoes or even homemade bast sandals. Their hasty training left soldiers unable to differentiate between the different officer ranks. They struck up conversations with generals and argued with officers. Commissars conducted no political education work and newspapers were unavailable. One sergeant is reported to have said, "In time of battle we never see our officers," insinuating shirking or worse. Their food was of poor quality and meager quantity. The result of this situation, said the men, was reflected in the fact that in their first engagement, thirty men went over to the Germans. To restore the situation the report simply recommended that the soldiers be properly clothed and fed, and appropriate political instruction be initiated.[50]

Political agitation often helped bolster morale. Regimental agitators and political workers were supposed to maintain a presence at the front-line battalions. There they passed on the latest official news, the latest heroic acts, the achievements of the regiment, i.e. how many Germans they had killed and captured recently, gave lectures on the current military situation, and Stalin's latest pronouncements.

The political apparatus strongly urged recognition of outstanding performance in combat with medals and awards and then spreading the word of the actions and awards among the other soldiers. Division newspapers spread the word of heroic exploits. The army passed out medals generously; between July 1941 and 1 January 1948 almost thirteen million people were given awards for their wartime efforts. In addition to medals, commanders sometimes presented soldiers with cash and presents for their efforts.[51]

In addition to personal awards, Stalin resurrected the Imperial Army's honorary title "Guards" for units that distinguished themselves in combat. Units so honored received new numerical designations with the title "Guards" in the forefront, new battle flags, and all the members of the unit had the title "Guards" placed before their title of rank, such as Guards Captain, Guards Sergeant, etc. The men were also granted higher pay. This "Guards" designation seems to have really motivated some men. They would write home about their desire for their unit to become a guards unit, or their pride at having become a Guards krasnoarmeets, or gvardeets. Despite its old regime origins, this morale booster was sought by older Bolshevik Civil War veterans – who certainly would have objected in 1919 – and young Komsomol battalion volunteers alike along with the ordinary peasant or worker.

The soldiers' perception of the quality of medical care also affected morale. Confidence in prompt and competent medical care bolstered morale, but knowledge of substandard care depressed men and resulted in more cautious behavior in combat. The quality of medical care for soldiers varied tremendously from front to front and division to division. The major factors affecting medical care were: medical personnel, in particular a chronic shortage of doctors and surgeons; command personnel whose attention to medical support varied; the availability of medical supplies; the availability of evacuation transport, the assignment of medical units and hospitals as required, and training of frontline medical personnel. In toto, the Red Army's medical service did its utmost to provide the best care it could, but major instances occurred throughout the war to undermine the soldiers' faith in the medical service's ability and their senior officers' concern for their welfare.

In the first days of the war there were great difficulties in treating and evacuating the wounded of the Northwestern Front because of poor planning and use of the railroads. Large numbers of wounded were abandoned on the field of battle, and only an insignificant number made it all the way back to the main hospital. Seven months later the ability of the Red Army to plan the care of its wounded had not markedly improved. A report from the Western Front in January 1942 illustrates just about everything that could go wrong with regard to medical support for the front-line soldier. Chief of the Political Administration of the Western Front, V. E. Makarov reported that in most units the front-line medics were performing heroically and saving hundreds of lives by treating soldiers under fire and taking many casualties themselves. In some units, however, medics and comrades more interested in self-preservation left men to lie unattended on the field of battle for hours. In one instance men were left for 20–30 hours under fire with no attempt to remove them.[52]

After being removed from the line of fire the soldiers were then taken to a higher level of care, usually a medical battalion. Yet, on the Western Front, Makarov reported that evacuation of the wounded by at least four rifle divisions was so poorly organized that they could not evacuate hundreds of men dozens of whom died. Makarov observed that the 20th Army had only one two-hundred-bed hospital, whereas regulations required it to have four. The one hospital, in December 1941, cared for 500–600 wounded which it put in peasant homes and village buildings. Its resources were spread thinly to the detriment of the medical treatment of the patients. The small number of evacuation points and the scarcity of medical transport vehicles hampered evacuation. Over a period of from three to five days a single brigade amassed 200 patients awaiting evacuation. Another 750 wounded from other units, scattered among three different villages, also waited to be evacuated. Many lightly injured gave up hope of being transported and walked to the hospital.[53] Such circumstances repeated themselves on every front.

Not only morale, but also the number of men available for combat were affected by the quality of care. In mid-1943 the medical staff of the First Ukrainian Front determined that the front-line strength was reduced by 20–23 percent due to soldiers seeking medical treatment in the rear because the lack of sufficient expertise at the front caused minor wounds and ailments to become serious and debilitating through improper medical treatment. The front stepped up the training of its front-line medical personnel in an intensive course which not only saved the lives of hundreds of soldiers, but also kept more men on the firing line.[54]

Supply

The supply situation greatly affected the Soviet experience of war. Dearth or plenty often determined the success of an attack or defense, lowered or raised morale, allowed or prevented training, and affected the health of soldiers. The material needs of the Red Army since its inception had never been met at 100 percent even in peacetime, which should come as no surprise considering the entire USSR existed in an economy of shortages until the day it collapsed.

Wartime exacerbated shortages because demands increased far above the level industry could produce. Allied Lend Lease helped mitigate the shortfall of equipment and supplies, but nothing could keep up with the enormous losses of weapons and equipment at the front. In the 1941 summer–fall campaign, the Soviet armed forces lost 20,500 armored vehicles, about 17,000 warplanes, and more than 60,000 artillery pieces and mortars. Defense production in the second half of 1941 could replace only 30 percent of rifles, 27 percent of tanks, 58 percent of guns and mortars, and 55 percent of warplanes. Opposing the renewed German effort to capture Moscow in October 1941 the crucial Western and Kalinin fronts had two-thirds of required rifles, and about one-third of required submachine guns and heavy machine guns. Defense production still struggled at the beginning of 1942. None of the GKO-set production quotas were met. Production of tanks reached only 45 percent of plan, aircraft – 65 percent. In January 1944, with most of the USSR cleared of the enemy, Soviet industry could provide adequate supplies for only four or five of the ten active fronts.[55]

Supply problems were exacerbated by the fact that not all production made it to the front. For a variety of reasons, from inadvertent misrouting of goods due to overtaxed railroads to incompetent supply officers, supplies frequently were delivered to the wrong place. The chaos in transportation that resulted from the demands of the war was not remedied until late February 1942 when the GKO set up a Transport Committee that coordinated basic transportation and planning of movement of military and civilian shipments. Although better planning eliminated chaos it could not guarantee adequate supplies because they never existed. The generally underdeveloped nature of the Soviet infrastructure, insufficient railroads, and poor roads that turned into quagmires during the fall rains and spring thaw, which prevented all but tracked mobility across the countryside, made timely delivery of goods nearly impossible.

From the very beginning of the war inadequate pre-war planning for supplies made itself felt. On the morning of 24 June 1941, the 8th Army already began to run short of gasoline. When the 8th Army commander requested fuel resupply from the front commander he was told, "make do."[56] Soldiers "made do" with no fuel by abandoning their vehicles. According to a July 1941 report, across the entire Russian front the artillery was short of shells and did not have enough for even one full day of combat. Anti-aircraft artillery ammunition was also in short supply making it difficult to counter German air attacks. In August 1941, General Zhukov, commander of a Reserve Front complained to Stavka of the many defects of the ten divisions of his 32nd and 33rd Armies. They did not have enough rifles. They had various artillery with the wrong kind of ammunition. They were not supplied with signal, engineer, nor chemical equipment. He put it bluntly, "In this state the divisions are not battleworthy."[57]

The ability of commanders of armies or fronts to acquire enough materiel in the second half of the war often spelled the difference between nominal and spectacular success. After Stalingrad the saying arose, "Where there is Zhukov there is success," but it may have been more tellingly rendered, "Where there is Zhukov there is surfeit of supplies." The front that Gabriel Temkin's division was part of seemed to be at the bottom of the pecking order when it came to supply until for one operation in 1944 it was placed under Zhukov. Then, heavy equipment, artillery, tanks, ammunition, engineer support, and aviation appeared in overwhelming quantities. At the conclusion of the offensive Zhukov was reassigned and the assets he had brought went with him. In the course of the war it seems that Stavka and the GKO gave up on the idea of keeping all units supplied at their authorized levels, but instead let units "make do" with less in order to keep back supplies to be used at critical moments or in vital strategic operations such as those at Stalingrad in 1942–43, Kursk in summer 1943, Operation Bagration in summer 1944, and the drive on Berlin in spring 1945.

Sometimes considerable portions of supplies were destroyed due to enemy action, especially in the first year of the war. German air attacks severely disrupted distribution of supplies and destroyed many dumps of vital supplies and munitions. In the first hours of the war, German-organized armed bands cut telephone and telegraph wires behind Soviet lines disrupting communications. In Poland and the Baltic states they attacked and destroyed supplies in Kaunas and Vilnius and other cities. Very quickly there developed a fuel shortage which immediately curtailed use of motor vehicles. Further hindering delivery of supplies was a shortage of horses from death by air attacks on transport units.[58]

To make up for its poor planning the Red Army often resorted to exploiting Soviet citizens every bit as ruthlessly as the Germans would. In Belorussia, in the first weeks of war, military authorities requisitioned 3,300 automobiles, 630 tractors, 35,900 head of cattle and swine, over 10,300 tons of cereal grains and more than 4,000 tons of food stuffs.[59]

When supplies, and especially food, failed to arrive morale plummeted. Men reacted in various ways, from grumbling to desertion, or just bitter humor as illustrated by a comment in the letter of Senior Sergeant Leonid S. Lezinskii to his family in November 1942, "I am able to suffer everything: hunger – like in the 1930s, cold – like in the Finnish war, but it is torture without a smoke."[60] When supplies arrived, especially resupply of personal items like new uniforms, boots and underwear, or winter clothing the mood of the soldiers dramatically improved. They often expressed childlike delight in the improvement of their personal lot.

Despite the Red Army's shift to large armored groups during the war, infantry forces, the *"Tsaritsa pole"* (queen of battle) remained the mainstay of the army throughout the war. From his experience in the *Tsaritsa pole* Temkin concluded:

> In general, it has been my impression that the ordinary Red Army rifle divisions of World War II were by themselves not much different from their Russian counterparts of World War I; they had probably many similar weaknesses and strengths. Among the first, I would mention a relative lack of military initiative and of military discipline, unless the latter was enforced with a firm hand.[61]

They did not benefit from the technological advances of Soviet power as did the armored forces. From the first to the last day of the war rifle divisions depended on horses for mobility. Their anti-tank guns and field artillery were pulled by horses, and the mortars were transported in horse-drawn carts. In Temkin's 78th Rifle Division the regiment commander, his staff, and the battalion commanders rode horses. Other officers often had horse-drawn carts for themselves and their equipment. There was not a single motor vehicle in his regiment until summer 1944. That summer the regiment commander and the chief of staff got jeep-like vehicles – not from Russian factories or lend lease – confiscated from the newly allied Romanian army. Those were the only motor vehicles the regiment had the whole war.

The poor training, high casualty cycle

Eventually, as historians John Erickson and David Glantz have demonstrated, the Soviet High Command mastered the art of large-scale combined arms operations, correctly placing the right types of units with sufficient numbers of men and material in the right places at the right times to yield success. What is not clear is whether or not the lower levels of the Red Army ever mastered modern warfare. The two fundamental factors that impeded men in the divisions from becoming experts at modern war were continual massive casualties that kept experience from accumulating, and consistently poor or nonexistent training of replacements and newly formed units. Gabriel Temkin relates that in March 1944, after his rifle division had two years of combat under its belt, "the Germans still had enough strength to inflict heavy casualties on us, and by skillful use of combined tank and air forces in their counterattacks were able to force us to flee in panic more than once."[62] The entire spring of 1944 his division suffered frightful casualties.

There are those Russian historians who now wish to spread the blame for the war's horrendous human toll from Stalin to include the generals. One such is V. E. Korol, who accuses most Soviet generals of consciously treating their soldiers as cannon fodder, concluding that: "V. Astaf'ev was correct when he declared, 'We simply did not know how to fight. We finished the war without knowing how to fight. We poured out our blood and threw back the enemy with our bodies'."[63] While some generals may indeed have been callous, incompetent, or lacked knowledge about modern war, it is unfair to place all the blame with them and not look at the wider picture, which must include the urgent need to get men to the front in 1941 and the consequences of the methods employed by the state and its ability to recruit, train, equip, and organize an army in the midst of total war. Given the history of the Red Army – and even the Imperial Army – one should not be surprised that training turned out to be the weakest link in the preparation of individuals and new units for battle (followed by weapons shortages) thus resulting in continuous high combat losses.

For the course of the war training took place when a unit formed or was pulled out of the line. Most units formed during the war went from inception to combat in only two months. During those two months training was conducted at the level of competence of the cadre, which varied widely. The material status of the unit affected the level of training as well. Obviously, training could not begin until sufficient supplies arrived. Invariably, the entire two months were not utilized for training as the leadership of new units had to attend to a plethora of administrative details as they processed the soldiers and distributed equipment, weapons, and supplies. With scant training of new units and replacement personnel it stands to reason that the lessons of the war were passed on to the rank and file in the shallowest manner or not at all. Poor training from the beginning – even before the German invasion – resulted in heavy casualties which necessitated quick reinforcement by large numbers of personnel and thus resulted in abbreviated training thereby creating a permanent cycle of poor training and high casualties, and excessive loss of materiel.

Gabriel Temkin's 78th Rifle Division was pulled out of the line only twice in 1943 – July and November. In July the division was replenished with several thousand replacements, but was granted only one month to train them before being recommitted to combat. In November, the division was again pulled out of the line. This time men received new uniforms and winter gear, but did very little military training.

Casualties sustained by the RKKA in 1944 and 1945 in Eastern Europe, and in China and Korea fighting the Japanese, according to official statistics – which probably represent a minimum number, rather than a definitive accounting – amount to 1,099,465 dead and missing, and 2,790,221 wounded and ill.[64] But, once the life of the USSR was secure in the second half of 1943, and particularly in 1944 when Soviet territory had been cleared of Germans, why did the high command not slow the pace of operations in order to better train and equip the Red Army and thereby reduce casualties? While no definitive answer is intended here, certain observations can be made. First, Stalin's view of postwar Europe dictated that as much of Europe as possible be occupied by Soviet troops before peace was made, which necessitated beating the armies of the Western Allies not only to the heart of Europe but Eastern Europe as well. This resulted in a quick pace of operations on a broad front. Second, habits once ingrained are not easily broken, and it is not known whether the Soviet high command recognized the correlation between high casualties, rapid turnover, and inadequate training and supply which would have led them to change their manning policies or conduct of operations.

The officer corps at war

As in peacetime, the army at war resorted to creative, non-traditional methods to fill leadership gaps with trained, semi-trained, and untrained personnel. To fill generals' positions, the army resorted to rapid promotion and appointment of non-military personnel, particularly in the rear services, and occasionally for *opolchenie* units. By and large the generals responded to the challenge of modern war particularly at the higher levels where they were not likely to become casualties. Many who survived the painful lessons of 1941 and 1942 went on to redeem themselves in 1943 and after.

Stalin's high expectations of his generals and marshals transcended friendship during this critical time. After giving his longtime friends Marshal Voroshilov and Marshal Kulik several important military commands which they botched he had them both transferred in disgrace to administrative duties. After the war he had Kulik executed. After directing several notorious and costly tactical failures, Stalin named Marshal Georgi Zhukov Deputy Supreme Commander and maintained for himself the active role of strategic oversight which he played with an iron fist, yet by and large he left the generals with the responsibility and initiative for tactical operations though he remained the final arbiter of all major operational decisions.

At the end of 1940, the Red Army had 407 generals; it began the war six months later with 994 generals and ended with 2,952, but as is so often the case in human affairs, as quantity increased, quality decreased. Of the 2,956 generals serving in mid-1944, only eighty had graduated from the Higher Military Academy, seventy-four from the Higher Military Academy short course, 768 from various other military academies, 318 from military academy short courses, 999 from special advanced courses, 494 from military schools but without advanced training, and 223 from various short courses of less intensity than military school. Generals of the rear services, political administration, and juridical service had no military education *per se*. In Stalin's opinion over half of the generals had not been properly prepared through the military education system. He claimed personal knowledge of 142 who did not have any military education whatsoever and added that the first thing to be done was to pull them out of their duties and give them appropriate military education.[65]

Similarly, Marshal Zhukov was not impressed at all by the majority of generals. In August 1944 he complained to the cadre section of the Commissariat of Defense that many commanders of armies, fronts, corps, and divisions were not at all well trained. He blamed it on the prewar years when the NKO did not prepare candidates for their higher positions, which also happened during the war. He did not mentioned his culpability as prewar Chief of the General Staff. Zhukov reported that many officers had been called from the reserves to command regiments or battalions who had never had command experience. They learned about war at the front at the price of much blood. He lamented that the reserve system did not actively train officers and keep their skills up or improve them in peacetime. He further decried the lack of culture and sophistication of the majority of high ranking officers. The officer corps was not up to the requirements of modern war, which, according to Zhukov, was eight-tenths technical. He thought the army needed officers who understood their own and the enemy's technical capacity, in particular artillery, tanks, and aviation – the crux of modern warfare. The Red Army suffered significant material and human losses because many officers were, in Zhukov's words, "technologically illiterate."[66] Furthermore, although many generals had passed through the military education system, Zhukov felt that the system, particularly the academies, did not prepare the officer corps to command in wartime. Finally, he saw a big problem with commanders not using their initiative, especially in the first part of the war. This having potential political ramifications, Zhukov put forth no suggestions on how to deal with it. There may be some hypocrisy in Zhukov's assessment, for as of yet no evidence has surfaced that Zhukov went out of his way to train his subordinate generals during the war.

The experience of war for officers below the rank of general was exceptionally difficult. In the initial period of the war casualties were so high and turnover so rapid, that when coupled with the continuing creation of new units, training was always abbreviated, which then perpetuated the high casualty rate, thus necessitating quick replacement which created a vicious cycle of inadequate training of replacement officers and high casualties for the duration of the war. The result was that a minority of officers in regiments had the chance to assimilate the lessons of war. Add into this equation rapid promotion of inadequately trained junior officers to battalion, regimental and brigade commands and casualties all around stayed high and mastery of the lessons of war remained low.

Russian historian B. V. Sokolov, gives unverified figures of losses of officers in all the armed forces due to death and capture in combat in 1941–45 as 1,023,093 men and women. Another 5,026 died from illness and other reasons, and 20,071 officers were sentenced to demotion by tribunals. The RKKA discharged 1,030,721 because of wounds. He maintains the ground forces alone lost 937,000 officers killed or captured.[67]

The rapid turnover of officers quickly led to a decrease in the ages of new officers. Before the beginning of the great expansion of the army in 1936–37 officers normally began military school at age eighteen and graduated at age twenty or twenty-one. During the war, training prior to commissioning usually lasted only two months and most new *mladshie leitenanty* took command of their platoons at age eighteen, and were often younger than many of their soldiers. So many young officers flooded the army that men like eighteen-year-old Lieutenant Oleg Rakhmanin and his fellow artillery school graduates, who reported for their first duty to participate in the Kursk–Orel offensive in July 1943, jokingly referred to men in the ages of twenty-five to thirty as "Elders" and "Fathers."[68]

From the beginning to end of the war an overwhelming number of units were commanded by officers of lower rank than the position called for. Dire straits found *mladshie leitenanty* commanding battalions in the defense of Moscow in 1941. It was normal even in 1945 to find companies commanded by lieutenants rather than captains, battalions commanded by captains rather than majors, and brigades and regiments led by majors rather than lieutenant colonels or colonels. In those cases when a division or corps commander and his staff had mastered the techniques of modern warfare, the lack of expertise in their subordinate regiments continued to keep combat losses excessive.

The Party and the Army in wartime

However reminiscent of a Soviet propaganda theme it may seem, the war probably reinforced the unity of the military political workers with the commanders, the process of which had certainly begun well before the war. On 10 July 1941, after two weeks of disaster on the battlefield, Stalin ordered the reinstitution of dual command as a sign of lack of faith in the military leadership. Subsequent elaboration of this order re-established that commissars answered together with the commander for fulfillment of a unit's military tasks making them equally liable for failure. When General Pavlov, commander of the Western Front, was executed in the summer of 1942, his commissar, Grigorev, was also shot. It stands to reason that commissars were equally as likely as commanders to find themselves in combat penal battalions if their unit fell apart and retreated. Finally, on 9 October 1942, dual command was abolished for the last time and *edinonachalie* permanently restored. The order encouraged the transfer to military command of those commissars with the best preparation and experience in combat and required deputy commanders for political affairs to be awarded appropriate military rank.

The issue of dual command or *edinonachalie* seems to have had little impact at the front. Relations between commanders and commissars usually remained strong for a variety of reasons. First, at the division level and higher, commanders personally chose their commissars so there was little likelihood of personality clashes. Second, just as in the prewar years, there was a constant exchange of personnel between PUR and the officer corps which served to diminish conflicting identities. In wartime the exchange of personnel, mostly from PUR to the officer corps, accelerated. Indications are that the Commissariat of Defense treated officers and commissars as a single manpower pool. Some men went back and forth between PUR and command assignments. Extreme battlefield conditions found some men acting as both commander and commissar: Private Timofei I. Morozov wrote to his daughter in October 1942 that he had been given two assignments: company *zampolit* and platoon commander. Vasilii V. Usanov, conscripted at the beginning of the war, began his service as *politruk* of a sapper battalion and within months was made a Senior Lieutenant and given command of his own sapper battalion.[69] Some commissars actively sought to become officers and a regular procedure was established to facilitate such transfers.

A third reason for harmonious relations between commanders and commissars was that they shared the perils of the front together. Commissars took part in combat and suffered massive casualties along with their officer peers. An example of a positive relation between commander and commissar, born of wartime conditions, was that of battalion *zampolit*, Larion L. Lega and his battalion commander. They had been together for about fourteen months when Lega was killed in action. On Larion's death his commander wrote to Lega's wife:

> Larion became more than a brother to me. We were together shoulder to shoulder, for a span of eight months on the road of war, together routed Germans, together enjoyed letters from our wives, together lay under exploding artillery and mortar shells, and bombs. We learned from each other and supported one another.[70]

Commissars, throughout the war, often made their presence felt in a positive way in the thick of battle, issuing orders and enforcing the orders of the commander. Indeed, commissars were expected to be at the forefront of battle. To reinforce the idea of the fighting role of commissars, in August 1941 PUR distributed a poster of a commissar, pistol in hand, leading some soldiers. The caption read: "The military commissar – father and soul of your unit." The pervasive and often heroic participation of political workers in battle gave many the informal credentials needed to make their commanders respect their opinions on military matters, or even to make independent military decisions when appropriate. Unfortunately, PUR, like the officer corps, suffered continual large-scale turnover due to death and injury which inhibited the accumulation of institutional knowledge.

Although it was not uncommon for officers to serve as commissars, PUR manned itself mostly by mobilizing party members, and recruiting men from within the ranks of soldiers. For military work the party did its best to find men with experience of organizational work in party organs. PUR tried to assign men to military political duties that corresponded to the level of their civilian duties. This resulted in many highly placed civilian party officials, including numerous Central Committee members, being assigned as commissars of divisions, corps, and armies very much as in the Civil War. Just as Stalin had been a front commissar during the Civil War, Nikita Khrushchev, as a Politburo member, served as commissar of a front during the Second World War. Training of these mobilized party members and Komsomols was haphazard. Some went straight to the front from civilian life, while others went to short political instructors' courses.

Party-political work during the war consisted of inspiring and encouraging the men before, during and after combat, recruiting new members to the party or Komsomol, communicating the party line, maintaining discipline, and bolstering morale. Attempts to inspire men before battle consisted mainly of speeches to large groups of soldiers. Gabriel Temkin recalled that in his regiment the Komsomol organizer,

> was generally liked, particularly by the younger soldiers, perhaps because his enthusiastic though naive speeches were genuine, strikingly sincere, and his optimism echoed their own dreams about the future. [He also acknowledged that some commissars] were quite capable of bringing about a desired improvement in mood and behavior, in raising the morale of the troops. I myself witnessed polit-propaganda officers who were not only able speakers but also had the gift of giving their speeches a spiritual meaning, infusing in their listeners a sense of honor, duty, and courage before major battles.[71]

Small group talks could be highly effective. Whenever possible, PUR recruited combat veterans of the units, sergeants and privates, who were party members or Komsomols, to act as "agitators," to give pep talks. After bàttle, to motivate soldiers for the next time, units held party meetings at which they decided who would get medals for their combat performance.

The unfortunate anti-religious policy of the communist regime – which was maintained in the army despite the partial rehabilitation of the Orthodox Church during the war – deprived the men of religious inspiration prior to battle or spiritual comfort when wounded or dying. Except for religion, the army and PUR used the universally standard methods to raise morale such as informational lectures, entertainment, education and propaganda. Travelling lecturers, troupes, and orchestras went from unit to unit providing a brief respite from the terror of combat and monotony of army life. In addition to entertainment the army did its best to provide the men with the daily "100," the euphemism for one hundred grams of vodka.

Recruiting new members to the party took on more significance than it had ever had before the war. On the one hand the regime desired some overt display of the army's continued loyalty, especially during the dark days of 1941; on the other hand, to keep party representation at a minimal level, there needed to be continuous replenishment of party members to replace the fallen. It is not easy to know who joined out of political or patriotic conviction and who for selfish reasons, hoping to get material benefits from party membership, but in letters home by men who had just been admitted to the party there is a general sense of accomplishment and happiness. To facilitate recruitment the Central Committee, in August 1941, reduced the candidacy period for party membership from three years to one year for men on active military service. In December 1941, the candidacy period for the best soldiers was reduced to three months. PUR closely monitored the process of recruitment to the party. It alternatively praised or condemned unit party organs for success or failure in recruiting and issuing party cards.[72]

Just as during the Civil War, the party considered Komsomols and party members to be more reliable soldiers and expected greater effort from them than non-party soldiers. These expectations became internalized by more than a few communists. One, Ivan A. Iuptaev, wrote home in 1943, "If more people would join the party then Hitler would be defeated more quickly."[73] The granting of a party or Komsomol card was intended to be done with ceremony to evoke a greater sense of commitment to the war on the part of the new recipients. Zoya Medvedeva remembered her induction into the Komsomol in 1942 thus:

> Just before the fierce fighting for Sevastopol started, we were admitted into the Komsomol. The distribution of the membership cards took place in the dugout of the HQ defence platoon. In front of a little table covered with a red cloth, political instructor Sergeyev handed out the cards and subsequently shook our hands firmly. In turn, we promised him to spare no effort in defending Sevastopol and, if necessary, sacrifice our very lives.[74]

The expectations of higher performance are reflected in a report of General-Major Emel'ianov, the chief of the political administration of the Primorskaia Army, in April 1944. The five divisions of the Primorskaia Army had just failed in their attempt to liberate Sevastopol, and Emel'ianov pinpointed the role of party-political work in the failure. The first important point that becomes clear is that General Emel'ianov expected better results in the next assault from having more party members and blamed the failed storming of the German defenses on 23 and 24 April on lax prebattle recruiting to the party. During the time the army had been in the Crimea up to the days of the attack and its preparation (20–25 April 1944) only 359 men had been admitted to the party and fewer than a third had been issued with their party cards. All the division political sections were considered to have fallen short of desirable performance, but one political section was singled out for not having issued a single party card to any of the forty men it had admitted.[75] Although the two days of fighting were sufficiently intense to produce over 1,150 Soviet casualties, Emel'ianov criticized the resolve of the men to take the city. In part he blamed the failure on the fact that "the political organs did not do everything to prepare individuals and especially the officers in their resolve to storm Sevastopol." The officers were criticized for poorly preparing for the attack, especially for their unwillingness to conduct hazardous reconnaissance patrols. The result was an attack with little knowledge of enemy defenses, which proved to be much stronger than anticipated. With no information about German positions, artillery fire had had little effect in the first attack. Ultimate victory, it was implied, would have to come through the efforts of the party organs, which would strengthen the men's resolve to take Sevastopol and get the officers to do a better job preparing for combat operations.

The Soviet Army in combat: 1941 and 1945

A conclusion that may have already been reached by the reader is that the Soviet people suffered so much during their war with Nazi Germany not only because their army was not ready at the outset of the war, but also because it was continually being remade during the war because of its losses. The level of tactical proficiency of the front-line regiments and divisions fluctuated up and down, but only within a narrow, rather low range of competence. Several official after battle reports highlight details of the Red Army's need to improve its training and its continual learning process.

In August 1941, after five weeks of disaster and retreat the Commissariat of Defense called for an investigation into the failure of the army's armored forces. On 5 August 1941, General-major Volskii submitted his report on the matter. All of Volskii's criticisms point to one root cause of the problems – officer training. Volskii criticized the assignment of mechanized corps to armies rather than to fronts because army commanders had no idea how to use them, and he considered the striking power of the corps to be of a strategic rather than a tactical nature, thus more effectively employed by the higher command. Volskii implies that front commanders possessed the requisite skill in the application of armor. Army commanders on several occasions had ordered tank and motorized forces to pull back and occupy fortified areas, or to man static linear defenses, which was a misuse of their mobility, depriving the army of inherent advantages of armor and in practice failing to achieve the desired result. Because of their lack of training, army commanders did not know how to combine infantry and armor together in operations and therefore employed them separately, thereby reducing the effectiveness of both. Army commanders usually sent tank units into battle with neither reconnaissance nor up-to-date intelligence on the enemy, nor information on adjacent units. Inexperienced corps commanders used their forces improperly, sending tanks into the fray not only in small groups but also as individual vehicles. The lack of familiarity with armored formations by senior officers and their staffs proved devastating to the armored vehicles themselves. Ignorant of the maintenance and resupply requirements of armored vehicles army staffs made no provisions in their battle plans for mechanized units to perform routine but vital maintenance and resupply their fuel and ammunition – a far more complex and time consuming undertaking for armored units than for the more familiar infantry. The special staff officers of army headquarters assigned to oversee the needs of mechanized forces failed to bring these needs to the attention of their commanders, who kept desperately throwing their armored forces into the breach with less effectiveness and greater losses each time. Frequently, armored units lost more vehicles by abandonment due to mechanical breakdown and lack of fuel than to enemy action.

Volskii severely criticized the lower level commanders who were supposed to have more intimate knowledge of the needs and use of their vehicles and units. He accused mechanized corps, tank division and tank regiment commanders and staffs of not having mastered the tactical and organizational skills required of armored unit commanders. They did not exercise initiative, nor did they exploit their forces' maneuverability. Moreover, as a rule commanders attacked the Germans head-on, rather than from the flanks, and neglected reconnaissance. Command and control by officers of the smallest to the largest armored formations were extremely poor.

General Volskii noted that before the war no one in the military school system had thought through what mechanized forces might encounter, not only by way of combat maneuver, but also of support needs and inter-arms coordination. This lack of foresight extended to the General Staff and Commissariat of Defense, where there was a complete lack of appreciation of the particular needs of large armored formations. Thus, Volskii summarized, "Some commanders in the mechanized corps were not up to their job and had completely no idea of how to command [their units]." It might be added that they were not always given the necessary means to get the most out of their men and machines either.

Some may be tempted to blame the 1937–39 purge of the officer corps for the lack of command experience with tanks, but not a single tank division commander or staff member was purged. The simple reason being that there were no tank divisions in those years. The RKKA did not begin forming its first tank divisions until 1940, hence the lack of training and experience. All of the armored units sent into battle in 1941 had been in existence only a matter of months. Subsequently, all tank units created during the war would exist for only a few months before being committed to battle.

A second report, also from August 1941, to Stalin from Chief of Red Army Artillery, General N. N. Voronov, is an evaluation of the performance of the 24th Army in the battles around El'nia from 20 July through

5 August.[76] In the report Voronov evaluates the performance of the 24th Army's infantry, artillery, and tanks, the supporting aviation, and enemy tactics in a battle that momentarily raised the hopes of Stavka that the string of German successes was nearly at an end. The section on infantry reads like a catalog of woes – all related to unpreparedness. The infantry did not know how to get the best use of their weapons; sections and platoons were not used properly by their leaders. The men did not know how to fire and maneuver using basic squad tactics. Infantry commanders and soldiers did not know how to bring artillery and mortar fire onto the enemy. They did not know how to time the use of their fire. On the other hand, the Germans knew how to attack under Soviet artillery and mortar fire. At the moment the Red Army did not know how to make use of its infantry in order to approach, attack and seize assigned objectives with the minimum of casualties. The infantry was slow to return fire, and slow to take up the use of camouflage.

Additionally, neighboring units did a poor job supporting each other. Under the slightest pressure soldiers were quick to withdraw. The infantry had a very unhealthy reaction to the appearance of enemy airplanes. The infantry did not have the means to engage enemy aircraft. Reconnaissance efforts were poorly organized. Without the help of local scouts they would not have learned anything of the enemy.

Voronov criticized front-line administration as well as combat performance. He observed that there was poor record keeping of killed and wounded. He wrote, "There is poor accountability for men in the companies which creates the appearance of large losses." He added that, "Evacuation of wounded from the field of battle is poorly organized, many instances leave much to be desired in the removal of wounded." Company logistics were in the hands of sergeants, who uniformly performed poorly.

About the artillery, his specialty, his comments were terse. Voronov noted that in many instances artillery men and officers were not thoroughly trained. Communications were not well maintained between the artillery and infantry and between superior and subordinate artillery units. The artillery was poorly supplied and its supply badly organized. The result was that, according to German prisoners, Red Army artillery caused few casualties.

Regarding armor he reported: "Tanks are employed in small numbers on a narrow front. The experience of fighting around El'nia shows the total pointlessness of using our KV and T-34 tanks in small numbers against organized enemy defenses." Voronov corroborates Volskii's observation that tank units were poorly prepared to work together with infantry and artillery. Furthermore, tanks often became separated from the infantry exposing them to fire from enemy anti-tank weapons.

In his comments on aviation General Voronov probably did not tell Stalin anything he did not already know: "For the entire period of activity enemy aviation clearly dominated the air . . . they inflicted losses and seriously hurt morale of our forces. Only in the last three days have our forces had a few successes and become a bit more active." That there was poor communication between air representatives in the divisions and the airfields, and poor coordination and cooperation with the ground forces should come as no surprise.

Still, despite Soviet shortcomings, Voronov saw some bright spots, writing that "In the area of El'nia from 5 August 1941 units of the enemy were sufficiently morally shocked and had large losses in personnel and material." As a result the Germans were denied the objectives they had sought to capture. Things would have worked out even better but, "Poor combat training of our forces, poor cooperation and low discipline did not produce the success necessary to assume the offensive." Specifically, poor administration from the top, and insufficient training of commanders and staff, made it impossible to exploit successes. Voronov particularly lamented the poor reconnaissance and intelligence gathering which "deprived us of the opportunity to act." Further success was precluded by the lack of necessary discipline, organization and purpose in the divisions. Once again, training at all levels seems to have been the key ingredient missing that would have reduced Soviet losses and prevented large-scale German success. That the Red Army was able to inflict serious damage on the Germans was indeed reason for optimism, but the similarity of these two reports to that of Voroshilov's 1940 post-winter war report did not speak well of the army's ability to learn quickly from its experiences and implement changes.

A report dated 31 March 1945 by Chief of the Political Administration of the 1st Belorussian Front, General-lieutenant Galadshev, to his superiors on the front military soviet and the Chief of PUR, on the battle for Poznan, Poland reflects the differences between the Red Army of 1941 and that of 1945. The battle took place during January and February 1945 and deserved a special report because Poznan turned out to be unexpectedly difficult to subdue. Unexpected, because the 8th Guards Army, commanded by General Vasilii Chuikov, was in the process of rampaging across northern Poland and into East Prussia at the time, sweeping all before it until it bumped up against the stubborn defenders of Poznan. The 8th Guards Army encircled Poznan on 22 January 1945 and, failing to take it from the march, left a corps to capture it as soon as possible.[77]

To begin, General-lieutenant Galadshev explained that the city was not taken initially because, "A check of workers of the political administration exposed serious shortcomings in the military work of units and formations and in party-political work which hampered the fulfillment of combat tasks." One of the main problems was that many commanders and political workers were thrilled by the previous victories of the winter and had ceased to take into account that the enemy still was able to mount serious resistance. This main deficiency led to such subsequent shortcomings as the cessation of coordination between the two rifle corps of two different armies operating in the vicinity of Poznan. The commanders of these corps failed to share information. As this problem was revealed, command of all units in Poznan devolved solely into the hands of General Chuikov. Before the first attack, the Soviet forces very poorly reconnoitered the German forces defending Poznan. One report said the city was defended by only five or six thousand men, another that it was protected by 20,000. It turned out to be defended by nearly 50,000 German soldiers. Ignorantly pushing against the fortified lines of an enemy of underestimated strength caused the majority of initial casualties. As a result, commanders stepped up reconnaissance and political workers stepped up propaganda work against enemy soldiers.

Another problem was that men began to shirk their combat duty. In the first days of the attack few men participated in the fighting. One rifle battalion of a guards rifle regiment mustered only 15–16 riflemen for the assault, whereas rosters indicated there were supposed to be some 157 men in this grossly depleted battalion. "Where were these people at the time of combat?" asked Galadshev rhetorically. He answered they were hanging out in the homes of the local Polish inhabitants, drunk. Other regiments reported equally low numbers of effectives. The front commander quickly ordered the military procuracy of the front to prosecute shirkers as a way of increasing discipline and the number of men in the front-lines.

The old problem of coordination and cooperation between the various arms surfaced in the attack on the city. The artillery fell behind the infantry and did not know what the infantry's objectives were. The artillery did not know which buildings were occupied by the Germans and which were not. There was a distinct lack of knowledge on how tanks, self-propelled guns and infantry were to cooperate in the street fighting. Galadshev then credits the political organs for addressing and overcoming the corps' problems in taking Poznan. The corps' political workers were ordered to quickly have veterans of Stalingrad teach the newer recruits. They canvassed the divisions for veterans of Stalingrad and battles in other cities and organized them to instruct the rest of the soldiers in the tactics and techniques of urban warfare.

At the suggestion of veterans of Stalingrad, rifle battalions were reinforced with tanks, artillery, and flamethrowers transforming them into battalion-sized storm detachments which were further subdivided into storm groups. Soldiers were grouped into five man assault teams. The corps' political organs organized some exclusively communist and Komsomol storm groups and sections. Groups were supported by direct fire from two or three self-propelled guns, two or three field guns and indirect fire from division artillery.

PUR organized a party cell and a Komsomol organization in each detachment. Communists and Komsomols were given intense motivational talks and indoctrination as to their role in leading and inspiring their detachment or group in preparation for the resumption of the attack. The report claims that Komsomols did most of the political education work in the storm groups and acted as role models fighting fanatically in storming enemy positions. Several communists in each storm group were designated agitators with the task of coming up with short two- or three-sentence slogans about the need to take the next objective. Detachments with large numbers of party members or Komsomols were assigned to spearhead most attacks. They correspondingly suffered heavy losses.

The main role assigned to party organs and bureaus of primary party organizations in street fighting was to keep the men motivated in the attack and to keep an eye out for and prevent drunkenness and looting, and to keep men from fading away from the firing lines. Officers were said to be unable to do this as they were preoccupied with the fight at the very front-lines. Party members were also to keep an eye out for valorous behavior so they could recruit those men into the party on the spot. Communist agitators used not only words, but also actions to inspire their fellow soldiers and officers. One common tactic was to carry the red flag of the USSR in the vanguard of assaults. When one attack on Poznan's citadel began to falter, a man holding a red flag leapt forward shouting, "For the Fatherland, for Stalin, forward!" and the rest of the detachment followed him. The political apparatus strongly urged immediate recognition of outstanding performance in combat with medals and awards and then spreading the word of the deeds among the other soldiers as a means of continuing to motivate the men in the midst of battle. Galadshev made great importance of the work of agitators in the victory at Poznan.

In street fighting regimental agitators and workers of political organizations were located with the battalions and storm groups. There they passed on the latest news from Sovinformbiuro, related the latest heroic acts, told how many Germans the regiments had killed and captured in the battle, gave lectures on the current military situation with the 8th Guards Army, and highlighted Stalin's latest pronouncements, etc. Agitators passed out the all-important newspapers to the front-line soldiers. Of course the agitators were not completely successful in motivating all soldiers. Galadshev included an incident in which three flamethrower operators showed cowardice by letting the compressed air out of their flamethrowers then claimed they did not work so they could be excused from the flamethrower detachment. They were immediately turned over to a court-martial. The report sums up the contributions of the political sections in overcoming the problems in the opening phase of the battle for Poznan enumerated earlier. At the top level, the 8th Guards Army political section served to facilitate communications between the various unit commanders. Corps and division political sections did the same at their level. Most significant perhaps was the work of *zampolits* in the rifle units and the support given them by higher political sections. They ensured communication and fulfillment of orders, helped man storm units and prepared them for fulfilling their tasks.

135

Most important, of course, was what happened at the front. Galadshev wrote, "The center of all party-political work was in the storm groups." It was given maximum attention by staffs and political sections. Komsomols and party members of all arms of storm groups held meetings to strengthen the combined arms work of the groups, increase the feeling of comradeship, and discuss how to coordinate their efforts. Division party commissions also kept up their work during the battle. The commission secretaries organized and held meetings to handle party business such as admitting applicants and examining infringements of party or military duties by party members. Another important job of senior party instructors was to keep track of casualties of communists.

At higher levels the party also had important practical work to do. Division political sections helped evacuate wounded and bury the dead. Political sections also combed the rear areas for supernumerary men, vehicles, and horses and sent them back to the front. One division political section flushed out nearly 300 men from the rear to send to the front in the last days of January, before the resumption of the attack on Poznan. Despite this success, Galadshev admitted that the work and organization of party and Komsomol organizations in the rear area was poor. For example, both the regimental supply point and the automotive company of one division went for over a month without holding meetings, and not a single man was admitted to the party in that time. In his conclusion General Galadshev stressed the role of the political apparatus and party members in assisting the military leadership in achieving victory in Poznan.

The most illuminating aspect of the report is how the Red Army was able to regroup and teach itself how to fight in the middle of a battle. One reason for this was the Red Army had the initiative, and in this instance could take the time to regroup and reorganize before returning to the attack. In 1941, front-line units seldom had the luxury of time for reappraisal, and, because the Germans had the initiative, generally spent most of their time reacting to German attacks. Another telling aspect was the especially active role of the party and political organs and communist and Komsomol soldiers and officers. These groups and individuals were far better organized and far more active and motivated in 1945 than in 1941. In most of 1941 and 1942 after action reports there were calls for greater political work, but in 1945 such work was more often than not highly integrated into the standard procedures of combat units and paid obvious dividends. On the purely military side, recurring problems with reconnaissance and coordination between units continued to result in unnecessary losses.

The story of the Red Army in the Second World War is essentially one of continuous death and rebirth. Most of the old army had disappeared in battle by January 1942 and most of the new army had an entirely different outlook on military service and reasons for fighting than had soldiers in service before

22 June 1941. Hundreds of thousands of patriotic, motivated, and educated urban party members and Komsomols volunteered to fight for a cause they deeply believed in. They were the type of soldier Lenin and Trotsky had dreamed of in 1917. Millions of others served willingly and faithfully, if not voluntarily, at the behest of the regime to defeat a hated and despised enemy. The army was united in a way it never had been before and never would be again, the political and party organs doing all they could to facilitate military success in cooperation with the officer corps. Unfortunately, the state took advantage of the people's willingness to fight and needlessly sent large numbers of people to their deaths through incompetence and desperation of both military and civilian leaders, rather than give sufficient training and equipment to ensure soldiers a fair chance for survival. In the end victory came through a combination of extensive human sacrifice, trial and error learning by the high command, selfless sacrifice on the homefront of male and female peasants and industrial workers, allied material aid, and the political leadership and organization of the wartime economy, to name only a few of the many components of the successful war effort. The final tribute must be ascribed, however, to the individual Soviet citizen who played his or her role and paid the price for the army's and regime's unpreparedness in 1941.

6

THE COLD WAR YEARS, 1946–91

The years of intense suffering by the Soviet people and their army that eventually resulted in victory greatly affected the army and society. For a generation Soviet society held the army in high regard making officer recruitment far easier than previously. Ironically, for the first ten years or so after the war the army had little need to recruit officer candidates because so many officers wanted to stay in the army. Indeed, until late 1953 the officer corps was bloated with officers to the point that it maintained a 1 : 4.5 ratio of officers to enlisted men, about twice as many as necessary.[1] The army became a fully motorized and mechanized army, with no more simple infantry divisions. Airborne divisions too, had air dropable armored fighting vehicles making the Soviet Army one of the most technologically advanced and mobile armies of the world. The price of the technical advance of the armed forces was borne both by society and the army. The military-industrial complex diverted scarce resources from civilian production and the generals diverted funds away from maintaining the soldiers' quality of life to high-tech weapons systems.

In the postwar years, especially after Stalin's death, the party and the army reached their peak of unity. The army's loyalty to the regime was unquestioned and unquestionable, and any idea that the army needed a watchdog died with Stalin. Unfortunately for the army, its close association with the party and government caused it to stagnate along with them in the 1960s, 1970s, and 1980s. The Second World War generation of officers held on to the top posts of command and administration well beyond their mental and physical limits. In 1990 the army still had thousands of generals who had started their careers during or before the 1941 German invasion. As a consequence of the lack of dynamic leadership and institutional stagnation the army lost touch with society becoming a world of its own. Officers lived as a superior caste apart from their men, which bred in them callousness and indifference leading some to physically abuse their men, the same way tsarist officers had.

Stalin and the army, 1945–53

In the aftermath of the war there seems to have been some tension between Stalin and his generals. On the part of the marshals and generals and many other officers and soldiers there was considerable resentment over Stalin having assumed all credit for the victory over fascism. Stalin could not have been unaware of this resentment and feared their acting against him. In particular he was uneasy with the popularity of many of the leading marshals and generals. In 1946, Stalin appointed Marshal Zhukov Supreme Commander of the Ground Forces and nominated him to the Central Committee – a post to which he was duly elected – yet the top military post in the government, that of Minister of Defense, went to Bulganin, a civilian. Later in 1946, secret police chief Lavrenti Beria arrested several officers close to Zhukov and coerced them into denouncing him as disloyal to Stalin. Ironically, Beria charged Zhukov with claiming more credit for victory in the Second World War than he deserved. Stalin dismissed Zhukov as Supreme Commander of the Ground Forces, transferred him to command the Odessa Military District, and removed him from the Central Committee. In 1947, more men who had at one time or another worked for Zhukov were arrested and coerced to denounce him as the leader of a military conspiracy against Stalin. As it turned out, Stalin did not consent to Zhukov's arrest and later had an assistant of Beria's arrested and shot. In October 1952 Stalin again nominated Zhukov to the Central Committee.

As long as Stalin continued to dictate the party line on the history of the war the military was unable to delve into the true strategic lessons of the war and had to confine themselves to studies of smaller operations and tactics. In 1956, three years after Stalin's death, the new General Secretary of the Communist Party, Nikita Khrushchev, asked Zhukov to write a report on Stalin's true role in the war. This report could have served as the basis for a general review of the strategic questions of the war, but instead Zhukov used it as a platform to denounce Stalin and blame all of the army's prewar and wartime shortcomings on him and his "cult of personality" rather than assessing each problem on its own merits. The only lesson advanced by inference was not to let the country or army fall under the sway of a dictator's cult of personality and everything would be fine.[2]

With Stalin's death the army took on an active role in politics it would not relinquish until well after the August coup of 1991. In order to secure power for themselves Khrushchev and Georgii Malenkov recruited Zhukov to a plot to eliminate Lavrenti Beria from the tentative triumvirate the three had formed. On 26 June 1953 Zhukov personally participated in the arrest of Beria and used military units under his control to guard the site where Beria was held until his execution. His reward was the post of Minister of Defense until Khrushchev abruptly dismissed him in 1957 fearing that Zhukov had designs on power.

Within months after Stalin's death and Beria's liquidation, Nikita Khrushchev began to drastically reduce the size of the armed forces in both personnel and units. He carried out this reduction in the armed forces over a period of six years and eventually pared the size of all of the Warsaw Treaty Organization (WTO) armies. He simultaneously withdrew many Soviet Army units from Eastern Europe. Between March 1953 and December 1958 the Soviet armed forces were reduced by 1.7 million men, from 5.3 million to 3.6 million. Khrushchev claimed he was able to do this because the USSR had expanded its nuclear forces to a degree making a large standing army unnecessary and because he felt sure of the loyalty of the Eastern bloc to communism and the Soviet Union. He also professed faith that the 1955 Geneva Conference obviated large peacetime armies. Furthermore, he claimed the need to shrink the army and pull back from Eastern Europe was an economizing measure. Supposedly at Zhukov's suggestion, officers' pay was cut saving the government even more money.[3] In 1960, Khrushchev proposed cutting another 1.2 million men from the armed forces. The reductions began, but were halted in 1961 due to the international crisis that resulted from the building of the Berlin Wall and were not resumed.

All branches of the armed forces gave up personnel and shrank their structures but the ground forces lost the most in absolute numbers. GlavPUR (as PUR was redesignated during the war) for its part eliminated 13,000 political workers from its ranks in 1955. The reduction of forces met with mixed reactions from the army. The rank and file expressed delight at the cuts, which sent many home before their two years were up, but officers who had plans for careers voiced negative feelings. On the one hand some saw the USSR returning to 1941 conditions of preparedness, which, in terms of numbers was quite true. On the other hand self-interest seems to have been the main source of distress. In 1957 and 1958 a total of 135,500 military and political officers ranging from generals to junior lieutenants were discharged from the service. Tens of thousands of them were not eligible for pensions, including many who had been in the service for nearly two decades. They felt a tremendous sense of injustice and betrayal, just as had those dismissed in the mass demobilization of officers in 1927. Additionally, those not eligible for pensions were also not guaranteed housing and had to fend for themselves. The lucky few transferred to the reserves could continue their careers there but still had to seek out civilian jobs. For the first time since 1927 the Soviet Army had so many officers it could scale back procurement and between 1956 and 1959 reduced the number of cadets in training by 22,000.[4] As a reflection of his reliance on nuclear weapons as a deterrent, Khrushchev established the Strategic Rocket Forces as a separate branch of the armed forces in 1960 and seemed to favor it as the premier service.

To maintain control over the Soviet empire it was essential for Khrushchev to be on good terms with the army. The first major test of loyalty came in 1956 with the crisis in Hungary. Encouraged by Khrushchev's thaw, the Hungarian Communist Party became factionalized into proreform and antireform wings with the proreform faction gaining the upper hand in mid-1956. Under Imre Nagy the reformers began to back away from Stalinist economics which made the Soviet Politburo feel threatened. Eventually, when the situation bordered on civil war in Hungary and the radical leadership proclaimed its intent to declare neutrality and withdraw from the Warsaw Pact, the Soviet leadership felt compelled to quash the Hungarian reform movement by force. On 4 November 1956 the USSR sent in some 30,000 men and a handful of armored, mechanized infantry, and airborne divisions. The invasion of Hungary, called "Operation Whirlwind" (carried out under the direction of Marshal Zhukov as Minister of Defense), resulted in ten days of fighting, mostly in Budapest, during which the Red Army killed some 2,000 Hungarians and wounded nearly 12,000 at a cost of 669 dead, 51 missing, and 1,540 wounded Soviet soldiers.[5] The army had come through for the party and government in its first cold war test.

Perhaps because of the new dependence of the party and government on the army there seems to have been much looser control over the military than under Stalin. The armed forces could count on representation in the Supreme Soviet, and the Central Committee (many of whose members were veterans of the Second World War) and often had either a candidate or full member on the Politburo.

Although the army could be relied on to suppress revolt in the satellite nations of the Eastern bloc, its willingness to kill Slavic Soviet citizens was not assured. A serious incident arose in Novocherkassk in the first week of June 1962. The incident started as a result of food shortages combined with wage cuts at a locomotive factory. Protests turned into rioting and troops of the local garrison were called in. Neither Lieutenant General Matvei Shaposhnikov, commander of some of the units in Novocherkassk, nor the garrison commander Major General Oleshko would order their men to fire on demonstrators, even when pressed in person by representatives of the Central Committee. Shaposhnikov's subordinate officers also acted with great restraint and reluctance and were fully in accord with his decision that it was neither necessary, nor appropriate, for the army to fire on unarmed citizens.

Eventually troops of a Ministry of Interior regiment did fire on the people. All told twenty-four civilians, including school children were killed. As evidence of the new political relation between the army and party neither Oleshko nor Shaposhnikov were punished at the time. However, in 1968, when Shaposhnikov requested that the Novocherkassk incident be reopened for investigation he was demoted and expelled from the party by the Brezhnev leadership.[6] This incident reflects the growing professionalization of the army in that it rebelled against being used as a police force, and until the late 1980s the regime refrained from putting the army in such a situation again. Knowledge and appreciation of this precedent of the army's unwillingness to use deadly force against unarmed Slavic Soviet citizens would have served the coup plotters of 1991 well.

Six years later the army was again put to the test of loyalty in service of ideological goals. Once again, this time in Czechoslovakia, a communist government had deviated from Soviet norms in the direction of internal economic and political reforms and radical external reforms. Like Hungary, the Czechs openly expressed an interest in withdrawing from the WTO and becoming a neutral country. The Soviet Union acted in predictable fashion organizing a multinational force of Warsaw Pact armies and invading on the night of 20–21 August 1968. Prague was seized so rapidly and with such overwhelming numbers that there was little fighting, even so ninety-six Soviet soldiers lost their lives, and perhaps two hundred Czechs and Slovaks were killed. Significant in this episode was not so much that the Soviet Army proved loyal in squashing its allies, nor that it had become proficient in invading peaceful nations, but that the army demonstrated distrust of its soldiers for this type of operation. A practice of lying to the men about the situation arose that would be repeated with disastrous consequences in Afghanistan eleven years later. The soldiers were not appraised of the true reason for the invasion, but were fed the wildest lies about threats from NATO. V. V. Nefedov, a private in the Seventh Guards Airborne Assault Division, related twenty years after the event:

> In our political classes, we had been told about events in Czechoslo-
> vakia: Extremists were trying to seize power, to wrest the republic
> from the socialist commonwealth and to restore capitalism. In early
> August we were suddenly put on alert, loaded on to trucks and
> taken to an airfield. We were told that right-wing elements in
> Czechoslovakia had stepped up their activities. We would have to
> provide assistance to the fraternal people. Before we flew out, our
> commanders distributed ammunition to us. We were told there was
> no way to know what to expect on landing. The border between
> Czechoslovakia and the FRG was now open, and we were to fore-
> stall a German invasion.[7]

As a result the soldiers were extremely confused about the hostile reception they received from the people they thought they were to help. Years later when the USSR experienced Czech-style reforms some felt remorseful and betrayed by their government.

Other significant actions by the armed forces during the cold war included instructing and advising the North Korean Army during the Korean War and providing fighter pilots. During the Vietnam war the Red Army again played an advisory role and for a year or so provided air defense crews to man North Vietnamese air defense missile batteries until the Vietnamese proved themselves proficient enough to employ them on their own. Soviet advisors could be found around the globe instructing and advising communist rebels in third world countries, as well as the armies of the anti-Israeli Arab governments in the Middle East. The Red Army held its own in numerous small- and large-scale border clashes with China in the late 1960s and early 1970s.

One result of the continuous military involvement combined with the cold war arms race with the West was that the armed forces maintained a relatively strong political position for resources in relation to its civilian competitors. This is not to say that the military had a privileged position, but that they had a highly visible one. Consequently, the Soviet regime diverted significant resources from civilian to military use. In 1952 nearly a quarter of state expenditure went to military purposes. It would never decline and steadily increased with the addition of the nuclear element until in the 1970s the growth could no longer be sustained and the amount spent on the armed forces leveled off – much to the military leadership's displeasure. Khrushchev, for example, boasted that he sacrificed numerous civilian social programs to build up the USSR's nuclear capacity on a par with the United States. After him, Brezhnev sought to gain nuclear superiority over the West at incredible and ill-advised expense to the Soviet Union's economy. Brezhnev also reversed Khrushchev's reduction of the armed forces and increased the manpower levels to nearly five million in 1970.[8]

By 1985, when Mikhail Gorbachev became General Secretary, the military–industrial complex annually absorbed 49 percent of the government's investment capital, 25 percent of the GNP, and employed four of every ten industrial workers.[9] Yet, even with consistently huge budgets, life in the army could not be considered easy. Little money went into maintaining or improving the quality of life of the officers and men – generals excepted – most found its way into the expensive nuclear program and high technology weapons development.

In many ways the peacetime army after the Second World War was quite different from the army before the war. As an institution it had finally come into its own as a result not only of the steady development since 1917, but obviously as an effect of the war years. Still, it took until the death of Stalin for the army to feel secure in its identity as an institution with interests to be represented and pursued in the political arena. This self-assurance was accompanied by broad social acceptance of the military as an honorable institution that attracted career officers. These positive changes from the prewar period were, however, accompanied by numerous negative characteristics, such as a caste mentality of officers, and the death of social idealism.

The officer corps

The ability of the army to recruit and retain officers helped create stability within the leadership and was only disrupted between 1953 and 1958 by the large-scale reduction in forces, yet even here there were positive elements in that the army used the downsizing to cull unfit members from the officer corps. Additionally, the officer corps was becoming more urban in social origin. In 1970, 54 percent of generals were peasants by social origin; at the same time, of the rising generation of officers – lieutenants and captains – only 18 percent were peasants. The army no longer depended on the party to bolster the officer corps and special mobilizations became a thing of the past. In a move that fostered elitism, the army ceased recruiting officer candidates from the ranks. All officers either entered the service through military schools or university. Many officers began their professional military training right out of high school at age fifteen as cadets in Suvorov military schools – established in 1943 as preparatory schools for military schools.

Stability was further enhanced, but perhaps to an unhealthy degree, by new terms of service for officers. Officers now were required to serve for twenty-five years and could only leave the service by transferring to the reserves at the discretion of the Ministry of Defense, or through discharge for disgraceful behavior which also required automatic revocation of party membership. Twenty years after the end of the war, however, the negative phenomenon of a caste outlook that had just emerged before the war had become solidified in the mentality of the officer corps. More and more officers came from career military families – and there were many military families as a result of the expansion of the officer corps in the Second World War. By the late 1980s the single largest group to provide officer candidates was military families.[10]

Forty years after the war, however, signs emerged that the Soviet Army leadership had become too stable – verging on stagnation. There was no mandatory retirement age and a great many officers simply refused to retire or transfer to the reserves and insisted on staying in active service into their sixties and seventies until they literally died at their posts. In this way the army became part and parcel of the era of stagnation. The army ususally assigned these elderly senior officers, all of them generals by now, as inspectors general in the Ministry of Defense's Group of Inspectors General. Inspectors general perform a very important function, they check that policies are faithfully and accurately implemented and usually have significant powers to set things right. Unfortunately, such a task requires a level of physical energy and mental alertness not often associated with octogenarians. The Soviet Army suffered inestimable harm in the 1980s because of this "old boy" system.

Prior to the Second World War army officers experienced a constant process of upward mobility due to the broad expansion of the army which continually created positions to be filled. After the war the process reversed, and there were fewer positions to be filled and plenty of officers to fill them. With generals holding on to their top jobs for years and years upward mobility slowed. This situation caused creeping stagnation and was exacerbated by the lack of a centrally controlled promotion and advancement system that put an officer's career completely in the hands of his immediate superior. Officers advanced by means of the efficiency report system.

There were no time limitations on how long an officer could fill a particular position, so commanders who were happy with a subordinate's performance could unfairly give him a low grade on efficiency reports preventing his promotion in order to retain his services. Conversely, officers who performed poorly would at times be cynically recommended for promotion in order to be disposed of. Even when a good officer was given high marks in his efficiency report, he might languish for years in his old job because his superior might not recommend him for promotion. Perhaps this is why future general and politician Alexander Lebed remained a captain and airborne school company commander for eight years, only leaving his unit by volunteering for duty in Afghanistan never having had command of a tactical unit.[11]

The practice that emerged in the crisis years before the Second World War of putting an officer of insufficient rank in charge of a unit oddly became enshrined as the desired procedure after the war when there was surfeit of officers. The promotion system became one of getting the higher position first, then earning the rank that went with it. Once the appropriate rank was earned the officer – with his commander's approval – was then allowed to begin casting about for the next higher position. From this situation developed career associations, or connections, to get ahead, rather than relying on professionalism and an impartial system. One officer referred to connections as "that cancer that afflicts our army." He bemoaned the fact that: "Competence and professionalism are qualities that seem to interest no one. The main thing is to have connections, in which case a high-ranking commander will take you along with him, into the apparatus or closer to Moscow, where conditions are incomparably better."[12] Consequently, practical preparation for higher command was virtually nonexistent. One either sank or swam as he learned on the job or was protected and advanced by powerful friends.

Higher military courses did exist and were required for promotion to lieutenant colonel yet, by the promotion system one held lieutenant colonel positions at the rank of major. Because of this arrangement, Alexander Lebed went from the routine of training airborne officer candidates to a battalion command in the war in Afghanistan with no practical or theoretical preparation whatsoever. He received his training for lieutenant colonel after he finished his tour of combat command. By the 1970s the regimen of advanced schools had slackened considerably. Staffed mainly by veterans of the Second World War who had "burned out" and saw their positions as sinecures rather than responsible assignments, the level of instruction fell precipitously. The students for their part were not blind to the prevailing attitude and took their time at military academies as vacations. Eventually, many top officers were simply unfit for command as the weeding out process succumbed to stagnation and indifference.[13]

With the elevation of their place in society and the complete absence of any revolutionary consciousness, officers' relations with their men became formal and distant – reminiscent of the officer-enlisted relations of the tsarist period. Physical violence, unheard of before the war, could be resorted to with impunity after the war by officers when dealing with subordinates. It was not at all unusual for officers to beat soldiers. According to one officer:

> Well, it is true that the officers beat the soldiers. Sometimes they beat them dreadfully. I saw it myself, though I didn't do it personally. I often tried to stop other officers, literally holding their hands. But I have never done it myself. Well, in rare cases, I did slap a soldier.[14]

Such behavior would never have been tolerated in the 1920s or 1930s.

Without fear of purges the negative traits of mutual protection, corruption and inefficiency bloomed. A former soldier who served in the mid-1980s wrote that he had experienced "an entire chain of violations on the part of my commanders," in particular their abuse of military equipment and soldiers' labor for personal gain. His unit commander:

> in order to have a wine cellar built for himself, arbitrarily kept soldiers "in the service" until June 19, despite the fact that an official discharge date of May 31 had already been stamped on their military cards.
>
> Another captain, the head of the motor pool, who had been put in charge of a truck that was supposed to transport weapons, spent his time drinking in a neighboring village. And he got away with it, despite the fact that the weapons were never delivered. I have also met soldiers who were forced to be servants for their commanders.
>
> My comrades coming back from the army confirm that there is a kind of mutual protection everywhere . . . which serves as a barrier against any attempt to reestablish real fairness.[15]

On the eve of the collapse of the USSR abuse of authority had reached its nadir. A deputy to the Peoples' Soviet of Deputies admitted in an interview:

> Today's Army is being consumed by favoritism, improper use of influence, and incompetence. I can't tell you how many letters we Deputies receive on that subject. [And that] The lack of legal principles governing military service creates a fertile soil for petty tyranny. It's no accident that military prosecutors' offices overturn about 30 percent of all orders issued by commanders at all levels.[16]

Living conditions

During the cold war the state gradually allowed the quality of life for officers to decline. The primary problems were nearly identical to those of the prewar period: low pay, poor quality and inadequate housing, inadequate social services, and deprived material conditions. The housing problem had not been solved before the war and was made worse by the destruction of property during the war. Postwar reconstruction included rebuilding military installations and their housing but never caught up with demand. The downsizing of the latter half of the 1950s did not significantly help the problem for the reason that, as a concession for the requirement of twenty-five years service, officers were guaranteed housing on retirement or transfer to the reserve. Thus, the discharge of tens of thousands of officers did not gain the army very much housing space because all those that retired or were transferred into the reserve were allocated housing out of the army's share of the national housing fund; and although the army's construction battalions built a considerable amount of housing, it had to turn over a great deal of it to trade unions and the party to allocate to their people.[17] The national housing fund remained decades behind fulfillment until it collapsed along with communism.

In the 1970s the army could not house tens of thousands of its officers and their families. In the 1980s the number of officers left to procure quarters at their own expense surged to 165,000 even as the army again reduced its forces. One officer wrote to the newspaper *Kommunist* complaining:

I feel ashamed where my wife and child are concerned: as a Soviet officer and a man, I am unable to provide them with elementary living conditions. I am concerned for my family and the future, and these concerns outweigh my fear of possible punishment for disobedience – for protesting openly against Army reality.

We live in a 1960-vintage plywood hut without any so-called amenities. There is no hot water – only cold, and it is out in the courtyard. True, they have put in steam heat, but there is not enough and every officer's family has two or three electric heaters. We bundle the kids up as best we can, otherwise they would freeze. No wonder they are constantly sick, and as for health care, there is nothing but one feldsher who cannot even provide medical advice, much less treatment. In my seven years of service, I have never had a physical. And what about our wives, who are deprived of even primitive gynecological care?

There are no day nurseries or kindergartens. The wives are forced to sit at home. And then there are the food concerns. When I was stationed on an island in the White Sea, we sometimes went for a month at a time without cooking oil, sugar and bread. But nobody seems particularly concerned about such things. When we do have a high-level inspection, the principal concern always seems to be whether to paint the fence green or gray and whether it should have a descending yellow stripe.[19]

Shortages of food existed at garrison stores in mainland USSR and inadequate food supplies from the military cooperatives. When food was available, officers or their wives had to wait in long lines for meager offerings.

Family issues particularly troubled officers. One unit commander reported that the kindergarten situation at his unit had become catastrophic. Previously the children of officers went to kindergarten at the local state farm (sovkhoz). The sovkhoz raised the cost by ten times and the unit officers fell 23,000 rubles into debt to the sovkhoz. A neighboring unit fell into such arrears that the local sovkhoz refused to allow the officers' children to attend kindergarten any more.[20]

Officers stationed in Eastern Germany suffered too. A captain serving in the Group of Soviet Forces in Germany complained that the apartment building he and twenty-nine other families lived in had not received any but cosmetic maintenance since it was built. He found especially troublesome the lack of heat in the winter. And this on the front-lines against capitalism.

NCOs and the rank and file

Training

In 1951, Osoaviakhim changed its name to Dosaaf (Voluntary Society for Assisting the Army, Air Force, and Navy) but its mission remained basically the same – prepare preconscription youth for military service. In addition to strictly military training Dosaaf became the umbrella organization running the USSR's sports clubs and youth programs geared to the twin goals of military preparedness and physical fitness. Through its automotive clubs Dosaaf claimed to have trained half of all motor vehicle drivers in the Soviet Union by 1985. In addition, Dosaaf trained harvester combine and tractor drivers, electricians, mechanics and radio specialists. In 1966, Dosaaf claimed ten million workers, kolkhozniks, white collar workers and others participated in its programs. In the 1970s the military aspect of the various youth programs waned considerably. Soviet youth began to understand Dosaaf activities as merely recreation programs and not preconscription training particularly when they constituted such non-military activities as soccer and motorcycle racing.

Eventually complacency and stagnation set in to the preconscription organs as is evidenced by the letter of a former soldier to the editor of a military periodical.

I was called up in 1965. I remember that all pre-conscripts were summoned by the military commissariat at least once a month on Saturdays or Sundays. We ran cross-country races, studied military equipment and weapons, and felt constant attention of commissariat workers who were also in the know about our home atmosphere. Such a preparation period strengthened the feeling of duty and helped our parents better understand the importance and necessity of the forthcoming service. But now nobody seems to care whether or not a young man is ready, physically and morally, for military service. My 17 year-old son is not "spoiled" by the commissariat's attention, as he hasn't been summoned a single time.[22]

This man went on to characterize the attitude of local military commissariats to preconscription training and call-up procedures in the 1980s as half-hearted. Such an interpretation is certainly in line with the overall lack of enthusiasm for military service that became manifest in the 1970s.

Unit training, and training of noncommissioned officers, continued much as before the Second World War. Basic training was to be imparted in the units within the first six months of a soldier's conscription and followed by large unit training in summer maneuvers. Soldiers drafted in the spring contingent, however, often attended their first summer maneuver period without having first completed their basic training.

Noncommissioned officers first attended a school for sergeants, usually six months in duration before joining their unit. In contrast to the prewar period, after 1945 the NCO schools were not run by regiments, but were centralized under a higher command, and candidates for NCO were identified by the military commissariats rather than the regiments. On completion of several months of training sergeants were assigned to troop units. Because of the combination of several factors such as low pay, poor living conditions, rudimentary training, and lack of professional status few sergeants desired to make the army a career. To the end the Soviet Army never succeeded in creating a dedicated longserving NCO corps, much to the detriment of discipline in the ranks.

Hazing and social control in the barracks

After the victory over Nazi Germany and the demobilization of the wartime army the military changed its conscription schedule from once a year to twice a year, spring and fall. Every six months a batch of new recruits arrived at their units just as the men who finished their two years of service departed. This created an atmosphere of instability as the turnover in personnel seemed almost constant.

An extremely negative, and in some cases debilitating, malady that emerged in the postwar period out of this new system of manning was *dedovshchina*, the rule of the grandfathers. Simply put *dedovshchina* was the hazing of the new recruits serving their first six months of service by the "grandfathers," or *stariki*, those serving their last six months. The soldiers serving their second and third six months spent their time licking their wounds and preparing to wreak havoc when they became the "grandfathers." Hazing manifested itself in numerous ways: physical abuse to assert the authority of the *stariki* followed by theft of the new recruits' possessions, forcing the recruits to do personal service as servants, making them do all the menial chores especially those assigned to the *stariki*, and extortion of money. Anatol Lieven evaluated the situation succinctly: "It [*dedovshchina*] humiliates men, weakens them physically, and breaks them down without 'building them up.' It is a general war of the strong against the weak, and it produces units riven by internal hatreds."[23] The widespread nature of *dedovshchina* is attested to by the literary thousands of letters to the editors of numerous military and civilian newspapers and periodicals after Gorbachev's policy of *glasnost* took effect in 1987.

The precise roots of *dedovshchina* have yet to be determined, but it might logically stem from the combination of several factors, the most important and obvious are: the rapid turnover and lack of cohesion among the rank and file; the lack of authority of sergeants over the men because the sergeants were short serving conscripts and often victims of *dedovshchina* as well; the economy of shortages that existed in the units which resulted in theft as the only means of replacing one's worn out uniform and gear; and the lack of involvement in enlisted men's lives by officers who routinely turned their back on the fratricidal warfare in the barracks. Finally, there is evidence that *dedovshchina* existed in civilian life as well, particularly in vocational–technical schools which many men attended after graduating school, but before military service.

In 1985, the first year for which statistics are available on *dedovshchina*, 4,000 soldiers were convicted of hazing.[24] This surely represents only the tip of the iceberg as soldiers themselves admitted few complained to the authorities and the cases of those that did were often covered up by the chain of command to avoid embarrassment. Some examples of *dedovshchina* give the reader a feel for the atmosphere that reigned in the army. One man wrote of his nephew's case.

> On the first day of his arrival the older boys stole everything from him so that he only had slippers left. They took everything, including his razor and a cake of soap. Nobody wanted to investigate the case. Alexander wrote a letter to his parents and his father brought him everything he asked him to bring . . . But a few days later he was beaten again and robbed. They took everything his father brought him.[25]

A private, under arrest for desertion, told a *Pravda* reporter he had fled his unit because:

> The sergeant always beat me and the other new recruits. One time he told us to write home and ask them to send fifty rubles. He took the money away from those who received it. I complained about the beatings, and I was called in to see the commander. He listened and said, "Don't write any more letters anywhere; the sergeant won't lay a hand on you." That very day he thrashed me good.[26]

The military procuracy recognized the harm *dedovshchina* inflicted on the army citing it as the cause of many desertions, suicides, and murders. The procuracy was helpless to intervene, however, as long as commanding officers refused to acknowledge the problem. Officers and *zampolits* hesitated to report crimes in their units because superiors interpreted undisciplined behavior as a reflection of poor leadership. The hierarchy often hindered the promotion of commanders with too many infractions in their units.

Alexander Lebed is a prime example of the ambivalence shown by officers to the problem of hazing. In his memoirs Lebed said he was aware of only one case of hazing in his military career and he handled that by beating up the offender. Elsewhere, however, he several times in a wry tone refers to "discipline by other means" to indicate hazing was a normal occurrence.

When called to account for *dedovshchina* the officer corps responded with many different and at time contradictory answers. The military judiciary fully acknowledged the problem yet some unit commanders denied it altogether. Others admitted it existed but claimed it did not constitute a problem. Still others tried to blame it on society and the quality of recruits, pointing out that many soldiers came from broken homes or had criminal records before entering the service, and had dropped out of school. Furthermore, such officers argued, it was unfair for the army to be blamed for a problem of society's making and the military ought not be expected to fix it. At other times, however, the army promoted itself as representative of the best of Soviet society. With such an array of opinions on the issue and different faces put on it by the army and supported by no central policy of reform it is no surprise that *dedovshchina* survived the collapse of communism and the Soviet empire to plague the new Russian Army.

Just how debilitating *dedovshchina* was to the army's combat readiness is unquantifiable. It certainly weakened the internal cohesion and generated hate and distrust. The experience of the war in Afghanistan, however, shows that units continued to function despite the hazing.

Ethnic and national minorities

Beginning in 1939, minorities began to form an integral part of the armed forces and grew in importance as a source of manpower as the Slavic birth-rate began to decline steadily in the postwar years. The integration of minorities was fraught with problems from the beginning, mainly those of language and racist feelings on the part of both Slavs and non-Slavs. The tensions created by these twin factors increased over the years as Russians became less dominant numerically and more dependent on minorities, particularly those from the Caucasus and Central Asia. The officer corps never ceased to be overwhelmingly Russian.

Before the Second World War Russians seldom accounted for less than three-quarters of a unit's personnel and often more. By the 1980s Russians were nearly always, depending on the type of unit, less than half, and some-times only a quarter of the personnel. In some corners of the army people recognized that the more multi-ethnic the military became, the more diffi-cult it would be to manage. What prevented the Soviet Army from ever achieving a socially integrated collective was the lack of central pressure to prevent discrimination and violence. The roots of the problem were entrenched racism and antagonism engendered by the imperial Russian/Soviet system, assumed Russian hegemony, and growing national awareness among minorities.

Certainly many soldiers and officers were able to get along in harmony, but it is clear that the overall environment in the postwar years was charac-terized by greater and greater resentment by the minorities of their treatment as inferiors by Slavs. The Red Army admitted, in a roundabout way, that this was a problem. As Lieutenant General Gennady Donskoi, Chief of the Political Administration, North Caucasus Military District pointed out, com-munists, Komsomols and officers in his military district were often "taken unawares by ethnic clashes and soldiers' and sergeants' reaction to them." Furthermore, "commanders and political officers often know little about that complicated sphere of Soviet life."[27] According to Donskoi, failure to address the problem would inevitably lead to deterioration of combat training, political education, discipline and overall combat readiness.

Language proved to be a particularly troublesome issue and sore spot for Russians, who took it for granted that the minorities ought to learn Russian and failure to do so was either an act of defiance or sign of ignorance. An interview with one Major Yelovets, a *zampolit* of a motorized rifle regiment is a case in point. He expressed the dominant Russian view that, given modern weaponry is complex and demands teamwork, "a perfect command of the Russian language is essential for all servicemen to learn the manuals and regulations, get command of military professions more quickly and adapt to the military environment more readily."[28] The underlying assumption was that the Soviet Army was essentially a Russian army. Yelovets went on to say, "It is important to bear in mind, however, that each year some of the enlisted men in multiethnic collectives find it difficult to associate with fellow servicemen and to make progress in training during the first months of service because they have a poor command of Russian." Assuming then that subsequent problems with integration were the fault of the minorities who had created an uncomfortable and challenging situation for the Russians. Naturally, under the circumstances, the nationalities tended to gravitate to their own kind and stick together, staying aloof from other nationalities with whom they could not communicate. The sociologist interviewing Major Yelovets added, "A man is apt to seek support among his own when he finds himself in a new, unfamiliar environment, *especially the army environment* [italics added]." The desire for support tended to result in "nationalistic isolation" and "nationalistic egocentrism."[29]

That "nationalistic egocentrism" did break out was common knowledge and may have contributed to the shape of *dedovshchina* in later years. The military procuracy suggested that in the 1980s hazing had taken on a decidedly racist content in many cases, estimating that as many as 25 percent of hazing incidents were racially motivated.[30]

Yuri A. Kravchenko, an army officer stationed in Sakhalin province, wrote the following letter to the editor of *Ogonek* in 1989 complaining of an observable increase in hostility toward everything Russian.

> Recently, more and more soldiers have been coming into the Army who don't know Russian. Very quickly, they master only those expressions which – in their opinion – are the most necessary: "My foot hurts," "My stomach hurts," "I have to go to the doctor." They use words in combination with "I want" a lot: "I want to sleep, eat, smoke, go to the store . . . ." And another expression has become very popular, and every one of them knows it: "No way!"
>
> It's very hard to command units containing these kinds of "mutes." Lots of problems arise even when there are only a few in the group. And what is someone like Captain N. Kanyshev supposed to do? In his company, a full third of the personnel doesn't know Russian. And I don't mean they just understand Russian *poorly*; they don't speak it at all![31]

Kravchenko noted he came across one company which had received four Armenians who spoke no Russian. After exhausting himself in attempts to communicate the *zampolit* tried addressing them in English. To his surprise the four Armenians all spoke English very proficiently, so they were able to communicate that way. Kravchenko seems to have been exasperated that these Soviets could speak English but not Russian.

The army could have recruited more female soldiers to gain more Russian speakers but chose not to. Immediately after the conquest of Germany the Ministry of Defense discharged nearly all the women from the armed forces. Only a handful of female officers and warrant officers remained. In the 1980s

153

the number of women in the army hovered around 20,000, most of them warrant officers. In 1991 the army had only 700 female officers. Despite the sexist attitude that prevailed women were allowed to serve in the war in Afghanistan as nurses, where at least a dozen were killed.[32]

Everyday living conditions

Conditions for officers were often far from ideal, but for enlisted men they could be absolutely horrendous. Alexander Lebed describes the garrison of the 331st Kostroma Airborne Regiment in 1985 when he first arrived to take command.

> It was colorless and wretched. The newest building was at least forty years old, and the base was a trash heap without a single visible trash can or dumpster.
>
> The wretched conditions of the barracks was especially striking. There were only two barracks on the base. The astonishing concentration of people fostered a total disregard for cleanliness. The toilets and sinks were broken, and three-fourths of the faucets were twisted off. The walls were covered with slime and mildew. Everything was overflowing, leaking, and smelled terrible. In the sleeping facilities, the side tables and stools were broken, and the entire hall had only two or three light bulbs, which were coated with dust.
>
> The senior enlisted personnel had adequate bedding, but the rest had to scavenge. Some of them had to use a second mattress instead of a blanket, while others had blankets but no sheets. Everything was bland, poor, and depressing. Boredom, hopelessness, and the desire to do something nasty, mean, and cruel to your neighbor hung in the air.[33]

Prior to Lebed's arrival, of the fifty-five crimes and accidents that had taken place within the division, twenty-seven had taken place in this regiment. Lebed blamed the departing commander who had simply shown no interest in his men's living conditions. Lebed claims he was able to reverse the conditions with considerable effort and time. As with most things in the Soviet Army the personality of the commander, his energy, and professionalism determined the quality of life of his subordinates. Unfortunately, evidence indicates that as the officer corps developed a caste mentality their consideration for the men weakened considerably.

Supplying soldiers with their basic needs did not markedly improve after the war, and this despite a major effort to reorganize the rear services and military production. The military economy was meant to be a planned economy just as the civilian economy but, like the civilian economy, was beset by the very poor flow of accurate or honest information from below regarding need for supplies, materials, and funds. The army intended there to be consequences for bad management but in reality there were none. Long-range planning was rare, particularly with regard to construction or maintenance of buildings. At the higher levels – military districts and branch administrations in particular – expenditures were irregular, rather than paced throughout the budget year. At the end of the year – typically the last quarter – all remaining funds would be spent in order not to have any left over at the end of the year as a way of protecting the budget. Therefore, the majority of a unit's funds would be spent at the end of the year but not necessarily on items the unit needed. The military administrators who spent the money most often used it on their needs, for example office supplies, but often well in excess of their requirements, and in the process neglected the needs of the line units for such basic items as new uniforms and boots, or for services such as recruits' haircuts.[34]

Having their material needs neglected eroded morale. A junior sergeant in a guards division complained in 1989 that he and his fellow soldiers drafted in 1987 were still wearing their initial issue of boots and uniforms and were eight months overdue for a new issue. He predicted they would be discharged soon wearing rags.[35] Under these circumstances some senior soldiers gave in to the temptation to assert their authority as "grandfathers" to rob new soldiers of their boots and uniforms, and anything else they needed.

Discipline and morale

With conditions of life and leadership varying from garrison to garrison and unit to unit discipline varied as well. Statistics for crime in the Soviet Army prior to 1985 are unavailable but the continued existence of disciplinary battalions indicates that there were always those who would challenge authority and resist conforming to military life. The numbers available from 1985 to 1990 show steady increases in infractions of rules and discipline. As with hazing, some in the army pointed to society as the culprit citing that every year in the 1980s the army took in 50,000 draftees with criminal records. In 1989, 19 percent of all conscripts had not completed middle school or vocational school. One-third of the men conscripted in 1989 had grown up as orphans, or in a one parent household, or in another situation without his birth parents.[36] In units without positive officer and noncommissioned officer intervention in the barracks and a reliance on "discipline by other means" true discipline and morale could only deteriorate.

Commanders frequently reassigned serious violators of discipline to disciplinary battalions (disbats). Just as with prewar disciplinary battalions they held men sentenced to from three months to three years. The majority of the men sentenced to them were in for fighting and beating up other soldiers. Drug abusers also could end up in disbats.[37]

Unlike the guardhouse or prison, disbats were not places of confinement. In most respects living conditions hardly differed from those in regular army units. Soldiers received their usual pay and were fed the same food as they had in their regular unit. The barracks were similar. Men were issued clean bedding, and shown films twice a week. On Saturdays they were given combat training and political education. Sundays they had the day off. During the week they were often used as labor on construction sites.[38]

Men assigned to disbats could be released back to their units for good behavior. Because time there counted as regular military duty most who served their full term were discharged directly into civilian life from the battalion. In 1991 the army had some 5,000 men doing time in disciplinary battalions.

The cold war army also had to cope with desertion, AWOL, and service avoidance. In the 1950s one can assume that social pressure, in addition to official sanction, helped keep desertion to a minimum. The reduction in the size of the armed forces meant that millions of young males never had to serve at all. This situation changed in 1967. A new law on universal military service went into effect to support the enlargement of the armed forces. The law lowered the age of conscription from nineteen to eighteen, the term of service was reduced from three to two years, the call-up would be twice rather than once a year, and more men were drafted. Consequently, in the 1960s, society became less supportive of military service as men who had never expected to serve – mostly university bound and professionally oriented – were called to the colors. Young men began to see service much as had their prewar, and even prerevolutionary, predecessors – unpleasant but normally unavoidable.[39]

Men with the means sought to avoid service by securing – for a price – bogus medical certificates exempting them from service, or securing deferments for university educations before performing military service. Once in university a male could become a reserve officer and subsequently never serve in the armed forces.[40] Routinely only 4 percent of reserve officers ever served, and then only for short periods. In this way tens of thousands of young men avoided service every year.

Desertion and absence without leave became common occurences in the 1970s and 1980s. It took until 1989, however, for the Ministry of Defense to reveal that, "desertion for the Armed Forces has become a 'widespread phenomenon' and that the deserters' parents often conceal them from military authorities." The Transbaikal Military District Prosecutor estimated that about 20 percent of all deserters left their units because of hazing, but most did so owing to an "unwillingness to do their military duty."[41] Few in the army high command ever admitted or understood that conditions in the armed services compelled men to desert and that deserters were not necessarily bad people.

Hunting down deserters came to occupy more and more of officers' time even to the point of having to leave training to pursue or retrieve runaways. In 1989 the army charged more than 2,000 men and ten officers with AWOL. In 1990 the numbers grew to over 4,000 men and nine officers. The first six months of 1991 saw 2,575 men and fifteen officers go AWOL. Figures for desertion were 250 men in 1989, 445 in 1990, and 402 in the first half of 1991. Draft evasion became a serious problem as well in the 1980s, particularly with the advent of the war in Afghanistan. Between 1989–91, 4,500 people were convicted of evading military service, and 7,000 were being sought. In Moscow alone, in the fall of 1990, 462 cases were pending trial for spring draft evasion by Muscovites. Self-mutilation to avoid service also became recognized as a problem.[42]

As in the past alcohol abuse was often associated with discipline problems, but in the postwar years drug abuse became an ever increasing problem as well. Drug abuse in the Soviet Army came to public attention during the war in Afghanistan and is popularly associated with that conflict, however, some officials in the Ministry of Internal Affairs maintained in 1988 that drug abuse in the military was not a recent phenomenon but had been identified as a problem in the 1960s by a number of army doctors and psychiatrists. They noted a large number of drug users among regular soldiers, particularly among those serving in Central Asia. Nearly 20 percent of Soviet drug abusers in the 1960s and 1970s are estimated to have begun their drug use in the armed forces. In the 1980s, according to military doctors and the procuracy, many soldiers who went on to commit crimes and use drugs, said that they started using drugs before entering the military.[43]

Economic work and military farming

Discipline and morale fluctuated up and down, from unit to unit and circumstance to circumstance, but one sure factor that served to depress morale and affect discipline was the use of soldiers for non-military tasks that demeaned their status as soldiers. One of these tasks, serving as agricultural labor, was a holdover from before the war. Yet the effect was different, worse, in the postwar era. Before the war agricultural labor was presented as heroic labor, as part of the Stalin revolution of industrialization and collec-tivization, not that everyone identified with that of course. In the 1950s and beyond, the rank and file recognized that they were just being exploited as cheap labor and nothing more. Such work conflicted with the public image of the glorious army that had defeated Nazism. As late as fall 1990 the Ministry of Defense reported that 23,000 troops of the Moscow Military District were working on area state and collective farms. Tens of thousands of soldiers in other military districts were also helping with the harvest. One tank division of the Moscow Military District sent out 1,500 soldiers every day to help collective farmers. They used the division's vehicles (and fuel) to haul harvested produce.[44]

In addition to working with peasants sowing the crops in spring and harvesting in autumn, a conscript stood a good chance of being assigned full- or part-time work on an army-owned farm. In 1991, the Ministry of Defense maintained eighty-three military state farms and 9,000 auxiliary farming operations for military units, organizations, and institutions. It also owned thirty-six military forestry enterprises and eighty-four military forestry sections.[45]

To run the eighty-three farms the army had its own career agronomists with the rank of warrant officer, but the auxiliary farming operations (unit farms) were often supervised by officers or *zampolits* detailed from other duties, with no special agricultural training. Most of the workers on military state farms were civilians, but unit farms employed soldiers' labor as much as possible. The goals of a military state farm were to feed itself and a military unit; the unit farms were to feed the unit and sell the surplus to officers.[46] Obviously the quality of the farm directly affected the nutrition of the unit. There were no guarantees that production goals would be met and often they were not. The army's farms faced the same difficulties common to all of Russian agriculture: lack of housing, lack of personnel, and desperately bad roads. Considering that far more soldiers were now from the urban areas than ever before such work may have been seen as especially degrading to the morale and self-image of these soldiers.

Besides working as free agricultural labor, army units were also legally and illegally used as a labor pool in the urban areas. A letter to the editor of *Argumenty i Fakty* from a staff member of a school for cooks highlights the abuse of soldiers' labor by the army itself.

> Students at the school of military chefs are assigned to work at various military and civilian organizations instead of learning the trade. In the morning, the school looks a lot like a labor exchange with teams of students being sent to many different places to do anything but study. Small wonder the graduates' skills leave a lot to be desired.
>
> Now, while so-called aid to other military units is something that can be excused, soldiers being sent to work at civilian organizations is a nonsense. A furniture-making plant "pays" the school in reject products. It won't be long before the lavatories will be finished in polished wood . . . !
>
> I would like to ask V. Marchenkov who is the commander of the school and a member of the Communist Party, how the pharmaceutical stores, the packaging shop, the commodities/purchases warehouse settle their accounts with the school, and whose pockets the money ends up in?[47]

He concluded, "I am convinced that my views are shared by thousands upon thousands of officers and NCOs . . ." and, realizing that this type of conduct by military officials was normal throughout the armed forces and that it seemed unlikely to change, he decided not to re-enlist.

Diversion of soldiers from training to serve as laborers seriously hindered their future military effectiveness. One senior lieutenant complained that every six months his anti-aircraft rocket battery received a fresh batch of sergeants from the school for NCOs, but they were not very well trained. The sergeants blamed it on the fact that in the school they had spent most of their time involved in economic activities and did not complete the course of instruction before being sent to the unit. The commander was then faced with the dilemma of what to do with them. They could not be given privates jobs because they were sergeants and none of the officers wanted to do the sergeants' job.[48]

An officer related in 1989 that at one point the Moscow City Soviet lost access to the temporary workers it used to bring in from outside and the city organizations began to scramble for workers.

> They pleaded with the USSR Council of Ministers for several military construction detachments. I happened to visit the city Party committee one day and thought I had entered General Staff headquarters by mistake. All I saw was a sea of uniforms: City officials were meeting with the commanders of their 'labor army'.[49]

That military service was often not military service at all, and often disenchanted the conscript with his service, is most clearly exemplified by the military construction units. Construction battalions were created in the immediate prewar years with the wartime tasks of constructing river crossings, bridges, trenches, etc. They were neither trained nor equipped for battlefield action. Their primary peacetime function was to build defense works, social facilities and assist with national economic needs. Essentially, they were nondisciplinary labor battalions with much less sophisticated training and equipment than engineer battalions. The battalions were manned by ordinary conscripts and their work assignments were under the direct charge of the Deputy Defense Minister for Construction and Quartering.

In the immediate aftermath of the Second World War the army's construction battalions were put to work rebuilding the USSR. They rebuilt the coal mines of the Donbas and the metallurgical industry in the Ukraine and helped rebuild such devastated cities as Stalingrad, Leningrad, Kiev, Minsk, and others. The civilian economy quickly became dependent on military labor and often relied on construction battalions for especially dirty or difficult work that it would have been difficult to get civilians to do. Eventually, construction battalion labor was incorporated into the five year planning process. One of the major long-term efforts of construction units was apartment building, but not exclusively for the military. Many special projects fell to the army. Military construction units did major work in preparing Moscow for the 1980 Olympics, building athletic venues and the hotel "Rossiia." They built the cosmodrome launch site at Baikonur, and much of the Baikal-Amur Railway in Siberia. Military construction units rebuilt the city of Leninakan after the 1988 earthquake in Armenia.[50]

The degree of dependence of the civilian economy on military labor is illustrated by the fact that in 1990 there were 501 military construction units with 329,000 soldiers working on civilian construction projects under the orders of twenty ministries and departments.[51] This, however, was not the extent of the military's involvement in civilian labor. Railroad troops, whose mission was to build railroads and bridges and organize communications in the event of war, actually spent the majority of their time serving the USSR Ministry of Transport construction. According to a *Pravda* report: "The ministry 'entrusts' the railroad troops with its least prestigious and lowest-paying jobs, and the soldiers can often be seen with crowbars and sledge-hammers doing work that civilian specialists won't touch." The railroad troops did fully 25 percent of all heavy work such as excavation and ballasting.[52]

Soldiers employed in non-military construction by civil agencies were often seriously neglected by the military chain of command and the "employing" civilian agency. According to the above *Pravda* report:

> Soldiers building a road for the Russian Republic Ministry of Motor Transport and Highways in Udmurtia last fall did not have enough tents, clothing or even dishes. Incidentally, these soldiers were not even military construction personnel; most were simply discipline violators who had been pulled together from various services and ordered to build a road, with virtually no training or equipment.

It is no wonder then, that the construction troops gained a reputation for having the worst discipline in the army. Construction units were said to be ridden with crime, desertion, and excessive hazing. This was compounded by the army's use of construction units as dumping grounds for many of their undesirable conscripts, notably those with criminal records and low intelligence. Minorities were overrepresented in the construction troops thus exacerbating racial tensions.[53]

For good reason morale was terrible in the construction battalions, the men were not trained as soldiers, were not treated like soldiers, but were expected to behave like soldiers. According to a General of the Military Procuracy:

> the Russian Republic Ministry of Construction in the Urals and Western Siberia has used only 50 percent of its military construction

workers for their intended purpose. The rest have worked in all manner of places – as auxiliary workers at a ski factory and a chemical plant, as dishwashers at cafeterias, as janitors and even as nannies in day-care centers. The picture is similar in other places.

Finally, in 1990, the Supreme Soviet recommended that the use of construction troops by civilian ministries be abolished by the end of the year, determining such use to be unconstitutional.[54]

The party and the army, 1945–85

The demise of Stalin caused no formal changes in the party's relation with the army. Khrushchev reaffirmed that the Central Committee headed the party's work in the armed forces and exercised its authority through GlavPUR. The army continued to be represented in the highest bodies of the government and Communist Party, e.g. the Supreme Soviet, Central Committee and the Poltiburo, by generals and the Minister of Defense – nearly always a general or Marshal of the Soviet Union. At the unit level, party organizations and *zampolits* still had the duty to support the military leadership especially in the areas of discipline, obedience to authority, and training.

Party and Komsomol membership remained steady until Gorbachev's reform era. In the 1970s, Komsomol membership in the armed forces hovered around 60 percent. A few units claimed 100 percent membership. In 1981, some GlavPUR sources reported that the officer corps had reached 80 percent party membership, and this turned out to be the height of officer party membership. Higher political levels sporadically complained – as they had before the war – that the primary cells did a poor job of checking on the backgrounds of people they nominated to the party. The primary party organizations were also periodically accused both of not doing a good enough job keeping up with their members through self-criticism and not insisting on high standards of personal conduct.[55]

Transferring between military officer duties and political duties declined remarkably after the Second World War, but the bond between commander and *zampolit* seems to have remained fairly strong. In matters of discipline, unfortunately, political officers more often than not colluded with their commander in covering up disciplinary crimes and malfeasance on the part of the commander in which the *zampolit* was often involved.[56]

After Stalin's death GlavPUR gave less emphasis to political education. GlavPUR mandated a total of five hours of political instruction per week. Twice a week political personnel delivered political reports lasting thirty minutes. *Zampolits* were supposed to hold formal political instruction in their units twice a week for two hours each time.[57] The content of political instruction gradually shifted away from Marxism–Leninism to cold war rhetoric emphasizing superpower antagonism and the threat of NATO and the United States to the Soviet Union. The soldiers were often reminded of their internationalist duty to protect the peace-loving nations of the socialist world from wanton capitalist aggression.

7

THE WAR IN AFGHANISTAN
AND THE GORBACHEV
ERA, 1979–91

In December 1979 the Soviet Army once again entered into combat, but this time it was an unpopular war with limited aims. The army failed to adequately prepare for this and the regime failed to mobilize national support for the army or soldiers. The prosecution of the war therefore suffered and the participants quickly became demoralized. In the 1980s, Mikhail Gorbachev's twin policies of *glasnost* and *perestroika* would do great damage to the relationship of society to the army by exposing its corruption, inefficiency, and brutality. It became widely known that for many military service was hellish rather than honorable. Under Gorbachev the regime acknowledged first to itself, and then to the Soviet people, that it could not win the war in Afghanistan. The realization that their sacrifices had been in vain angered many and shattered the image of the all victorious Red Army that had been maintained since 1945. When people saw how the army no longer represented the ideals of honor, duty, and socialist equality they lost faith and withdrew support for it. When the army was used against Soviet citizens during nationalist disturbances in 1988 and afterwards, people began to turn against it. Finally, reactionary elements of the army turned against Gorbachev in a failed coup attempt that ironically destroyed the remnants of a system they had hoped to save.

The war in Afghanistan, December 1979–February 1989:
a peacetime army at war

The mass infusion of Soviet troops into Afghanistan in December 1979, which popularly dates the beginning of the war, represented the culmination of decades of peaceful relations during which a series of Afghan governments drew closer to the USSR. In the 1970s a series of coups brought communist leaders into control of the government, which had been a limited monarchy with little actual control outside of the urban areas, first Nur M. Taraki in April 1978, then Hafizallah Amin in September 1979, who proceeded to initiate a program of soviet-style socialism in their country. Here began the problems for the Afghan government and eventually the Soviet Union. The program of socialization, which involved coercive elements of anti-religion and class warfare in an attempt to modernize and bring under firm state control the disparate ethnic and tribal groupings, ran counter to everything the traditional and independent Islamic Afghan village stood for. It invited a violent response, not only in the isolated mountain valleys, but in cities as well. In 1978, a massive antigovernment riot broke out in Herat which was bloodily suppressed. By this time the Afghan army was relying on nearly 3,000 Soviet military advisors to help maintain government control in the face of serious challenges. In the course of 1978 and 1979 both Taraki's and Amin's communist Afghan governments, on sixteen separate occasions, requested the Soviet government to intervene with military forces.

Finally, in spring 1979, under orders from Leonid Brezhnev, General Secretary of the Communist Party, and the Politburo, the Soviet Army began preparing for a large-scale infusion of military units, not to conquer Afghanistan and turn it into a satellite state, but to suppress the resistance movements long enough for the Afghan government to gain a secure hold over the population so it could survive on its own. Prior to the actual introduction of forces into Afghanistan and throughout the conflict the party leadership remained determined to limit the level of Soviet military commitment.

The first acts of the incursion were the Soviet's 40th Army's seizure of control over the single road into Afghanistan from the Soviet Union through the Salang Pass, as well as a bridgehead over the Amu Dariya River on 25 December 1979. Next, on 27 December, Red Army paratroops and a special KGB unit assassinated Amin, toppled his government, and replaced him with Babrak Karmal. Simultaneously, Soviet forces seized important posts in Kabul and attempted to neutralize the elements of the Afghan Army loyal to Amin, which involved heavy fighting between Red Army airborne units and Afghan army units in Kabul.

From the invasion until the final withdrawal of the 40th Army in 1989 the Red Army's strategy centered on accomplishing three major objectives: first, defending Kabul, and keeping the roads open between that city and the cities of Kandahar and Herat, and keeping the Salang highway open between Kabul and Termez in the USSR. In pursuit of this objective the Soviet Army established outposts on the above roads and devoted extra efforts to "pacify" the provinces north of Kabul and those bordering the USSR. The second objective was to take the war to the resistance in the form of sweeps of Mujahideen held territory with large mechanized forces, and aerial bombing of suspected rebel villages. After only a few years these tactics had compelled around five million Afghan civilians to flee to Iran or Pakistan for the duration of the conflict. The army's third objective was to close the Afghan–Pakistan border to prevent the resupply of the resistance by foreign powers and to keep Pakistan from becoming a base of operations for the resistance movement – in this the army failed utterly.[1]

In 1980, 1981 and 1982, the 40th Army conducted large-scale search and destroy missions into the hills and valleys. The Panjshir Valley, only forty miles from Kabul received special attention. The pattern that quickly developed after the Mujahideen suffered heavy losses trying to fight conventionally, was that the rebels, organized into detachments of from twenty to two hundred, would slowly retreat in the face of superior Russian numbers and firepower avoiding pitched battles, but ambushing and harassing the advancing troops with fire from rifles, machine guns, mortars and hand-held rockets as they withdrew.[2] They always returned after the Soviet and Afghan government forces left.

For their part, the Mujahideen did not launch offensives but sought to remind the Afghan communists and 40th Army of their presence through small-scale action. Throughout the war the favorite targets of the Mujahideen were road-bound vehicular convoys. The guerillas would ambush the column, first disabling the lead and rear vehicles and bringing the rest to a halt, then chopping it into isolated pieces. According to a Russian infantry battalion commander, "To talk about the *dukhi's* tactics, however, is to over-generalize. Each band of rebels has its own style of fighting. And despite a common headquarters, each has its own interests and views on conducting combat operations."[3] He had high regard for the Mujahideen's combat capabilities and their capacity to learn from the Soviets.

In 1982, the Red Army began to use battalion-size heliborne operations against the Mujahideen, which sometimes resulted in local successes but never had a chance to change the course of the war. While in control of villages thought to be sympathetic to the resistance the Soviet Army adopted a policy of laying waste to the infrastructure, crops, and livestock to make it worthless to guerillas. This behavior contributed to the exodus of civilians to Pakistan and Iran, but engendered greater hatred among the people to see the war through to the end and to send their sons to fight the Soviet Army when they came of age.

Throughout the war, the Soviet Air Force had undisputed control of the air because the resistance had no aircraft, but the Mujahideen could affect the use of air power, both airplanes and helicopters, with anti-aircraft weapons such as heavy machine guns and anti-aircraft missiles captured from the Red Army, or supplied by the United States. The American missiles in particular, after 1986, seriously reduced the effectiveness of Soviet air power by forcing fighter-bombers to fly higher, thus reducing the accuracy of bombing and forcing helicopter units to adopt less aggressive tactics. As pilots became more cautious so did the ground troops they supported, reducing overall the pressure on the Mujahideen.

Vladislav Tamarov, a soldier in the 103rd Airborne Division, described three different levels of operations in which his unit participated. The largest were major operations in which the division, with elements of the 40th Army, supported by artillery and aircraft and accompanied by Afghan army units, sought large groups of Mujahideen in specific areas. These operations developed in stages and lasted for several weeks.

The next level of operations were smaller and usually consisted of only one airborne regiment deployed in helicopters and/or armored personnel carriers with artillery and air support. These smaller operations aimed to destroy a specifically identified group of guerillas, whose location had been determined by Afghan intelligence. These operations lasted from around a week to ten days. As part of large and small operations soldiers often combed villages in search of caches of weapons or Mujahideen hospitals. Small operations conducted solely with helicopters lasted only three to five days because of difficulties of supply.

The third level of operations were the ambushes carried out by a few score soldiers. Small units conducted ambushes at night along roads and mountain trails thought to be frequented by the Mujahideen, and near villages suspected of harboring guerillas. According to Tamarov, combat had a seasonal rhythm to it, being at its most intense in spring and summer, but tending to slacken off in the winter when many Mujahideen went home to their villages or to Pakistan.[4]

The total number of Soviet soldiers in Afghanistan on an annual basis fluctuated between 80,000 and 115,000. Some additional units sortied out of Termez in the USSR. Many fighter and bomber units operated from the USSR into Afghanistan. The peak total of Soviet troops operating in the conflict in any given year was approximately 150,000. Altogether approximately 642,000 Soviet soldiers served in the war between 1979–89. Twice a year the USSR sent replacements to the 40th Army: in the fall came the men called up in the spring, and in the spring came the men called up in the fall. Despite continual reinforcements units always operated below strength with anywhere from one-quarter to one-third of the men on sick call or hospitalized with some serious disease or malady (hepatitis, typhus, malaria, dysentery, or meningitis mostly) at any given time.[5]

At war's end the Soviet Union claimed a death toll of 12,854 soldiers and 1,979 officers, and 35,478 wounded in action. In addition, 330 people, including twenty-one officers, were taken prisoner or declared missing in action. More than 26,000 Afghan Army soldiers lost their lives. Almost immediately after the government released these figures Soviet citizens began to question them, suspecting them to be too low. Some claimed the army had ways of categorizing deaths so they would not fall into the category of combat or noncombat losses in Afghanistan, for instance those who died of their wounds in hospitals in the USSR, or those who fought in Afghanistan but were stationed in the USSR.[6]

Another 469,685 soldiers became casualties from non-fatal wounds and disease. Of these 415,932 were from disease, and of these one-quarter suffered from infectious hepatitis. Due to combat wounds and disease 10,751 soldiers became invalids. Equipment losses amounted to 114 airplanes, 332 helicopters, 147 tanks, 1,314 armored personnel carriers, 433 artillery pieces and mortars, 510 engineering vehicles, and 11,369 trucks.[7]

Luckily for the Soviet Army, the Mujahideen resistance remained fragmented along tribal and ethnic lines preventing a coherent unified armed struggle that would have been even more costly for the Soviet Union than it was. Mujahideen numbers are estimated at between 20,000 and 100,000 full-time fighters and another 150,000 part-time fighters. Specific numbers of Mujahideen casualties are unknown, however, among all nongovernment Afghanis the losses may have run over a million.

The Afghan government's army, which the Soviet Army was to reinforce, numbered 100,000 in 1979 but dwindled to around only 25,000 in 1980 due to desertion and defection to the Mujahideen. It took until 1986 for the government to get it back up to 40,000 — a strength it never surpassed — leaving the Soviet Army to bear the brunt of the fighting. Throughout the war defections and desertion plagued the Afghan Army. Officially the Afghan Army was declared a fraternal army but the officers and men of the 40th Army never really trusted their counterparts, considering them all potential security risks. The exception to this was the Afghan intelligence service, which at times reliably served to pinpoint Mujahideen enclaves for destruction.[8]

In 1986, for reasons as yet unknown, the Soviet Union replaced Afghan President Babrak Karmal with Dr Najibullah Admadzi. The same year, the USSR began the process of turning the war over to the Afghan Army, which it had been trying to build up through training for the past few years. This was the prelude to eventual Soviet withdrawal from the war in Afghanistan. The pull out began in earnest in 1988 and was completed by 15 February 1989.

The experience of the Afghanistan War was in many ways different from that of the Second World War. The main differences were that Afghanistan was a counterinsurgency war, soldiers were only in the combat zone for roughly eighteen months and then rotated home for demobilization, and the soldiers in Afghanistan quickly realized they had no idea why they were fighting the war, nor who was friend or foe among the population. The psychological preparation for the invasion of the original troops and for subsequent reinforcements was for the most part amateurish and counterproductive, as well as reminiscent of the explanations given for intervention in Hungary in 1956, and Czechoslovakia in 1968. Soviet veterans of the war revealed that explanations for intervention had no factual basis whatsoever. One soldier said: "We were told that we would have to help the Afghan people defend their revolution from foreign mercenaries. They said that there were many mercenaries from Pakistan, China, and the United States in the country." Another cliamed that, "Just before we went to Kabul, we were informed by our *zampolit* that we would have to fight Iranian and Pakistani forces that had entered the country from outside." One soldier was told his unit would be fighting Chinese mercenaries dressed as Afghans. A fourth related that: "The political officer gave this lecture about the international situation: he told us that Soviet forces had forestalled the American Green Berets airborne invasion of Afghanistan by just one hour. It was so incessantly drummed into us that this was a sacred 'international duty' that eventually we believed it."[9] The explanation closest to the truth that Soviet soldiers were ever given was that they were to help the Afghans build socialism.

The soldiers of the initial invasion force had absolutely no special military or psychological preparation at all. One private, Malkov, who had been in the army only a few months, said after the war that he and his comrades were told they were going to Afghanistan for joint exercises with the Afghan Army and although they were issued with live ammunition no one suspected they were going into battle. He was in the Democratic Republic of Afghanistan (DRA) for two days before, "the truth hit me like thunder!"[10] In three more days his unit came under enemy fire and took casualties.

The lack of truthful information about the nature of the war cost the lives of numerous Soviet soldiers. Malkov tells the horrible tale of the death of a friend, the shock of which was magnified by its unexpectedness.

> Four of us came there to collect water. While we were filling tanks and flasks, Valera Zhitskikh said: "Now, boys, while you're here, I'll drop [in] at the market. I'm short of film to make snapshots." He took his submachine gun and marched away. He was some fifty meters away, and we somehow had lost sight of him, deep in our work.
>
> Suddenly we heard a terrifying scream. We stood frozen with fright. Valera, gunless, was running towards our APC, his head falling back. Blood was spurting from his throat. It'd been cut from ear to ear. He'd been running some twenty meters more, then collapsed.
>
> We seized our guns. But whom to shoot? Bursting with rage, we were nearly blind with hatred. We kept combing this g__damn market again and again to its bottom but no good came of it. We never found the killer and Valera's gun.
>
> That day we realized that the enemies were not only in the Pakistan gangs or among those who hid high up in the mountains. They may also be among people living next door to our camp. Any time, any place they could stab you or shoot a bullet right in our faces. Thus, in a natural way, I was confronted with a question: whom were we defending here? and from whom? where was the enemy?[11]

Racial differences, the language barrier, and nature of the war caused mistrust and suspicion to dominate the relationship between Slavic soldiers and Afghans. Consequently the environment was ripe for atrocities and mistreatment of civilians. Mistreatment took two forms, official and unofficial. Official mistreatment included bombing and shelling known civilian targets, taking and executing hostages, and ambushing peaceful caravans. Unofficial mistreatment included murder and looting by soldiers without permission. These acts were discouraged and their perpetrators usually punished. Despite the prohibitions, Soviet soldiers developed the habit of looting and stealing from Afghan civilians. According to one soldier: "during combat operations we would go through a village and take anything we wanted. We would simply go in and say, 'Give me hashish,' or whatever else." If the Afghan did not comply he or she was often beaten or sometimes killed.[12]

Atrocities were not uncommon. On the one hand they seemed to have been sanctioned during operations, but were strictly forbidden otherwise and severely punished. A soldier who admitted to participating in an atrocity told that:

> I was on a military mission for eighteen days. I had to go hungry and to carry corpses. So many soldiers in our company died that it was horrible. They shot my best friend, so afterwards we went through the houses and shot all the residents one after the other: women, children, everybody.[13]

Sometimes Soviet Army atrocities were in direct response to Mujahideen barbarity. The aforementioned private Malkov and his battalion, in their first major sweep of the Panjshir valley in August 1980, were cut off from their regiment and had to fight their way out losing several men dead and missing. The battalion commander organized a search party to locate the missing men. Malkov relates:

> For three days we'd been pursuing the gang. At last we'd caught a glimpse of smoke rising from the ravine near the village. The coals were still warm when we'd come up. We shuddered at what we saw. Three burnt boys' bodies were lying near the fire. The fourth was put above the fire like in a grill. Cut off tongues, ears, picked out eyes were spread around. I thought that my heart would never bear such a terror, it would explode like a grenade.[14]

In their fury Malkov's unit rushed the village and killed everyone.

The above atrocities took place in the heat of battle but the following incident was one of many carried out in cold blood.

One of the atrocities that I witnessed personally took place on the day of the October Revolution anniversary. We caught four Afghans who were tied, laid on the road, and run over with a BMP [tracked armored personnel carrier]. One of the Afghans was a priest with a beard and they spared him. But the next morning the officer ordered one of the soldiers to pour gasoline over him and set him on fire. The soldier couldn't do it and started screaming. The officer got really upset and said, "I've had enough of this. Watch how it's done." And he grabbed the Afghan by the throat and slit it.[15]

Throughout the war few prisoners were taken by either side, especially if it inconvenienced mobility. The Mujahideen routinely murdered downed Soviet pilots and helicopter crews. Going into battle Soviet soldiers and Mujahideen fighters came neither to expect nor give quarter.

Although planning for the move into Afghanistan began six months before the introduction of troops the army made no attempt to specially train the units for the type of combat – desert, mountain, and counterinsurgency – the soldiers would face. This may have been done out of the need for secrecy. The Turkestan Military District, which had originally organized the 40th Army and spearheaded the intervention, did not get the operations order until two weeks before it had to act. The army soon remedied this situation by setting up special desert warfare training centers in the Turkestan Military District for those bound for the DRA. There the climate and terrain resembled Afghanistan. The army founded mountain warfare training centers in Azerbaidzhan and Tajikistan.

The training at those centers was not optimal even though the army ended up putting considerable thought and resources into it. According to Tamarov the training produced a herd mentality, the routine of which defeated the weak men. The officers were indifferent to them because: "Their assignment was to prepare cannon fodder to be sent to Afghanistan. They knew that during three or four months of boot camp they couldn't make us into anything much. Only a few tried to teach us at least something: hand-to-hand combat or marksmanship." Another soldier related that: "The first week we worked in a refrigeration plant, loading and unloading bottles of lemonade. Then we were sent to work on officers' homes – I did all the bricklaying for one of them. We spent a fortnight putting a roof on a pigsty."[16] In his entire period of training he went to the live fire range only twice, once to fire nine rounds, and the second to throw one hand grenade. This inexcusable and negligent attitude toward training cost some men their lives and kept the combat efficiency of the units low.

The experience of war in Afghanistan was made worse for the soldiers by the continuing practice of *dedovshchina* in the units. Theoretically, there should have been no *dedovshchina* in the DRA because after the initial invasion replacements were not supposed to be sent there until they had finished six months of training, thus placing them into the intermediate category of soldiers. However, the army routinely sent men into Afghanistan with only three or four months of service making them vulnerable to hazing. Additionally, a new demension of *dedovshchina* was added by the soldiers in Afghanistan, that of including all soldiers new to the war in the bottom rung of the pecking order for six months to a year, no matter how much time they had already served in the army. Normally, the veterans hassled and humiliated the new soldiers, the "greens," having them do the dirtiest work, run errands, launder their uniforms, and so on. New arrivals would be stripped of their personal possessions and beaten if they resisted. Uniform items would be "confiscated" by the veterans on an as needed basis to replace their worn out clothes.[17] Obviously such behavior did nothing to reinforce cohesion and trust between soldiers of a unit, but tended to generate friction instead.

Sometimes those who were abused in the *dedovshchina* system struck back fatally, as illustrated by the following incident related by a veteran.

> This happened at one of the Soviet roadblocks on the Kabul–Jelalabad road. There were three *stariki* and a young soldier serving in a tank. I knew the young soldier very well; his name was Aleksei. When he would come to the base, he used to tell me that the *stariki* were abusing him viciously, beating him constantly and making him do the hardest work. If he couldn't accomplish it, the three *dedushki* would beat him twice as hard. He told me that they forced him to stand guard every night until dawn; he seldom slept more than two or three hours. They even tried to molest him sexually. His face was always marked by beatings. What could I advise him? I just told him, "Hang in there Alyosha hang in there." Well, in the end, he couldn't take it anymore, and one night while the *dedushki* were sleeping sweetly he emptied an entire magazine into them and killed all three of them. He got eight years for that.[18]

In other instances young soldiers killed their tormentors during battle or at night with handgrenades.

Amazingly, when it counted the most, officers turned a blind eye to it all, perhaps because their treatment of the men was often no better. According to one soldier:

> When I first got to the unit in Jelalabad, the commander of our platoon . . . would yell and cuss people out all the time. He would also hit people and even knocked a *starik's* teeth out. So one day when we were out in the mountains on operations, two of the *stariki* just pushed him over a cliff. They said that he had slipped, and even though most of the platoon saw them, nobody reported them. Everybody hated his guts and was happy to get rid of him.[19]

Other soldiers murdered their officers in front of their units. In one instance, according to Artyom Borovik, a Russian journalist: "A senior lieutenant noticed that a soldier's hair was too long, so he straddled him like a horse and gave him a haircut. He dismounted, made sure that the length of the soldier's hair met military regulations, and shook his index finger at him." The soldier retrieved his rifle and shot the lieutenant then and there, killing him. In another incident an old timer attempted to murder his platoon commander for having reprimanded him in front of the other soldiers.[20] Clearly, officer–enlisted relations had fallen away from the revolutionary ideal.

The Red Army took its poor race relations with it to Afghanistan. Most of the initial ground forces deployed into Afghanistan were from the Turkestan Military District and were brought to full strength with local reservists and transfers from construction battalions. These people were mostly Central Asians, and those from the construction troops were poorly prepared or entirely untrained for combat. As a result they diminished, rather than enhanced, the combat capacity of the units. Perhaps because of sympathy for the Afghans and antipathy for Russians, or simply due to Russian mistrust, the army soon withdrew Muslim soldiers from the initial force. Eventually, over one hundred Muslim soldiers defected to the Mujahideen, not for religious or political motives, but because of the unbearable conditions in the Soviet Army. For the rest of the war the army kept Muslims to a minimum in the combat forces. Muslims did, however, serve in large numbers in support units, especially construction units. Consequently, life for Russians in construction battalions or any unit in which they were the minority, could be very brutal. Overall, 70 percent of the soldiers (and casualties) in the war were Slavs – vastly overrepresented in relation to their numbers in society.[21]

Living conditions, seldom good in the USSR, were often abysmal in the DRA. Most important, the camps lacked adequate plumbing. Hygiene suffered accordingly. Not only were the soldiers kept isolated from the local inhabitants, but their refuges were breeding grounds for disease. The Red Army suffered thousands upon thousands of cases of jaundice, dysentery, hepatitis, typhus, and skin diseases endemic to the region. It is possible that the death toll from these has been greatly under reported. The army's medical service seems to have been unprepared to tackle the health requirements of a third world nation and did not rise to the occasion. A military doctor in a medical battalion lamented that in 1985 his staff performed 264 amputations and in 1988 fifty saying about the ability of the unit to perform its duties, "It hit us hard, especially considering that [in 1985] we didn't – and still don't have [in 1988] – a single piece of factory-made medical equipment or a conventional operating room."[22] The military had only one major hospital in the DRA in Kabul; most serious cases had to be treated in the USSR.

The soldiers only got ten rubles a month and usually spent it on food to supplement their rations or substitute for army food that simply was so bad the men would not eat it. In desperation soldiers bought food directly from Afghans. They were not allowed alcohol or beer. Additionally, morale suffered from boredom and lack of diversion. Soldiers not stationed in Kabul were not allowed to go into the city. Seldom were men given leaves to go home during their two years' service.

To cope with the boredom, fear, and general misery, many soldiers turned to drug use. Readily available, drugs could be obtained for money or barter. The three most popular drugs were hashish, opium and marijuana. Boredom and isolation were major reasons for drug use. Often soldiers would take drugs when off duty or just after combat to soothe their nerves. Sometimes, however, soldiers would go on operations under the influence of narcotics impairing their military efficiency occasionally at the cost of lives. Some soldiers thought drugs enhanced their ability to cope in combat. According to one man: "When you're stoned, you don't notice that you're tired. You run up and down the mountains and the *kishlaks* like a billy goat, without ever stopping."[23] Officers and warrant officers were more likely to abuse alcohol because they had easier access to it. Vodka was hard for soldiers to get. Those who could not cope with the death, deprivation, or hazing committed suicide.[24]

To support their desire or need for drugs and additional food soldiers commonly resorted to theft of government property for sale or trade to Afghan civilians. Soldiers would sell automotive spare parts, tires, and even rifles, rocket propelled grenades and ammunition. A soldier confessed: "In my unit, which was guarding the *komandatura* in Kabul, we had a lot vehicles, so we sold gasoline mostly but also boots and uniforms. I smoked hashish so I needed the money."[25] Soldiers in construction battalions found a lucrative market for their building materials. The lure of easy money also attracted officers. The trade in stolen military goods became such a regular feature that a special bazaar in Kabul sprang up to facilitate the business.

Inspite of the myriad problems confronting the 40th Army and the individual soldier and officer the Soviet forces gave a good account of themselves. Commanding officers, particularly in the airborne and air assault units, experimented and devised innovative tactics to deal with expected and unexpected situations. Men fought courageously, used initiative and ingenuity to accomplish missions and to survive. From the personal narratives now coming out about the war we learn that unlike the war against Nazi Germany, in Afghanistan the soldiers did not fight for their country or freedom, or any ideal at all, but in a more basic sense the war for them was a process in which one strove to overcome hardship, pulled one's weight, showed appropriate courage, and responded to the need to be seen as a man in the eyes of his peers; and then left with a tortured soul wondering "why?".

The Gorbachev era

Mikhail Gorbachev's ascendence to the position of General Secretary of the Communist Party in 1985 began the last identifiable stage of the Soviet Army's existence. Under his leadership the USSR disengaged from the war in Afghanistan, seeking a Vietnam-style peace with honor which recognized their inability to bring about victory for Afghan socialism. Gorbachev picked up where his predecessors left off, making a serious bid to end the arms race which included the reduction of both nuclear and conventional forces. His era of "new thinking" resulted in the reduction of Soviet Armed forces in Eastern Europe and a slashing of the defense budget.

Simultaneous with these actions were Gorbachev's twin policies of *perestroika* and *glasnost* which opened the army to public scrutiny and criticism. *Glasnost* and *perestroika* also created an environment in the USSR of national minority unrest which affected the army in two significant ways: first, it was often called on to suppress unrest; second, the army suffered from the refusal of minorities to serve outside their home areas and finally to serve at all. The scrutiny made *dedovshchina* a public issue and prompted many to evade the draft out of fear of victimization. The loss of the war, added to the scandal of *dedovshchina* and substandard living conditions endured by the military, once and for all destroyed the proud image the army had maintained since the Second World War. Finally, *glasnost* and *perestroika* and the disintegration of the Soviet empire prompted reaction within the armed forces that led to military participation in a coup against Gorbachev in August 1991.

Winding down the cold war: reducing the Soviet military

Gorbachev's negotiations with United States President Ronald Reagan began to bear fruit in 1989. First, the Soviet Army successfully ended its involvement in the war in Afghanistan on 15 Februry 1989. Next, intent on reducing the military–industrial complex's drag on the Soviet economy and the cost of the military presence in Eastern Europe Gorbachev announced sweeping cuts in personnel, weapons, and occupation forces. In consultation with the Politburo and the Ministry of Defense, Gorbachev declared in 1989 that the armed forces budget would be cut by 14.2 percent; the size of the armed forces by 12 percent; and the manufacture of weapons and military hardware by 19.5 percent. Specifically, the armed forces would be reduced by a total of 500,000 men over two years (1989–90), 240,000 from Europe, 200,000 from the Far East and Mongolia, and 60,000 from inside Russia. One hundred thousand of these men were to be officers. By July 1990, twenty-one divisions had been demobilized and two military districts were combined into one. Such measures allowed for the abolition of 1,400 posts for generals and 11,000 for colonels by the end of 1989. On 1 January

1990 the personnel strength of the armed forces was projected to stand at 3.9 million with more cuts to follow. Gorbachev pledged to remove 10,000 tanks from Europe, of which 5,000 were to be destroyed. Additionally, 8,500 artillery pieces and 820 combat aircraft would be decommissioned by the end of 1991. Gorbachev also indicated that the armed forces would need to develop a new military doctrine – a defensive doctrine.[26]

The reduction of forces caused dismay in some circles, particularly the older generation of generals, but the reality was that by mid-1990 the army found itself unable to fully man its remaining divisions. Demographics posed a problem in that there were fewer eighteen-year-old males in the latter half of the 1980s than there had been a decade before. Minister of Defense General Dmitrii Iazov claimed the army was short 400,000 soldiers due to obstruction of conscription. Another problem, ascribed to public pressure possible only under conditions of *glasnost*, was that in 1989 the Ministry of Defense reinstated educational deferments, a practice that had been suspended during the 1970s. The army claimed this cost them 200,000 men in 1989–90. In July 1990, the Ministry of Defense claimed the army was short 536,000 men and would be short 700,000 in the fall. In 1990, the USSR had three million draft age men, but fully half had been deferred because of higher education, their family situation, health, or employment in basic industry.[27]

The other half of the problem was draft evasion because of growing, open, and militant nationalism on the part of minorities and desertion due to *dedovshchina*. Draft evasion had first become a significant problem during the war in Afghanistan when military commissariats took bribes to exempt men from service. From that the problem began to grow along national lines. In 1989, the first calls were heard for nationalities to serve only in their home-lands or be granted alternative forms of local service. The Baltic republics began this movement suggesting the creation of territorially based divisions and even the re-creation of former divisions such as the 16th Lithuanian Division of Second World War heritage, or the Latvian Rifle division of Civil War fame. The idea for local service was subsequently picked up by the Transcaucasus republics. National extremists called on young men to avoid the draft completely. Blind to the depth of these movements, the high command rejected all these suggestions as unhealthily nationalistic. Hoping to keep its young men at home, in 1990 the Supreme Soviet of Latvia presented a draft law on alternative service for Latvian males aged 18–26 with pacifist or religious objections which did not allow any form of military service anywhere, but was more like public service.

The first active show of resistance to conscription came in November 1989 in Tbilisi, Georgia SSR in the form of a sit-down strike by potential conscripts and some men already in uniform absent from their units without permission. They demanded either alternative or regular service, but only in Georgia. In 1990 the army responded by authorizing 25 percent of the fall call up in the Transcaucasus and the Baltic republics to serve locally, but only if they were married, had children, or had difficult family circumstances. This did not satisfy the Baltic and Transcaucasus peoples one bit, but inflamed Russians who complained of being sent to minority areas where they were harrassed. Furthermore, Armenians claimed that 40 percent of their conscripts were sent to construction units. The Ministry of Defense responded that the actual number was 20 percent but promised to cut that in half.[28]

In 1990, the President of the Moldavian SSR passed a decree saying that Moldavian men could only be called to serve in the Soviet Armed Forces if the individual man applied for conscription in writing and had the written permission of his parents. Ukraine declared it would call up citizens for service only in Ukraine. Uzbekistan likewise would not let its young men serve in construction units outside Uzbekistan. Armenia required that all service be on its soil unless individual soldiers requested otherwise. A particular concern of Armenians was to keep their men out of the hands of Azeris and vice versa because ethnic tension had already flared into large-scale violence over the issue of Nagorno-Karabakh.[29]

Minority compliance with conscription orders was very poor in 1989, but 1990 saw the worst showing for conscription since the Civil War. Neither the spring nor fall quota of recruits were met. The quota for Latvia was met at only about 25 percent and most of those were ethnic Russians living in Latvia. Conscription rates were only 7.5 percent of quota for Armenia, and 28 percent for Georgia.[30]

In the country as a whole only 79 percent of those summoned reported for duty. Many of those subsequently deserted. The majority of those who did answer the call for military service were ethnic Russians. The draft in spring 1991 yielded similar results.[31]

According to General Iazov, in 1990, "for the first time, we ran into organized attempts to disrupt call-ups into the armed forces. This was manifested in an especially sharp way in Armenia, where fulfillment of the USSR Law on Universal Military Service was blocked and the spring call-up was virtually thwarted."[32] The problem, according to Iazov, was not merely that men did not want to serve, but that local authorities, the party, and members of military commissariats aided and abetted men in avoiding service based on nationalistic motives. Such conduct had the potential to cause the collapse of the entire non-Russian conscription organization. In November 1990, the head of the political department of the Georgian SSR military registration and enlistment office said that for more than a year they had been unable to conduct regular military training, and the appropriate organizations had begun to forget the "science of mobilization and how to deal with the tasks of preparing young people for the army."[33] With conscription in such disarray preconscription preparation had also fallen by the wayside in the Baltics and Caucasus.

For the first time in forty years, the army began to experience difficulty in recruiting and retaining officers. In 1989, despite lowered quotas, military schools and academies failed to enrol a full complement of students. Simultaneously, effective January 1990, the Ministry of Defense offered to let any officers resign their commissions and leave the military with no penalty. So many officers submitted their resignations that the offer had to be rescinded. One officer estimated that had it not been recinded the Turkestan Military District would have been reduced to only one officer per company.

To determine the cause of the mass desire to leave the service the Ministry of Defense launched a broad inquiry, in one instance surveying 1,800 officers, 250 warrant officers, 300 officers' and warrant officers' wives and 150 cadets. The primary motivation cited for leaving the service was the low and falling quality of life. Lack of free military housing and the cost of providing one's own quarters proved to be a common complaint. The dearth of jobs for wives, and kindergartens for children also troubled many. The army determined that as of the end of December 1990, 165,000 officers provided quarters for themselves at their own expense and that this would rise to 200,000 by the end of 1991. At the same time per capita earnings of military families had shrunk to 30 percent lower than those of workers' families because of Gorbachev's economic reforms. Fully half of all officers' wives who wanted jobs could not obtain one. These conditions worsened rather than improved over the next year.[34]

Many officers felt angry over being reclassified to a lower grade during the process of downsizing, which cost them status and pay. According to the army's report: "Ninety-one percent of those polled admitted that with today's inflation and shortages, their wages do not correspond to their expenditures of physical and moral effort and their colossal workloads. After all, officers, especially young ones, have to be on duty 13–15 hours a day, and they get days off only once a month, or even less." As a consequence large numbers of junior officers had filed requests to be discharged into the reserves, many under pressure from their wives. Nearly two-thirds of officers polled complained that the army's organization was becoming unraveled and officers were given assignments "not befitting combat officers." Statements such as "There's no combat training or political training. They've turned the regiment into a guard unit;" and "We're becoming construction-site foremen and security guards," were widespread. The overall drop in the armed forces' prestige in society concerned many officers too. A different, smaller poll revealed that 91 percent of those wishing out were 30 years old or younger; 65 percent were communists and 21 percent Komsomols.[35]

When *glasnost* made information from and about the West more accessible officers and their families were able to compare their situation to those of their NATO adversaries. In every category the Soviet Armed Forces came up the loser, especially in quality of life issues, pay, and conditions of service. Such open comparison accelerated the declining prestige of the military and inhibited officer recruiting. A major and USSR People's Deputy saw the army's image become distinctly negative in popular opinion saying:

> Past are the legends about high material well-being of officer families. Add to this the housing problem in remote garrisons with no guarantee of receiving any apartment after leaving the forces, miserable social benefits of the dependents, immense moral discomfort caused due to some decisions of different ministries and other state institutions to involve the army in non-combat activities as a cheap labor force.[36]

In 1990, conditions of life for officers and their families were identical to those of the 1930s as were recruiting problems. The difference was that no-one seriously looked to the party for a special mobilization or any other intervention.

The army's prestige dropped furthest among the national minorities due to increased nationalism, opposition to their second class status in the service, and because of the recent use of the armed forces by the regime against demonstrations in the Caucasus. Unlike in Novocherkassk in 1962, the army willingly used violence against non-Slavic citizens which resulted in injuries and numerous civilian deaths. An open letter to General Iazov from a Georgian man, following the April 1989 killings of civilians in Tbilisi, was indicative of the growing attitude of people toward the Soviet Army.

> "The Red Army is the strongest." We've known that for a long time, but we never imagined how strong it could be against unarmed people (we've seen how strong it was against *armed* people in Afghanistan). By killing women with shovels, your soldiers showed true heroism.
>
> I'm sure that if my people have the strength to start a civil war, you will fall face first into s__t, just like in Afghanistan.[37]

More disturbing for the regime than the lack of respect was the population's growing lack of fear of the armed forces.

Public criticism of the military, particularly treatment of servicemen by their superiors, surfaced for the first time in Soviet history, courtesy of *glasnost*. One result of the new openness regarding military affairs was the founding congress of the Union for the Social Protection of Servicemen, Reservists and Members of their Families, popularly named "Shield" in October 1989. It professed as some of its basic principles to make radical cuts in the number of generals and in the Ministry of Defense's administrative structures; to eventually abolish political organs at the division and army levels; and to abolish the institution of company political officers.[38]

Another civilian watchdog organization, the Committee of Soldiers' Mothers, was founded in 1990. An unofficial organization of soldiers' mothers who were afraid for their sons' safety in the service, it represented not only those with sons in service, but also the interests of mothers whose sons were or soon would be of draft age. They did without a doubt gain the attention of the Ministry of Defense which was eventually forced to acknowledge the Committee's interest when they threatened to call a national boycott of conscription unless their concerns were addressed. Their major concerns were *dedovshchina*; violence at the hands of superiors; violence related to ethnic issues; the desire for good training and improved living conditions; holding superiors responsible for mistreatment of their sons; greater protection of servicemen's legal rights; and compensation for death of a serviceman. They also expressed the desire to disband construction units. Gorbachev eventually passed a decree to satisfy the above issues giving the Committee credit. The Ministry of Defense, however, dragged its feet on implementing the decree.[39]

Another problem *glasnost* caused for the army was that when the Soviet populace got a true look at the world it no longer seemed so threatening. For some the West actually appeared inviting, hence the following letter to a military periodical:

> Yes, I mean it − I want to live in Australia. Not long ago Soviet television showed a film about that country, and I liked everything there − wonderful shops with lots of goods, and many cars, cafes and restaurants.
>
> Before army service I lived in Pskov oblast. What good is there about that place? Mud everywhere in rainy weather, the club closed for months, newspapers and magazines delivered a week late. And the shops? Their empty shelves make me sick. One has to go to Pskov for sausage, and queue for hours to buy it. Is this any way to live?
>
> I am still young and want to live well. That is why I dream of going to Australia. When I complete my army service I will request a permit to leave the country. I am not going to betray my homeland or anything like that. There is just nothing here for me to do. I did not sign my name because they will start "educating" me, and I have already had enough of that.[40]

A host of patriotic responses − mostly from aging veterans − followed the printing of this letter. Some referred to the writer as scum, but for his generation he was not out of line, or out of step. Other educated youths considered military service a waste of time for intelligent men with futures in the civilian economy − an opinion that if voiced before 1985 could easily have led to arrest.[41]

Perestroika

Some in the army, usually the younger officers, courageously acknowledged the army's defects and sought to expose them and offered ways to remedy them. One significant category of problems was the officer – particularly the commanding officer – relationship with the soldiers and sergeants. Commanders held themselves aloof from their men and junior officers. They tended to view and treat all subordinates as an anonymous mass, rather than as individuals. Commanding officers were known to act rudely, arrogantly, tactlessly, and were inattentive to subordinates' complaints and requests. The solution was for officers to become more approachable. One officer declared: "Every leader must feel the inner need to associate with human beings, trying to be a compassionate yet demanding senior comrade and not merely a 'commanding officer.' Neither slogans nor lip service will do. Everyday hard work aimed at particular individuals and not at 'the masses' is the ticket."[42] He went on to declare what was becoming a popular idea, that the army needed democratization through democratic institutions such as the Komsomol, officers' assemblies and courts of honor, and enlisted men's assemblies to make decisions, or help commanders make decisions regarding promotions and assignments, awards and commendations, pasttime activities, and furthering education. Democratic institutions using *glasnost*, in his words, should target "faults, abuses, cruelty, neglect of particular human beings and offenses against military discipline." Clearly, self-criticism within party cells had failed.

Naturally some resisted change and lashed out against it. An example of the intransigence of senior officers and political personnel is illustrated in a letter of complaint to the military procuracy in 1989 from a detachment of civilian employees of the army in East Germany. With the men lined up in formation:

> the unit commanders came and began spouting abuse and threats at them. The head of the political department [told us]: "Freedom is democracy, democracy is power, and power is dictatorship. Restructuring is only inside the Soviet Union, and it's already coming to a dead end even there. Here there has been and will be no restructuring. Here, restructuring for you means having short haircuts." The deputy commander for rear services expressed himself even more bluntly: "The time of people marching about with placards in the Soviet Union is already coming to an end, and as for you restructuring hasn't arrived and isn't going to." The officer ended his speech with the vilest unprintable abuse.[43]

This letter had sixty-one signatures on it and concluded, "How long will moral and ethical norms continue to be flouted, and an 'anything goes' atmosphere continue to flourish?" Truly, this was no army of a new type.

From the above example one can easily understand the increased calls within the military for independent tribunals to insure justice in units because the arbitrariness and abuse of power of commanders was not checked by tribunals which were made up of local officers sympathetic to the power of senior commanders over everybody. Others proposed that legal advisors be attached to units to advise both officers and men of their power and rights in an effort to promote the rule of law.[44]

Perestroika affected the political administration in ways similar to the military, and in unique ways too. Relations between senior political personnel and their subordinates reflected those of the military – distant and uninvolved. Calls for this to change abounded from lower level *zampolits*. A Major Vinogradov complained that his political department, like all the others, "have been following the obsolete pattern: the directive – a plan or measure – then the report, with people being mere performers." There had been no real change in the way political personnel or departments had related as human beings to the soldiers despite official decrees and announcements. The GlavPUR apparatus continued to overrule party organizations in units and formations. He saw elections to the leading bodies of GlavPUR as the solution, giving real power to the primary party organizations in the units so that majority rule could determine GlavPUR policy – revolutionary indeed. He also suggested eliminating areas closed to criticism, letting the light of *glasnost* shine everywhere. Particular problems with criticism were indifference or outright persecution by commanders.[45]

The overall politicization of Soviet society caused by *glasnost* and *perestroika* posed a particular problem for GlavPUR in that it stood to lose its monopoly over politics. As freedom of speech became a reality the party line became less and less relevant and often irrelevant. Political parties forming in civil society attracted the attention of the rank and file and officers alike. The role of GlavPUR and its existence became the subject of discussion by 1989. The leadership of GlavPUR swore the leading role of the party would never be given up and declared the work of noncommunist parties and soldiers' membership in them illegal. Nevertheless, servicemen did join noncommunist parties and voted in elections. At first the Communist Party prevailed in the military, electing seventy-four officers and two civilian employees, all of them communists or Komsomols, to the first Congress of People's Deputies in 1989 and 114 in 1990. The elections in spring 1991, however, which put nearly 9,000 servicemen in soviets of all levels, local, Republic, and the Supreme Soviet, produced many noncommunists.[46]

In 1990, civilians and servicemen began to call for the abolition of GlavPUR. Under intense pressure from the public and reformers in high party offices GlavPUR, in summer 1990, began to formulate plans to make party organizations in the army completely independent of GlavPUR. Then began a process of working with "public–political" organizations, literally accepting a multiparty status for the army. This effectively put the jobs of 100,000 GlavPUR personnel at risk, much to their dismay.

In January 1991, GlavPUR lost its status as an independent organization within the military. Gorbachev severed its relationship with the Central Committee. By Presidential decree GlavPUR became a subordinate body of the Ministry of Defense answerable to its policies and governance. It was no longer a party organization. As a result of this decree, military–political agencies began organizing educational work with consideration for soldiers' political views, ethnic characteristics and attitudes toward religion.

The army and the coup, 19–21 August 1991

The centrifugal forces unleashed by *glasnost* and *perestroika* were unmistakably tearing apart the fabric of the Soviet Union, causing economic and social turmoil, and destroying the place of the army in politics and society. In response to Gorbachev's sometimes unwillingness and other times inability to stop the disintegration a cabal of ultraconservatives plotted to overthrow him for the purpose of restoring the power of the party, the army, and the Russian nationality over the rest of the Union.

The Soviet Army's involvement in the August 1991 coup against Gorbachev can be traced to Minister of Defense Iazov. The head of the conspiracy to create the State Committee for State Security, KGB chief Kriuchkov, knew that without the army the revolt had no chance and therefore enlisted the reluctant participation of Iazov whose main thought was to preserve the disintegrating Soviet empire. Only through his influence were other important generals such as commander of army ground forces General Varennikov, Deputy Defense Minister Achalov, commander of the Airborne forces General Grachev, and commander of the Air Force General Shaposhnikov brought into the scheme. Most of these men had serious doubts about the coup and for a time acted only out of a sense of loyalty to their immediate superior – Iazov. Acting under the orders of Varennikov and Grachev, elements of two army tank divisions and some airborne units dutifully rolled into Moscow on 19–20 August with quite vague instructions and no clear mission.[47]

Iazov was caught off guard, because the people of Moscow, like the peoples of the Caucasus, did not back down from confrontation with the army. Instead, it was the soldiers who proved irresolute; and like in Novocherkassk in 1962, the generals were unwilling to order shooting. Because the people of Moscow were unintimidated, Iazov, fearing to create a civil war, and on the advice of his generals, decided on 21 August to withdraw the troops from Moscow, whereupon the coup collapsed.

Marshal Sergei Akhromeev, personal military advisor to Gorbachev, and Chief of the General Staff until 1988, committed suicide by hanging himself in his Kremlin office shortly after the failed coup attempt. His suicide note included the following sentiment shared by many top-ranking officers, "everything I have devoted my whole life to building is collapsing."[48] Subsequently Gorbachev named Marshal of Aviation E. I. Shaposhnikov the new Minister of Defense. He promptly resigned from the Communist Party, dismissed General Moiseev, the Chief of Staff of the Army, for "compromising" himself during the coup, and purged the Ministry of Defense of the majority of its deputy ministers and heads of departments and administrations.

The failure of the coup resulted in the virtual death of the Communist Party in the USSR and the abolition of GlavPUR in the army. Three days after the coup Gorbachev, in a Presidential decree, announced the termination of the activity of political parties and political movements in the armed forces. Military personnel could participate in political parties and movements on their own time. A week later the Ministry of Defense officially abolished GlavPUR. Political personnel who wanted to stay in the armed forces could petition to be transferred to military-educational duties. Overall, though, many were discharged, especially those of higher rank. The army ordered all former GlavPUR personnel who had twenty-five or more years of service discharged by 1 December 1991. That amounted to more than 3,000 political workers. Shaposhnikov promised that only five or six of GlavPUR's thirty-two generals would remain in service.

Boris Yeltsin's ascendancy to the leadership of a new Russia and the formal dissolution of the Soviet Union in December 1991 saw to the final demise of the Soviet Army and its immediate resurrection as a restructured Russian Army built on the shaky foundations of its predecessor.

CONCLUSION

The Red Army began with a worthy vision that included voluntarism, comradely brotherhood, and even democracy. Yet, the Red Army fell away from some of its ideals very quickly and the rest by 1941 and created – or recreated – an organization/institution that relied on coercion and lies. The rest of Soviet society experienced the same coercion and lies and when the state relaxed its grip and truth became available Soviet society and the army could no longer stand as they had, but demanded radical reorganization. The process of reorganization of the Soviet state led to its collapse and the army could not save it.

The army, ironically, started out as a suspect institution, one distrusted by Bolsheviks on principle, but grew to become an essential pillar of the Soviet state. As an integral part of the regime the army reflected the positive and negative qualities of Soviet government and society. At first the positives outweighed the negatives. Between 1922 and 1941 the army was a significant avenue of social mobility for peasants and workers. It was a place where illiterates could learn to read and write. The army taught men advanced farming and vocational skills, useful in postmilitary employment. Men were treated with dignity. Eventually, however, the evils of the old army crept into the Red Army.

From 1945 onward there were only pretensions that the Soviet Army was an army of a new type. It had become an army of the old type and the leadership wanted it that way. Officers became elitist, as did party and government officials. Soldiers reverted to the status of anonymous, insignificant beings as did the majority of Soviet citizens. Living conditions in and out of the army were always trying and they worsened in the end until they became intolerable. Under conditions of constant threat from capitalist powers the army high command could claim a position above society to justify its internal practices and demands on resources. When "peace broke out" between the USSR and the United States in the late 1980s the army, party, and government leadership lost their claims to being above society. Then all aspects of military service and social integration that had been held together by external threat or internal coercion began to unravel.

The national minorities began to break away from the Union. Minority soldiers began to break away from the army. Aging officers and civilian leaders inflexibly tried to hold on to the past, but were challenged by younger men pushing reforms and change. There was no concensus in the army or party. Men began to desert or evade military service because they saw no point in the suffering service entailed. Hundreds of thousands of party members turned in their membership cards recognizing that the party was part of the problem, not the solution for the USSR.

The army as an institution could not help but be discredited along with the party because it had forfeited its credit when it turned its back on its founding ideals: when it refused responsibility for its members' safety and ignored *dedovshchina*; when it treated its men as cannon fodder; when it made its men and junior officers live in hellish conditions while colonels and generals lived in luxury. It deserved criticism for its excessive demands on the economy that left civilians in equally as bad living conditions as its soldiers. It deserved no credit for sending men to battle unprepared physically, or mentally, feeding them lies rather than truth. Like party bosses, many officers deserved condemnation for their corruption and abuse of power.

The Red Army managed to defeat one of the most powerful armies of the twentieth century, but in the end could not resist its own hostile population and weakened government. The half-hearted support of the August Coup showed that, in 1991, the army was no longer a defender of the legitimate government, but neither was it a force that would promote alternatives. The Soviet Army was in limbo – politically useless, and socially unpopular. In many ways it had become a liability for the USSR, and an easy target for criticism and budget cuts. By the time it was renamed the Russian Army, it was no longer Soviet, or Red; and that had been the problem for fifty years.

NOTES

1 The birth of the Red Army

1 Rex A. Wade, *Red Guards and Workers' Militias in the Russian Revolution* (Stanford, Cal.: Stanford University Press, 1984), 329–31.
2 Francesco Benvenuti, *The Bolsheviks and the Red Army, 1918–1922* (Cambridge: Cambridge University Press, 1988), 215.
3 Leon Trotsky, *The Military Writings and Speeches of Leon Trotsky, vol. 1, 1918: How the Revolution Armed* (London: New Park, 1979), 47–8. Hereafter cited as *How the Revolution Armed*.
4 Sergei I. Gusev, *Grazhdanskaia voina i Krasnaia Armiia: sbornik statei* (Moscow: Voenizdat, 1958), 111, 112–13.
5 Mark Von Hagen, *Soldiers in the Proletarian Dictatorship: the Red Army and the Soviet Socialist State, 1917–1930* (Ithaca, NY: Cornell University Press, 1990), 28–9.
6 Orlando Figes, "The Red Army and mass mobilization during the Russian Civil War, 1918–1920," *Past and Present*, no. 129 (November 1990), 199.
7 Trotsky, *How the Revolution Armed*, vol. 1, 487–8.
8 Figes, "The Red Army and mass mobilization," 206.
9 *Ibid.*, 170–1, 172–3, 190–1.
10 Trotsky, *How the Revolution Armed, vol. 1*, 482.
11 Trotsky, *How the Revolution Armed, vol. 2*, 105–14.
12 Eduard M. Dune, *Notes of a Red Guard* (Urbana, Ill.: University of Illinois Press, 1993), 131.
13 Orlando Figes, *Peasant Russia, Civil War: the Volga countryside in revolution (1917–1921)* (Oxford: Oxford University Press, 1989), 181–2.
14 Isaac Babel, *1920 Diary* (New Haven, Conn.: Yale University Press, 1995), 97.
15 *Ibid.*, 46–7, 50.
16 *Ibid.*, 69, 90.
17 Arthur E. Adams, *Bolsheviks in the Ukraine: the Second Campaign, 1918–1919* (New Haven, Conn.: Yale University Press, 1963), 149–85, 188–9, 190, 307, 311, 312.
18 David Footman, *Civil War in Russia* (New York: Praeger, 1961), 258–62, 273, 275, 285.
19 *Ibid.*, 291, 292–3, 294–301.
20 Evan Mawdsley, *The Russian Civil War* (Boston: Allen & Unwin, 1987), 183.
21 Benvenuti, *The Bolsheviks and the Red Army*, 32–3.
22 *Ibid.*, 42.
23 Trotsky, *How the Revolution Armed, vol. 2*, 115–20.

24 Babel, *1920 Diary*, 18.
25 *Ibid.*, 50, 89.
26 Trotsky, *How the Revolution Armed, vol. 2*, 272.

2 The Civil War, and Polish–Soviet War, 1917–21

1 Trotsky, *How the Revolution Armed, vol. 1*, 313; *vol. 2*, 75.
2 Benvenuti, *The Bolsheviks and the Red Army*, 109–18.
3 Dmitrii F. White, *The Growth of the Red Army* (Princeton: Princeton University Press, 1944), 92–8.
4 Von Hagen, *Soldiers in the Proletarian Dictatorship, 1917–1930*, 41–2, 43.
5 Trotsky, *How the Revolution Armed, vol. 1*, 242.
6 Dune, *Notes of a Red Guard*, 126.
7 *Ibid.*, 128–9.
8 Figes, *Peasant Russia, Civil War*, 324–33, 327, 328, 332.
9 *Ibid.*, 335–40.
10 Babel, *1920 Diary*, 12, 23, 28.
11 *Ibid.*, 21.
12 *Ibid.*, 55, 65, 68, 82, 91.
13 Adams, *Bolsheviks in the Ukraine*, 347.
14 Stephen Brown, "Communists and the Red Cavalry: the political education of the *Konarmiia* in the Russian Civil War, 1918–1920," *Slavonic and East European Review*, vol. 73, no. 1 (January 1995), 88.
15 *Ibid.*, 86.
16 *Ibid.*, 93, 94.
17 Adams, *Bolsheviks in the Ukraine*, 343.
18 Babel, *1920 Diary*, 4.
19 *Ibid.*, 51.
20 *Ibid.*, 73.
21 Dune, *Notes of a Red Guard*, 142–3; Trotsky, *How the Revolution Armed, vol. 2*, 340–1, 522–3, 578–9.
22 John Erickson, "The origins of the Red Army," in Richard Pipes, ed., *Revolutionary Russia* (Cambridge, Mass.: Harvard University Press, 1968), 245, 250.
23 Peter Kenez, *Civil War in South Russia: the first year of the Volunteer Army* (Berkeley, Cal.: University of California Press, 1971), 170–3, 185–8.
24 Adams, *Bolsheviks in the Ukraine*, 25.
25 *Ibid.*, 35–6, 38–40.
26 *Ibid.*, 36, 38.
27 *Ibid.*, 50–1.
28 *Ibid.*, 51–3.
29 *Ibid.*, 68–74.
30 Figes, "The Red Army and mass mobilization," 206–7, 208.
31 Adams, *Bolsheviks in the Ukraine*, 350–85; Kenez, *Civil War in South Russia*, 39–44, 142, 169, 172.
32 A. M. Ageev, "Vzaimodeistvie reguliarnykh sovetskikh voisk s partizanskimi formirovaniiami v nastuplenii Vostochnogo fronta v 1919–1920 gg.," *Voenno-istoricheskii zhurnal*, no. 1 (1987), 66–8.
33 Norman Davies, *White Eagle, Red Star: the Polish-Soviet War, 1919–20* (London: Orbis, 1983), 27.
34 Adam Zamoyski, *The Battle for the Marchlands* (Boulder, Colo.: East European Monographs, 1981), 83, fn.
35 *Ibid.*, 135.

36 Davies, *White Eagle, Red Star*, 210–22; *Direktivy Glavnogo Komandovaniia Krasnoi Armii (1917–1920): Sbornik dokumentov* (Moscow: Voenizdat, 1969), 548–54; John Erickson, *The Soviet High Command: a military-political history, 1918–1941* (New York: St Martin's Press, 1962), 94–5.

37 Davies, *White Eagle, Red Star*, 236, 237, 249–51, 258–9; Iu. V. Ivanov, "Zadolgo do Katyni: Krasnoarmeitsy v adu Pol'skikh kontslagerei," *Voenno-istoricheskii zhurnal*, no. 12 (1993), 22–6; G. F. Krivosheev, *Grif sekretnosti sniat: Poteri Vooruzhennykh Sil SSSR v voinakh, boevykh deistviiakh i voennykh konfliktakh: Statisticheskoe issledovanie* (Moscow: Voenizdat, 1993), 28.

38 Krivosheev, *Grif sekretnosti sniat*, 30–1, 36.

3 The Red Army between the wars, 1922–39

1 For a detailed treatment of the political infighting around the establishment of the mixed regular–territorial system see Francesco Benvenuti, *The Bolsheviks and the Red Army, 1918–1922* (New York: Cambridge University Press, 1988), 168–75; and Mark Von Hagen, *Soldiers in the Proletarian Dictatorship: the Red Army and the Soviet Socialist State, 1917–1930* (Ithaca, NY: Cornell University Press, 1990), 137–52.

2 Mikhail V. Frunze, *Sobranie Sochinenii*, vol. 1 (Moscow/Leningrad: Gosizdat, 1929), 211.

3 Leon Trotsky, *Military Writings* (New York: Merit Publisher, 1979), 106–8.

4 Sergei I. Gusev, *Grazhdanskaia voina i Krasnaia Armiia: sbornik statei* (Moscow: Voenizdat, 1958), 121–7.

5 Lars T. Lih, Oleg V. Naumov, and Oleg V. Khlevniuk, eds, *Stalin's Letters to Molotov* (New Haven, Conn.: Yale University Press, 1995), 85.

6 Harriet F. Scott and William F. Scott, *Soviet Military Doctrine: continuity, formulation, and dissemination* (Boulder, Colo.: Westview Press, 1988), 13, 14.

7 Iurii Rybalkin, "Moskva, Nastas'inskii, 13", *Rodina* no. 9 (Fall 1996), 68.

8 Il'ia Berkhin, "O territorial'no-militsionnom stroitel'stve v Sovetskoi Armii," *Voenno–istoricheskii zhurnal*, no. 12 (1960), 16; *Krasnaia zvezda*, 15 July 1925.

9 Victor Kravchenko, *I Chose Freedom* (New York: Charles Scribner's Sons, 1946), 47.

10 Rossiiskii gosudarstvennyi voennyi arkhiv (hereafter cited as RGVA) f. 9, op. 26, d. 487, ll. 80–85; d. 490, l. 41.

11 Leon Trotsky, *Military Writings* (New York: Merit Publishers, 1969), 69.

12 *Dlia distsipliny net melochei* (Moscow: Gosizdat, 1927), 1–3, 9–11.

13 *Metodika Takticheskoi Podgotovki Pekhoty-33 chast' I* and *Metodika Takticheskoi Podgotovki Pekhoty-33 chast' II* (Moscow: Voenizdat, 1933).

14 Koniukhovskii, *Territorial'naia sistema voennogo stroitel'stva* (Moscow: Voenizdat, 1961), 41.

15 Berkhin, "O territorial'no-militsionnom stroitel'stve v Sovetskoi Armii", 16.

16 Iosif I. Geller, *Pod krasnoi zvezdoi: Krasnaia Armiia na fronte kollektivizatsii* (Samara: Gosizdat, 1931), 69; *Vsearmeiskie sovershchaniia politrabotnikov 1918–1940* (Moscow: Nauka, 1984), 176–7.

17 *Krasnaia zvezda*, 17 February, 5 March 1933.

18 Aleksandr A. Svechin, *Strategy*, Kent D. Lee, ed., a translation of *Strategiia* ([Moscow: Voennyi vestnik, 1927], Minneapolis, Minn.: East View Publications, 1992), 204–5.

19 British Foreign Office File 371: Russia Correspondence 1927, vol. 12585, 18–20; hereafter cited as *BFO 371*.

20 Georgi K. Zhukov, *Vospominaniia i Razmyshleniia*, vol. 1, 11th edn, *dopolnennoe po rukopisi avtora* (Moscow: Novosti, 1992), 192.
21 *Krasnaia zvezda*, 3 December 1932; Nikolai Iakovlev, *Ob artillerii i nemnogo o sebe* (Moscow: Voenizdat, 1981), 29.
22 RGVA f. 9, op. 26, d. 490, l. 2; f. 25893, op. 1, d. 292, l. 129.
23 Vladlen S. Izmozik, "Voices from the Twenties: Private Correspondence Intercepted by the OGPU," *Russian Review*, vol. 55, no. 2 (1996), 306, 307.
24 *Krasnaia zvezda*, 12 November, 9 December 1932; 17 March 1933.
25 *Krasnaia zvezda*, 4, 5 August 1932.
26 *Krasnaia zvezda*, 3 October 1933.
27 Vladimir F. Klochkov, *Krasnaia Armiia – shkola kommunisticheskogo vospitaniia sovetskikh voinov, 1918–1941* (Moscow: Nauka, 1984), 204, 205.
28 Oleg Suvenirov, "Vsearmeiskaia Tragediia," *Voenno-istoricheskii zhurnal*, no. 3 (1989), 43.
29 K. E. Voroshilov and M. V. Frunze, *O molodezhi* (Moscow: Partizdat, 1936), 139; K. E. Voroshilov, *O molodezhi* (Leningrad: Molodaia gvardiia 1937), 16–17.
30 Harold J. Berman and Miroslav Kerner, *Documents on Soviet Military Law & Administration* (Cambridge, Mass.: Harvard University Press, 1958), 85–94.

4 PUR and the Army: the political side of military service

1 Pavlovskii, *Kak Krasnaia armiia gotovit boitsa-grazhdanina* (Moscow/Leningrad: Gosizdat, 1929), 12.
2 Benvenuti, *The Bolsheviks and the Red Army*, 155, 183.
3 I. Petukhov, *Partiinaia organizatsiia i partiinaia rabota v RKKA* (Moscow/Leningrad: Gosizdat, 1928), 75; Iurii P. Petrov, *Stroitel'stvo politorganov partiinykh i komsomol'skikh organizatsii armii i flota (1918–1968)* (Moscow: Voenizdat, 1968), 244.
4 RGVA f. 37837, op. 21, d. 23, l. 19, 20; f. 54, op. 1, d. 1235, l. 17; Petrov, *Stroitel'stvo politorganov partiinykh i komsomol'skikh organizatsii armii i flota*, 233; Iu. I. Korablev, *KPSS i stroitel'stvo Vooruzhennykh Sil SSSR* (Moscow: Voenizdat, 1959), 469.
5 *U.S. MID Report*, "Political training in the Red Army, 1931–32", Reel 4, 344.
6 Mikhail Soloviev, *My Nine Lives in the Red Army* (New York: David McKay, 1955), 95–7.
7 *Krasnaia zvezda*, 15 November 1928.
8 *Krasnaia zvezda*, 2 June 1935; *Dvadtsat let raboche-krest'ianskoi krasnoi armii i voenno-morskogo flota* (Leningrad: Lenoblizdat, 1938), 95.
9 *Harvard University Refugee Interview Project: Soviet Interview Project Archives*, 1980–1987 (University of Illinois Archives: Record Series 24/2/50-51), #18 RF, A3, p. 15.
10 "Chistka partii i zadachi partorganizatsii VVS," *Vestnik Vozdushnogo Flota* no. 10 (1933), 9–11; RGVA f. 887, op. 1, d. 86, ll. 6–7; f. 1293, op. 5782, d. 6, l. 25; *Krasnaia zvezda*, 6 September 1929, 17 May 1934.
11 Roger Reese, "Red Army opposition to forced collectivization, 1929–1930: the Army wavers," *Slavic Review*, vol. 55, no. 1 (1996), 25–45.
12 RGVA f. 9, op. 26, d. 487, l. 109.
13 RGVA f. 9, op. 26, d. 487, l. 26; d. 490, l. 44; f. 37837, op. 21, d. 23, l. 143.
14 RGVA f. 9, op. 26, d. 487, l. 51, 56–8; d. 490, l. 27, 82, 113.
15 RGVA f. 9, op. 26, d. 487, ll. 26–9; d. 490, ll. 10, 22, 104–10, 121–8; Document 171, "Report from the commander of the Siberian Military District to

Voroshilov regarding directives forbidding use of the military in operations against the kulaks," in Diane P. Koenker and Ronald D. Bachman, eds, *Revelations from the Russian Archives: Documents in English Translation* (Washington, DC: Library of Congress, 1997), 383.

16 RGVA f. 9, op. 26, d. 490, ll. 17, 23–4; f. 887, op. 1, d. 86, l. 6; f. 25893, op. 1, d. 292, ll. 40, 47–9, 75; Oleg F. Suvenirov, "Narkomat oborony i NKVD v predvoennyi gody," *Voenno–istoricheskii zhurnal*, no. 6 (1991), 26.

17 Aleksei Iovlev, *Deiatel'nost KPSS po podogotovke voennykh kadrov* (Moscow: Voenizdat, 1976), 98; Viktor F. Loboda, *Komandnye kadry i zakonodatel'stvo o kadrakh razvitii vooruzhennykh sil SSSR* (Moscow: Voenizdat, 1960), 53; *Krasnaia zvezda*, 4 February 1934; *Pravda*, 31 January 1935.

18 RGVA f. 4, op. 1, d. 1120, ll. 4, 10, 13–15; K. E. Voroshilov, *O molodezhi*, 19, 53, 141; *Krasnaia zvezda*, 17 February 1933, 4 February 1934; *Pravda*, 31 January 1935.

19 *XV let Krasnoi Armii* (Arkhangel'sk: severnoe kraevoe gosizdat, 1933), 11.

20 Timothy Colton, *Commissars, Commanders and Civilian Authority* (Princeton: Princeton University Press, 1979), 59.

21 Vladimir Unishevsky, *Red Pilot: Memoirs of a Soviet Airman* (London: Hurst & Blackett, 1939), 26–42.

22 K. Voroshilov, *O molodezhi*, 53, 54.

23 RGVA f. 4, op. 1, d. 1134, ll. 2, 3.

24 RGVA f. 37837, op. 21, d. 23, ll. 49, 177, 194, 200, 201, 211.

25 Iovlev, "Podgotovka komandnykh i politicheskikh kadrov Sovetskoi Armii," 65.

26 RGVA f. 37837, op. 21, d. 23, l. 18; Boris Tel'pukhovskii, *KPSS vo glave stroitel'stva Vooruzhennykh Sil SSSR* (Moscow: Izdatpolit, 1983), 115; D. A. Voropaev and A. M. Iovlev, *Bor'ba KPSS za sozdanie voennykh kadrov, 1918–1941* (Moscow: Voenizdat, 1960), 132.

27 RGVA f. 37837, op. 21, d. 23, l. 64; "O Nakoplenii Nachal'stvuiushchego sostava i popolnenii im Raboche' – Krest'ianskaia Krasnoi Armii: Iz spravki-doklada nachal'nika Upravleniia po nachal'stvuiushchemu sostavu RKKA Narkomata Oborony SSSR E. A. Shchadenko, 20 Marta 1940 g.," *Izvestiia TsK KPSS*, no. 1 (1990), 178.

28 *U.S. MID Reports*, "Red Army discipline and morale, November 1, 1927", Reel III, 898.

29 *Krasnaia zvezda*, 1 September–30 December 1929.

30 *Izvestiia*, 10 December 1926; V. A. Lebedev, "Stenogramma Fevral'sko-Martovskogo (1937 g.) Plenuma TsK VKP (b) (23 Fevralia–5 Marta 1937 g.)" *Voenno-istoricheskii zhurnal*, no. 1 (1993), 61.

31 E. H. Carr, *Foundations of a Planned Economy 1926–1929* (New York: MacMillan, 1969), vol. 1, 129; Donald Filtzer, *Soviet Workers and Stalinist Industrialization* (London: Pluto Press, 1986), 212–22; Solomon Schwarz, *Labor in the Soviet Union* (New York: Praeger, 1951), 152.

32 RGVA f. 9, op. 26, d. 487, l. 60; f. 37837, op. 21, d. 23, l. 16; *Krasnaia zvezda*, 16 April 1932, 27 April 1933.

33 *Krasnaia zvezda*, 5 August 1932.

34 RGVA f. 9, op. 26, d. 487, l. 60; *Krasnaia zvezda*, 24 July 1933.

35 Lebedev, "Stenogramma Fevral'sko-Martovskogo (1937 g.) Plenuma TsK VKP(b)," 61; Iu. B. Rubtsov, "Unichtozhat', kak beshenykh sobak," *Voenno-istoricheskii zhurnal*, no. 4 (1994), 76; Robert W. Thurston, *Life and Terror in Stalin's Russia, 1934–1941* (New Haven, Conn.: Yale University Press, 1996), 51–6.

36 Roger Reese, "The Red Army and the Great Purges," in J. Arch Getty and Roberta Manning, eds, *Stalinist Terror: New Perspectives* (Cambridge: Cambridge University Press, 1993), 199.
37 Lebedev, "Stenogramma Fevral'sko-Martovskogo (1937 g.) Plenuma TsK VKP (b)," 61.
38 "O rabote za 1939 god: Iz otcheta nachal'nika Upravleniia po nachal'stvuiush-chemu sostavu RKKA Narkomata Oborony SSSR, E. A. Shchadenko, 5 Maia 1940," *Izvestiia TsK KPSS*, vol. 2, no. 1 (1990), 188; A. T. Ukolov and V. I. Ivkin, "O masshtabakh repressii v Krasnoi Armii v predvoennye gody," *Voenno-istoricheskii zhurnal*, no. 1 (1993), 57, 58.
39 F. B. Komal, "Voennye Kadry Nakanune Voiny," *Voenno–istoricheskii zhurnal*, no. 2 (1990), 21; "O Nakoplenii Nachal'stvuiushchego sostava i popolnenii im Raboche-Krest'ianskoi Krasnoi Armii . . . ," 178–80. "Ob otbore 4000 kommu-nistov na politrabotu v RKKA 29 Avgusta 1939 g." *Izvestiia TsK KPSS*, no. 1 (1990), 174–5.
40 Document 54 "Order by Marshal Voroshilov, People's Commissar of Defense, to the Red Army, June 7, 1937, concerning another counterrevolutionary fascist organization uncovered within the military by the NKVD," in Koenker and Bachman, *Revelations from the Russian Archives*, 112–14.
41 Document 58 "Politburo announcement of VKP(b) Central Committee expul-sions and arrests, signed by Stalin, December 1937," in Koenker and Bachman, *Revelations from the Russian Archives*, 119.
42 RGVA f. 37837, op. 21, d. 23, ll. 44, 45; op. 22, d. 41, ll. 73–6, f. 896, op. 3, d. 10, ll. 9–15; Oleg Suvenirov, "Narkomat oborony i NKVD v predvoennye gody," *Voprosy Istorii*, no. 6 (1991), 29–34.
43 Lebedev, "Stenogramma Fevral'sko-Martovskogo (1937 g.) Plenuma TsK VKP(b)," 61–2.
44 Oleg F. Suvenirov, "Esli b ne ta vakkhanaliia," *Voenno-istoricheskii zhurnal*, no. 2 (1989), 57, 58; K. Voroshilov, L. Mekhlis, S. Budenny, G. Stern, *The Red Army Today, Speeches Delivered at the Eighteenth Congress of the CPSU (B) March 10–21, 1939* (Moscow: Foreign Language Publishing House, 1939).
45 Colton, *Commissars, Commanders and Civilian Authority*, 58–60; *Krasnaia zvezda*, 29 August 1937.
46 *Krasnaia zvezda*, 14 May 1938.
47 Mark Von Hagen, "Soviet soldiers and officers on the eve of the German invasion: towards a description of social psychology and political attitudes," *Soviet Union/Union Sovetique*, vol. 18, nos. 1–3 (1991), 90–4.
48 *Krasnaia zvezda*, 15 January, 2, 14, 17, 26, 28 February, 20 April 1937; Matvei V. Zakharov, *General'nyi shtab v predvoennye gody* (Moscow: Voenizdat, 1989), 100, 101.
49 "O rabote za 1939 god: Iz otcheta nachal'nika Upravleniia po nachal'stvuiush-chemu sostava RKKA Narkomata Oborony SSSR, E. A. Shchadenko, 5 Maia 1940," *Izvestiia TsK KPSS*, no. 1 (1990), 186.
50 "O Nakoplenii Nachal'stvuiushchego sostava i popolnenii im Raboche-Krest'ianskoi Krasnoi Armii . . . ," 178; "O vydvizhenii nachal'stvuiushchego sostava RKKA, 25 Marta 1940 g.," *Izvestiia TsK KPSS*, no. 1 (1990), 179.
51 *Krasnaia zvezda*, 6 August, 30 December 1937; 30 January, 15 February, 22, 27 May, 30 July, 27 August, 1938.
52 A. Cheremnykh, "Razvite Voenno-uchebnykh Zavedenii v predvoennyi period (1937–1941 gg.)," *Voenno-istoricheskii zhurnal*, no. 8 (1982), 75; "O Nakoplenii Nachal'stvuiushchego sostava i popolnenii im Raboche-Krest'ianskoi Krasnoi Armii . . . ," 180.

53 "O Nakoplenii Nachal'stvuiushchego sostava i popolnenii im Raboche-Krest'ianskoi Krasnoi Armii . . . ," 179.

5 The Red Army and the Second World War, 1939–45

1 Harriet F. Scott and William F. Scott, *Soviet Military Doctrine: continuity, formulation, and dissemination* (Boulder, Colo.: Westview Press, 1988), 17.
2 RGVA f. 25880, op. 4, d. 5, ll. 555–6; A. G. Khor'kov, "Tekhnicheskoe perevooruchenie Sovetskii Armii nakanune Velikoi Otechestvennoi voiny," *Voenno-istoricheskii zhurnal,* no. 6 (1987), 22.
3 RGVA f. 25880, op. 4, d. 5, ll. 145, 146, 182, 183, 220, 345.
4 RGVA f. 25880, op. 4, d. 4, ll. 16–20, 196, 197, 268–70, 290; d. 5, ll. 301, 303–7, 316–24, 328, 545, 547, 595, 597.
5 *Krasnaia zvezda,* 27 June 1940.
6 A. T. Ukolov and V. I. Ivkin, "O Masshtabakh Repressii v Krasnoi Armii v predvoennye godu," *Voenno-istoricheskii zhurnal,* no. 1 (1993), 59.
7 RGVA f. 25880, op. 4, d. 5, ll. 382–6; V. E. Bystrov, ed., *Sovetskie polkovodtsy i voenachal'niki* (Moscow: Molodaia gvardiia, 1988), 242–55, 306–14.
8 *Pravda,* 25 August 1940.
9 Petro Grigorenko, *Memoirs* (New York: W. W. Norton, 1982), 108, 109; Marshal G. K. Zhukov, *Vospominaniia i razmyshleniia,* 11th edn (Moscow: Novosti, 1992), vol. 1, 249–87; Amnon Sella, "Khalkhin-Gol: The Forgotten War," *Journal of Contemporary History,* vol. 18 (1983), 658–62, 663, 667; G. F. Krivosheev, *Grif Sekretnosti Sniat: Poteri Vooruzhennykh Sil SSSR v voinakh, voevykh deistviiakh i voennykh konfliktakh* (Moscow: Prosveshchenie, 1992), 76–85.
10 Krivosheev, *Grif Sekretnosti Sniat,* 93–126; "O Nakoplenii Nachal'stvuiushchego sostava im Raboche-Krest'ianskoi Krasnoi Armii: Iz spravki-doklada Upravleniia po nachal'stvuiushchemu sostavu RKKA Narkomata Oborony SSSR E. A. Shchadenko, 20 Marta 1940 g.," *Izvestiia TsK KPSS,* no. 1 (1990), 181.
11 Iurii G. Perechnev, "O nekotorikh problemakh podgotovki strany i Vooruzhennykh Sil k otrazheniiu fashistskoi agressii," *Voenno-istoricheskii zhurnal,* no. 4 (1988), 46.
12 "Akt o Prieme Narkomata Oborony Soiuza SSR tov. Timoshenko S. K. ot tov. Voroshilov K. E.," *Izvestiia TsK KPSS,* no. 1 (1990), 193–205.
13 *KPSS o vooruzhennykh silakh Sovetskogo Soiuza: dokumenty 1917–1968* (Moscow: Voenizdat, 1969), 277, 278, 302.
14 Amnon Sella, *The Value of Human Life in Soviet Warfare* (New York: Routledge, 1992), 108, 156.
15 "Postanovlenie Voennogo Soveta Severnogo fronta, 28 iiunia 1941 g., g. Leningrad," V. V. Cherepanov, "Shli na front dobrovol'no: O narodnom opolchenii iazykom dokumentov," *Voenno-istoricheskii zhurnal,* no. 1 (1996), 10; "Postanovlenie Biuro Leningradskogo Gorkoma VKP(b), 29 iiuna 1941 g.: O formirovanii v gorode Leningrade armii dobrovol'tsev" and "Plan organizatsii 200-tysiachnoi armii dobrovol'tsev g. Leningrada," in Cherepanov, "Shli na front dobrovol'no," 11.
16 *Istoriia ordena Lenina Leningradskogo voennogo okruga,* 3rd edn (Moscow: Voenizdat, 1988), 172; Stepan Bardin, "Chest' svoiu ne uronili", in V. P. Bogdanov, ed., *Zhivaia Pamiat': Velikaia Otechestvennaia: pravda o voine v trekh tomakh* (Moscow: Sovet veteranov zhurnalistiki Rossii Soiuz Zhurnalistov RF, 1995), vol. 1, 218–19.

17 "Chrezvychainaia Troika Provodit Dobrovol'nuiu Mobilizatsiiu," *Istochnik: dokumenty russkoi istorii*, no. 2 (1995), 100–2.
18 Cherepanov, "Shli na front dobrovol'no," 12, 13; Vladimir Baskakov, "Opolchentsy," in Bogdanov, ed., *Zhivaia Pamiat'*, vol. 1, 138.
19 "Doklad ob itogakh proverki sostoianiia divizii narodnogo opolcheniia 32-i i 33-i Rezervnykh Armii, 3 Sentiabria 1941 g.", in Cherepanov, "Shli na front dobrovol'no," 13.
20 "Doklad ob itogakh proverki sostoianiia divizii narodongo opolcheniia," in Cherepanov, "Shli na front dobrovol'no," 13; Georgii Kumanev "Krakh operatsii,'" 'Taifun in Bogdanov, ed., *Zhivaia Pamiat'*, vol. 1, 164.
21 *Krasnoznamennyi Belorusskii voennyi okrug*, 2nd edn (Moscow: Voenizdat, 1983), 120; "Organizuetsia narodnoe opolchenie: Telegramma iz Kieva, 5 iiulia 1941 g." *Izvestiia TsK KPSS*, no. 7 (1990), 198.
22 Andrei Gorshkov, "Tuliaki srazhaiotsia s Guderianom," in Bogdanov, ed., *Zhivaia Pamiat'*, vol. 1, 186–9.
23 "V TsK VKP(b) t. Shembergu Politinformatsiia Altaiskogo Kraikoma VKP(b), 20 avgusta 1942 g., Ob itogakh komplektovaniia pervoi osoboi dobrovol'cheskoi Stalinskoi Brigady Altaiskogo kraia," in Cherepanov, "Shli na front dobrovol'no," 14, 15; *Poslednie pis'ma s fronta, 1942* (Moscow: Voenizdat, 1991), 74–5, 120–1.
24 G. F. Krivosheev, "Podgotovka voennoobuchennykh rezervov dlia Sovetskoi Armii v predvoennye gody i v khode Velikoi Otechestvennoi voiny," *Voenno-istoricheskii zhurnal*, no. 1 (1988), 48–51.
25 Gabriel Temkin, *My Just War: the memoir of a Jewish Red Army soldier in World War II* (Novato, Cal.: Presidio, 1998), 103–4.
26 *Ibid.*, 112–13, 115, 116.
27 "Postanovlenie GKO no. 2470, 3 noiabria 1942 g., O formirovanii zhenskoi dobrovol'cheskoi strelkovoi brigady," in Cherepanov, "Shli na front dobrovol'no," 15.
28 Zoya Matveyevna Smirnova-Medvedeva, *On the Road to Stalingrad: Memoirs of a Soviet Woman Machine Gunner*, edited and translated by Kazimiera Janina (Cottam, Toronto: Legas, 1996), 18.
29 Temkin, *My Just War*, 202.
30 Leonid Piterskii, "Deti na Voine," *Istochnik: Dokumenty russkoi istorii*, no. 1 (1994), 55; and "Syn polka," *Rodina* no. 2 (1995), 63–8.
31 K. Khromova, "Synov'ia Polkov," *Sovetskii voin*, no. 5 (1989), 50.
32 B. V. Sokolov, "The cost of war: human losses for the USSR and Germany, 1939–1945" (translated by Dr Harold S. Orenstein, originally published as *Tsena voiny: Liudskie poteri SSSR i Germanii, 1939–1945 gg.) The Journal of Slavic Military Studies*, vol. 9, no. 1 (March 1996), 166.
33 V. Litovkin, *Izvestiia*, 8 May 1990, 3.
34 RGVA, f. 25880, op. 4, d. 4, l. 439–40, 441–4, 448.
35 Sella, *The Value of Human Life in Soviet Warfare*, 194.
36 "Politdonesenie otdela politpropagandy 11-i armii v UPP Severo-Zapadnogo fronta," in Semin, Sigachev, and Chuvashin, "Na linii fronta," *Istoricheskii arkhiv*, no. 2 (1995), 44.
37 *Poslednie pis'ma s fronta, 1942*, 424.
38 "Donesenie politupravleniia Zapadnogo fronta v GlavPU RKKA," in Semin, Sigachev, and Chuvashin, "Na linii fronta," *Istoricheskii arkhiv*, no. 2 (1995), 61–2.
39 "Poslednie pis'ma s fronta," *Voenno-istoricheskii zhurnal*, no. 6 (1989), 66.
40 *Poslednie pis'ma s fronta, 1942*, 79, 186–90, 238.

41 Omer Bartov, *Hitler's Army: Soldiers, Nazis, and War in the Third Reich* (Oxford: Oxford University Press, 1992), 84–8; "Politdonesenie upravleniia politpropagandy Zapadnogo fronta v GlavPU RKKA," in Semin, Sigachev, and Chuvashin, "Na linii fronta," *Istoricheskii arkhiv*, no. 2 (1995), 43–4.

42 "Prikaz Narodnogo Komissara Oborony soiuza SSSR no. 227," in Bogdanov, ed., *Zhivaia Pamiat'*, vol. 1, 303–6; Sella, *The Value of Human Life in Soviet Warfare*, 153, 158–9.

43 Semen Borzunov, "Na Donu, pod Voronezhem: Iz dnevnika frontovogo Korrespondenta," in Bogdanov, ed., *Zhivaia Pamiat'*, vol. 2, 84.

44 *Poslednie pis'ma s fronta, 1942*, 533.

45 S. Khomenko, "Disciplinary Battalion Joins Battle," *Soviet Soldier*, no. 11 (1990), 36–8.

46 G. S. Beloborodov, "Brali vraga Ezhovymi rukavitsami: Vnutrennie voiska NKVD v gody Velikoi Otechestvennoi voiny," *Voenno-istoricheskii zhurnal*, no. 9 (1993), 12; "Politdonesenie politupravleniia Iugo-Zapadnogo fronta v GlavPU RKKA," in Semin, Sigachev, and Chuvashin, "Na linii fronta," *Istoricheskii arkhiv*, no. 2 (1995), 51.

47 Temkin, *My Just War*, 178–9; *Poslednie pis'ma s fronta, 1942*, 247.

48 *Poslednie pis'ma s fronta, 1942*, 74, 523; *Poslednie pis'ma s fronta, 1944*, 444.

49 "Politdonesenie Politupravleniia 1-go Belorusskogo fronta v GlavPU RKKA i Voennyi sovet fronta 'O politicheskom obespechenii boev za g. Poznan'," in Semin, Sigachev, and Chuvashin, "Na linii fronta," *Istoricheskii arkhiv*, no. 3 (1995), 33; "Politdonesenie politupravleniia Iugo-Zapadnogo fronta v GlavPU RKKA", Semin, Sigachev, and Chuvashin, "Na linii fronta," *Istoricheskii arkhiv*, no. 2 (1995), 51.

50 "Donesenie upolnomochennogo Gosudarstvennogo Komiteta Oborony po Smolenskoi oblasti I. S. Khokhlova v GKO o polozhenii v osvobozhdennykh raionakh i v voiskakh 30 armii," in S. A. Mel'chin, Iu. v. Sigachev, A. S. Stepanov, "Zharkoe leto sorok pervogo goda: Dokumenty GKO i Stavki perioda Smolenskogo srazhenia. Iiul' – sentiabr' 1941 g.," *Istoricheskii arkhiv*, no. 1 (1993), 65.

51 Semin, Sigachev, and Chuvashin, "Na linii fronta," *Istoricheskii arkhiv*, no. 2 (1995), 40–1.

52 "Politdonesenie otdela politpropagandy 11-i armii v UPP Severo–Zapadnogo fronta," and "Donesenie politupravleniia Zapadnogo fronta v GlavPU RKKA," in Semin, Sigachev, Chuvashin, "Na linii fronta," *Istoricheskii arkhiv*, no. 2 (1995), 46, 57.

53 "Donesenie politupravleniia Zapadnogo fronta v GlavPU RKKA," 57, 58.

54 Magomed Inderbiev, ". . . A tovarishcha vyruchai!," in V. P. Bogdanov, ed., *Zhivaia Pamiat'*, vol. 2, 421.

55 Georgii Kumanev, "Krakh Operatsii 'Taifun'," in Bogdanov, ed., *Zhivaia Pamiat'*, vol. 1, 164, 167.

56 Viacheslav Grinevskii, "Pomnit Neman," in Bogdanov, ed., *Zhivaia Pamiat'*, vol. 1, 81.

57 "Doklada zapiska komanduiushchego rezervnym frontom G. K. Zhukova, 7 avgusta 1941 g.," in Cherepanov, "Shli na front dobrovol'no," 12.

58 "Politdonesenie otdela politpropagandy 11-i armii v UPP Severo–Zapadnogo fronta," in Semin, Sigachev, and Chuvashin, "Na linii fronta," *Istoricheskii arkhiv*, no. 2 (1995), 43, 45, 46.

59 *Krasnoznamennyi Belorusskii voennyi okrug*, 2nd edn, 121.

60 *Poslednie pis'ma s fronta, 1942*, 110.

61 Temkin, *My Just War*, 139, 141, 190.

62 *Ibid.*, 174–5, 182.
63 V. E. Korol, "The price of victory: myths and reality" (translated by David M. Glantz), *The Journal of Slavic Military Studies*, vol. 9, no. 2 (June 1996), 422. For the quote Korol cites, *Literaturnaia Rossiia*, 16 May 1988.
64 Krivosheev, *Grif sekretnosti sniat*, 323–7.
65 "My raspolagaem samymi luchshimi kadrami: Zapiski o poslevoennom ustroistve armii," *Istochnik: Dokumenty russkoi istorii*, no. 2 (1996), 132–6, 139, 141, 142, 143, 148, 149.
66 *Ibid.*, 137–8.
67 B. V. Sokolov, "The cost of war: human losses for the USSR and Germany, 1939–1945," 167.
68 Oleg Rakhmanin, "Ne Shchadia zhizni," in V. P. Bogdanov, ed., *Zhivaia Pamiat'*, vol. 2, 280.
69 *Poslednie pis'ma s fronta, 1942*, 15–19, 438–42; "Poslednie pis'ma s fronta," *Voenno-istoricheskii zhurnal*, no. 6 (1989), 66.
70 *Poslednie pis'ma s fronta, 1942*, 91.
71 Temkin, *My Just War*, 131–2.
72 "Politdonesenie politupravleniia Iugo–Zapadnogo fronta v GlavPU RKKA," Semin, Sigachev, and Chuvashin, "Na linii fronta . . .," *Istoricheskii arkhiv*, no. 2 (1995), 48–51.
73 *Poslednie pis'ma s fronta, 1943*, 34.
74 Smirnova-Medvedeva, *On the Road to Stalingrad*, 38.
75 "Donesenie politotdela Primorskoi armii nachal'niku politupravleniia 4-go Ukrainskogo fronta M. M. Proninu 'O nastupatel'nykh deistviiakh voisk armii i partiino-politicheskoi rabote za 20–25 aprelia 1944 goda,'" Semin, Sigachev, and Chuvashin, "Na linii fronta.," *Istoricheskii arkhiv,* no. 3 (1995), 26.
76 "Ob opyte boev chastei 24 armii v raione g. El'nia v period s 20 iiulia po 5 avgusta 1941 g.," "Chasti Protivnika Moral'no Potriaseny," *Istochnik: Dokumenty russkoi istorii*, no. 2 (1995), 108–11.
77 "Politdonesenie Politupravleniia 1–go Belorusskogo fronta v GlavPU RKKA i Voennyi sovet fronta 'O politicheskom obespechenii boev za g. Poznan,'" in Semin, Sigachev, and Chuvashin, "Na linii fronta," *Istoricheskii arkhiv*, no. 3 (1995), 31–52.

6 The cold war years, 1946–91

1 "Spravka-doklad G. K. Zhukov o sokrashchenii Vooruzhennykh Sil 12 avgusta 1955 g.," in *Voennye Arkhivy Rossii*, no. 1 (1993), 280–1.
2 Liubov' Kievskia, Vladimir Lebedev, Sergei Mel'chin, Iurii Murin, Anatolii Chernev, "'Chego Stoiat Polkovodcheskie Kachestva Stalina,' Neproiznesennaia rech' marshala G. K. Zhukova," *Vestnik* no. 2 (1995), 143–59.
3 Nikita Khrushchev, *Khrushchev Remembers*, translated and edited by Strobe Talbot (Boston: Little, Brown, & Co., 1970), 514–17; "Sovet Ministerov Soiuza SSR: postanovlenie 12 avgusta 1955 goda no. 1481-825cc. 'O sokrashchenii chislennosti Vooruzhennykh Sil'," in *Voennye Arkhivy Rossii*, no. 1 (1993), 273.
4 "Zapiska I. Koneva i A. Zheltova v TsK KPSS ob otnoshenii v armii k Zaiavleniiu Sovetskogo pravitel'stva po voprosu o razoruzhenii, 1 iiunia 1956 g.;" "Zapiska I. Serova v TsK KPSS o nedovol'stve nekotorykh ofitserov Zabaikal'skogo voennogo okruga organizatsionnymu meropriiatiiami po sokrashcheniiu Vooruzhennykh Sil;" and "Zapiska R. Malinovskogo v TsK KPSS o rabote po sokrashcheniiu Vooruzhennykh Sil, 8 ianvaria 1959 g.;" and "Zapiska R. Malinovskogo i V. Sokolovskogo v TsK KPSS s predlozheniiami po

dal'neishemu sokrashcheniiu Vooruzhennykh Sil SSSR, 3 ianvaria 1956 g.," in *Voennye Arkhivy Rossii*, no. 1 (1993), 292–306.

5 E. I. Malashenko, "Osobyi korpus v ogne Budapeshta: Operatsiia 'Vikhr'," *Voenno-istoricheskii zhurnal*, no. 1 (1994), 31–6; *Grif sekretnosti sniat*, 36.

6 Iuri Bespalov and Valery Konovalov, "Novocherkassk 1962," *Komsomolskaia pravda*, 2 June 1989, 4; N. Trubin, *Pravda*, 3 June 1991, 4.

7 Leonid Shinkarev, *Izvestiia*, 19 August 1989, 5.

8 D. Derk Swain, "The Soviet military sector: how it is defined and measured," in Henry S. Rowen and Charles Wolf, Jr, eds, *The Impoverished Superpower: Perestroika and the Soviet Military Burden* (San Francisco: ICS Press, 1990), 103–6; Leo Cooper, *The Political Economy of Soviet Military Power* (New York: St Martin's, 1989), 49.

9 Rowen and Wolf, *The Impoverished Superpower*, 1–7.

10 V. Zolotukhin, "The Army needs reform," *Soviet Soldier*, no. 8 (1990), 6–7.

11 Ellen Jones, *Red Army and Society* (Boston: Allen & Unwin, 1985), 89; Alexander Lebed, *General Alexander Lebed: my life and my country* (Washington, DC: Regnery Publishing, 1997), 49–51.

12 V. Dymarsky and Ye. Shashkov, *Kommunist*, no. 3 (January 1990), 51–8.

13 Patrick Cronin, "Perestroika and Soviet military personnel," in William C. Green and Theodore Karasik, eds, *Gorbachev and His Generals: the reform of Soviet military doctrine* (Boulder, Colo.: Westview Press, 1990), 134–7.

14 Alexander Alexiev, *Inside the Soviet Army in Afghanistan* (Santa Monica, Cal.: Rand Corporation, 1988), 40.

15 V. Chaplinsky, "A barrier against fairness," in Christopher Cerf and Marina Albee, *Small Fires: letters from the Soviet people to Ogonyok Magazine 1987–1990* (New York: Simon & Schuster, 1990), 175.

16 Anatoly Ivanov, "Judge the Army objectively," *Soviet Military Review*, no. 11 (1989), 4.

17 N. Chechikov, "V neravnykh usloviiakh," *Sovetskii voin*, no. 9 (1989).

18 "Dvattsat' tysiach beskvartirnykh," *Krasnaia zvezda*, 6 April 1990, 1.

19 V. Dymarsky and Ye. Shashkov, *Kommunist*, no. 3 (January 1990), 51–8.

20 M. Boltunov, "Kak vyzhit' garnizonu?" *Sovetskii voin*, no. 10 (1991), 6–8.

21 A. Shuvaev, "Zhivut zhe liudi . . . ," *Krasnaia zvezda*, 27 June 1989, 2.

22 V. Lesnikov, "As the call, so the echo," *Soviet Soldier*, no. 6 (1990), 37.

23 Anatol Lieven, "Disarmed and dangerous," *The New Republic*, 22 December 1997, 22.

24 V. Litovkin, *Izvestiia*, 9 August 1990, 6.

25 Ron McKay, *Letters to Gorbachev: life in Russia through the postbag of Argumenty i Fakty* (London: Michael Joseph, 1991), 187.

26 N. Senchev, *Pravda*, 12 September 1990, 6.

27 "School of internationalism," *Soviet Military Review*, no. 8 (1989), 3.

28 Iuri Deriugin, "Multiethnic military collective," *Soviet Military Review*, no. 12 (1987), 5–6.

29 *Ibid.*, 6.

30 V. Mukhin, "Neustavnye otnosheniia: chto budet zavtra?" *Kommunist Vooruzhennykh Sil*, no. 1 (1991), 12–13.

31 "Military communication," in Cerf and Albee, *Small Fires*, 202–4.

32 I. Ivanov and L. Iakutin, "Shuravi Khanum," *Sovetskii voin*, no. 6 (1988), 12–13; N. Kartashov, "Madonny . . . V potonakh," *Kommunist Vooruzhennykh Sil*, no. 4 (1991), 33–45.

33 Lebed, *My Life and My Country*, 149.

34 Laure Després, "The economic planning and management of the *Tyl* in the Soviet Armed Forces," *Europe-Asia Studies*, vol. 48, no. 5 (1996), 770–2.

35 I. Medvedev, "Ekh, sapogi soldatskie . . . ," *Sovetskii voin*, no. 9 (1989).

36 V. Mukhin, "Neustavnye otnosheniia: chto budet zavtra?" *Kommunist Vooruzhennykh Sil*, no. 1 (1991), 11–14.

37 S. Vorob'ev, "Kakim byt' disbatu?" *Kommunist Vooruzhennykh Sil*, no. 20 (1990), 11–12.

38 Viktor Badurkin, "Confinement shall be commuted to . . . ," *Soviet Military Review*, no. 7 (1989), 36–8.

39 Richard A. Gabriel, *The Mind of the Soviet Fighting Man: a quantitative survey of Soviet soldiers, sailors, and airmen* (Westport, Conn.: Greenwood Press, 1984), 5–8, 49–51, 91–4.

40 William Zimmerman and Michael L. Berbaum, "Soviet military manpower policy in the Brezhnev era: regime goals, social origins and 'Working the System,'" *Europe-Asia Studies*, vol. 45, no. 2 (1993), 281–9.

41 Gabriel, *The Mind of the Soviet Fighting Man*, 37–9, 80–3, 126–7; *Krasnaia zvezda*, 14 October 1989, 4.

42 S. Chugaev, *Izvestiia*, 5 November 1991, 2; 4 October 1990, 3.

43 Boris Kalachev, *Literaturnaia gazeta*, 26 October 1988, 12.

44 "Davai, Davai, soldatushki," *Krasnaia zvezda*, 23 September 1990, 4.

45 *Pravda*, 11 January 1991, 3.

46 I. Esiutin, "Khleb Maiora Senchenko," *Sovetskii voin*, no. 4 (1989), 74–5; *Krasnaia zvezda*, 29 August 1990, 4.

47 Ron McKay, *Letters to Gorbachev*, 194–5.

48 A. Krivonos, "Nedouchki ne nuzhny!" *Kommunist Vooruzhennykh Sil*, no. 19 (1990), 24.

49 Evgeny Sorokin, *Pravda*, 26 April 1989, 3.

50 "Voennye stroiteli – piatiletke," *Krasnaia zvezda*, 13 August 1988, 1; O. Vladimirov, "Posle tragedii," *Sovetskii voin*, no. 4 (1990); V. Ermokhin, "Net mesta v paradnom stroiu?" *Kommunist Vooruzhennykh Sil*, no. 14 (1990), 11–12.

51 *Izvestiia*, 12 June 1990, 3.

52 Evgeny Sorokin, *Pravda*, 26 April 1989, 3.

53 V. Litovkin, *Izvestiia*, 1 November 1989, 6.

54 V. Litovkin, *Izvestiia*, 1 November 1989, 6; 12 June 1990, 3.

55 L. Iakhno, "Pochemu peresmotreno personal'noe delo," *Kommunist Vooruzhennykh Sil*, no. 3 (1961), 60–1; "O ser'eznykh nedostatkakh v rabote partiinykh organizatsii i politorganov Odesskogo voennogo Okruga i Krasnoznamennogo Baltiiskogo Flota po priemu v partiiu i vospitaniiu molodykh kommunistov: Iz postanovleniia TsK KPSS," in *KPSS o vooruzhennykh silakh Sovetskogo Soiuza: dokumenty 1917–1968* (Moscow: Voenizdat, 1969), 377–8; Jones, *Red Army and Society*, 126, 127.

56 I. Rogatin and A. Kolinichenko, "Kogda miriatsia s nedostatkami," *Kommunist Vooruzhennykh Sil*, no. 12 (1961), 72–4; Jones, *Red Army and Society*, 140–1.

57 M. Kalashnik, "Political education in the Soviet Armed Forces," *Soviet Military Review*, no. 10 (1965), 12–16.

7 The war Afghanistan and the Gorbachev era, 1979–91

1 Robert F. Baumann, *Russian-Soviet Unconventional Wars in the Caucasus, Central Asia, and Afghanistan* (Ft Leavenworth, Kans: Combat Studies Institute, 1993), 136; Oleg Sarin and Lev Dvoretsky, *The Afghan Syndrome: the Soviet Union's Vietnam* (Novato, Cal.: Presidio, 1993), 101.

2 Aleksandr Liakhovskii, *Tragediia i doblest' Afgana* (Moscow: GPI Iskona, 1995), 174–8, 180–5.
3 Artyom Borovik, *The Hidden War: a Russian journalist's account of the Soviet war in Afghanistan* (New York: Atlantic Monthly, 1990), 81.
4 Vladislav Tamarov, *Afghanistan: Soviet Vietnam* (San Francisco, Cal.: Mercury House, 1992), 20.
5 Baumann, *Russian-Soviet Unconventional Wars*, 149; Lester W. Grau, ed., *The Bear Went Over the Mountain: Soviet combat tactics in Afghanistan* (Washington, DC: National Defense University Press, n.d.), xiv, 202.
6 V. Izgarshev, *Pravda*, 17 August 1989, 6; *Argumenty i fakti*, no. 4, 4–10 November 1989, 7; Liakhovskii, *Tragediia i doblest' Afgana*, Appendix 14.
7 Liakhovskii, *Tragediia i doblest' Afgana*, Appendix 14.
8 Baumann, *Russian-Soviet Unconventional Wars*, 166.
9 Alexiev, *Inside the Soviet Army in Afghanistan*, 19–20; Svetlana Alexievich, *Zinky Boys: Soviet Voices from the Afghanistan War* (New York: W.W. Norton, 1990), 43–4.
10 G. Ustiuzhanin, "An omen proved true," *Soviet Soldier*, no. 3 (1991), 38.
11 *Ibid.*, 38–9.
12 Alexiev, *Inside the Soviet Army in Afghanistan*, 56.
13 *Ibid.*, 58.
14 Ustiuzhanin, "An omen proved true," 38–9.
15 Alexiev, *Inside the Soviet Army in Afghanistan*, 59.
16 Tamarov, *Afghanistan: Soviet Vietnam*, 12; Alexievich, *Zinky Boys,* 168–9; Sarin and Dvoretsky, *The Afghan Syndrome,* 89–91.
17 Alexievich, *Zinky Boys*, 49–50, 58, 116, 120.
18 Alexiev, *Inside the Soviet Army in Afghanistan*, 38.
19 *Ibid.*, 40.
20 Borovik, *The Hidden War*, 121–2.
21 Baumann, *Russian-Soviet Unconventional Wars*, 149; Alexiev, *Inside the Soviet Army in Afghanistan*, 43; Borovik, *The Hidden War*, 154, 215.
22 Borovik, *The Hidden War*, 134, 135.
23 Alexievich, *Zinky Boys*, 25; Borovik, *The Hidden War*, 186.
24 Borovik, *The Hidden War*, 121.
25 Alexievich, *Zinky Boys*, 53.
26 *Izvestiia*, 12 August 1989, 2–3; *Pravda*, 16 December 1989, 5; 5 July 1990, 4.
27 Valery Vyzhutovich, *Izvestiia*, 15 July 1991, 1; *Krasnaia zvezda*, 18 July 1991, 1.
28 *Krasnaia zvezda*, 19 November 1989, 4.
29 *Pravda*, 13 September 1990, 2; *Izvestiia*, 2 October 1990, 2; *Krasnaia zvezda*, 7 March 1990, 4.
30 V. Kaushanskii, *Krasnaia zvezda*, 10 November 1989, 2; *Izvestiia*, 4 October 1990, 3; *Izvestiia*, 7 January 1991, 1.
31 *Izvestiia*, 8 January 1991, 2; V. Litovkin, *Izvestiia*, 22 July 1991, 2.
32 *Pravda*, 5 July 1990, 4.
33 *Pravda*, 16 November 1990, 1, 3.
34 V. Zolotukhin, "The Army needs reform," *Soviet Soldier*, no. 8 (1990), 6–7; "Kak zhivesh', ofitserskaia sem'ia?" *Kommunist Vooruzhennykh Sil*, no. 4 (1991), 17–24.
35 S. Taranov, *Izvestiia*, 20 October 1989, 2; S. Sedin in McKay, *Letters to Gorbachev*, 177–8.
36 V. Zolotukhin, "The Army needs reform," 6–7; Aleksandr Mikhailov, "Chelovek v voennom forme," *Kommunist Vooruzhennykh Sil*, no. 9 (1990), 14–27.

37 I. Artilavka, "An open letter to Minister of Defense of the USSR Yazov," in Cerf and Albee, *Small Fires*, 219.
38 A. P. Moskovskii, *Novosti*, no. 44, 29 October 1989, 2.
39 *Pravda*, 16 November 1990, 1; *Izvestiia*, 11 January 1991.
40 Ie. Aleksei, "Khochu zhit' v Avstralii," *Sovetskii voin*, no. 12 (1989), 47.
41 T. Volodia, "Armiia ne dlia menia," *Sovetskii voin*, no. 5 (1989), 47.
42 Valentin Khrobostov, "The crucial factor," *Soviet Military Review*, no. 11 (1989), 5–7.
43 *Izvestiia*, 24 October 1989, 2.
44 "No more management by Orders and Decrees," *Soviet Military Review*, no. 1 (1989), 28; N. Beliaev "Ne oslabliaite kriticheskii nastroi," *Kommunist Vooruzhennykh Sil*, no. 14 (1990), 8.
45 "No more management by Orders and Decrees," 27, 28.
46 V. Nechaev, *Krasnaia zvezda*, 9 April 1989, 2; 30 March 1991, 1–2; "Neskol'ko partii v odnom polku?" *Kommunist Vooruzhennykh Sil*, no. 1 (1991), 15–20.
47 James H. Brusstar and Ellen Jones, *The Russian Military's Role in Politics* (Washington, DC: National Defense University, 1995), 12–16; E. Maksimova, *Izvestiia*, 9 September 1991, 8. The two divisions that entered Moscow during the coup, the 4th Kantemir Tank Division, and the 2nd Taman Motorized Rifle Division, went in at only 20 percent strength. The rest of the men were in field training, or participating in the harvest of potatoes.
48 *Komsomolskaia pravda*, 27 August 1991, 3.

SELECT BIBLIOGRAPHY

General works

Colton, Timothy. *Commissars, Commanders and Civilian Authority*. Princeton: Princeton University Press, 1979.

Erickson, John. *The Soviet High Command: A Military-Political History, 1918–1941*. New York: St Martin's Press, 1962.

Krivosheev, G. F. *Grif Sekretnosti Sniat: Poteri Vooruzhennykh Sil SSSR v voinakh, voevykh deistviiakh i voennykh konfliktakh*. Moscow: Prosveshchenie, 1992.

The Civil War

Adams, Arthur E. *Bolsheviks in the Ukraine: The Second Campaign, 1918–1919*. New Haven, Conn.: Yale University Press, 1963.

Babel, Isaac. *1920 Diary*. New Haven, Conn.: Yale University Press, 1995.

Benvenuti, Francesco. *The Bolsheviks and the Red Army 1918–1922*. Cambridge: Cambridge University Press, 1988.

Brown, Stephen. "Communists and the Red Cavalry: the political education of the Konarmia in the Russian civil war, 1918–1920," *Slavonic and East European Review*, vol. 73, no. 1, January 1995.

Davies, Norman. *White Eagle, Red Star: the Polish-Soviet War, 1919–20*. London: Orbis, 1983.

Dune, Eduard. *Notes of a Red Guard*. Urbana, Ill.: University of Illinois Press, 1993.

Figes, Orlando. "The Red Army and mass mobilization during the Russian Civil War, 1918–1920," *Past and Present*, no. 129, November 1990.

Footman, David. *Civil War in Russia*. New York: Praeger, 1961.

Kenez, Peter. *Civil War in South Russia: The first year of the Volunteer Army*. Berkeley, Cal.: University of California Press, 1971.

Mawdsley, Evan. *The Russian Civil War*. Boston: Allen & Unwin, 1987.

Meijer, Jan M., ed., *The Trotsky Papers, 1917–1922*. London: Mouton, 1964.

Trotsky, Leon. *The Military Writings and Speeches of Leon Trotsky, vol. one, 1918: How the Revolution armed*. London: New Park, 1979.

Between the wars

Reese, Roger R. *Stalin's Reluctant Soldiers: a social history of the Red Army, 1925–1941*. Lawrence, Kans: University Press of Kansas, 1996.

—— "Red Army opposition to forced collectivization, 1929–30: the army wavers," *Slavic Review*, vol. 55, no. 1 (Spring 1996), 24–45.

Von Hagen, Mark. *Soldiers in the Proletarian Dictatorship: The Red Army and the Soviet Socialist State, 1917–1930*. Ithaca, NY: Cornell University Press, 1990.

—— "Soviet soldiers and officers on the eve of the German invasion: towards a description of social psychology and political attitudes", *Soviet Union/Union Soviétique*, vol. 18, nos 1–3 (1991), 79–101.

White, Dmitrii F. *The Growth of the Red Army*. Princeton: Princeton University Press, 1944.

The Second World War

Bogdanov, V. L., ed., *Zhivaia Pamiat': Velikaia Otechestvennaia: pravda o voine*. 3 vols. Moscow: Sovet veteranov zhurnalistiki Rossii Soiuz zhurnalistov RF, 1995.

Erickson, John. *The Road to Stalingrad: Stalin's war with Germany*. London: Weidenfeld & Nicolson, 1975.

—— *The Road to Berlin*. Boulder, Colo.: Westview, 1983.

Glantz, David and House, Jonathan. *When Titans Clashed: how the Red Army stopped Hitler*. Lawrence, Kans: University Press of Kansas, 1995

Poslednie pis'ma s fronta. 5 vols, 1941–45. Moscow: Voenizdat, 1990–92.

Sella, Amnon. *The Value of Human Life in Soviet Warfare*. New York: Routledge, 1992.

Temkin, Gabriel. *My Just War: the memoir of a Jewish Red Army soldier in World War II*. Novato, Cal.: Presidio, 1998.

The cold war and Afghanistan

Alexiev, Alexander. *Inside the Soviet Army in Afghanistan*. Santa Monica, Cal.: Rand, 1988.

Alexievich, Svetlana. *Zinky Boys: Soviet voices from the Afghanistan war*. New York: W.W. Norton, 1990.

Baumann, Robert F. *Russian-Soviet Unconventional Wars in the Caucasus, Central Asia, and Afghanistan*. Ft Leavenworth, Kans: Combat Studies Institute, 1993.

Borovik, Artyom. *The Hidden War: a Russian journalist's account of the Soviet war in Afghanistan*. New York: Atlantic Monthly Press, 1990.

Brusstar, James H. and Jones, Ellen. *The Russian Military's Role in Politics*, Washington, DC: National Defense University, 1995.

Gabriel, Richard A. *The Mind of the Soviet Fighting Man: a quantitative survey of Soviet soldiers, sailors, and airmen*. Westport, Conn.: Greenwood Press, 1984.

Grau, Lester W., ed., *The Bear Went Over the Mountain: Soviet combat tactics in Afghanistan*. Washington, DC: National Defense University Press, n.d.

Jones, Ellen. *Red Army and Society*. Boston: Allen & Unwin, 1985.

Lebed, Alexander. *General Alexander Lebed: my life and my country*. Washington, DC: Regnery Publishing, 1997.

Liakhovskii, Aleksandr. *Tragediia i doblest' Afgana*. Moscow: GPI Iskona, 1995.

Sarin, Oleg and Dvoretsky, L. *The Afghan Syndrome: the Soviet Union's Vietnam*. Novato, Cal.: Presidio, 1993.

Tamarov, Vladislav. *Afghanistan: Soviet Vietnam*. San Francisco, Cal.: Mercury House, 1992.

Published documents

Cherepanov, V. V. "Shli na front dobrovol'no: O narodnom opolchenii iazykom dokumentov," in *Voenno-istoricheskii zhurnal*, no. 1 (1996), 9–16.

"Chrezvychainaia Troika Provodit Dobrovol'nuiu Mobilizatsiiu," in *Istochnik: dokumenty russkoi istorii*, no. 2 (1995), 100–2.

Direktivy Glavnogo Komandovaniia Krasnoi Armii (1917–1920): Sbornik dokumentov. Moscow: Voenizdat, 1969.

Koenker, Diane and Bachman, Ronald., eds. *Revelations from the Russian Archives: Documents in English Translation*. Washington, DC: Library of Congress, 1997.

KPSS o vooruzhennykh silakh Sovetskogo Soiuza: dokumenty 1917–1968. Moscow: Voenizdat, 1969.

Mel'chin, S. A, Sigachev, Iu. V. and Stepanov, A. S. "Zharkoe leto sorok pervogo goda: Dokumenty GKO i Stavki perioda Smolenskogo srazhenia. Iiul' – sentiabr' 1941 g.", *Istoricheskii arkhiv*, no. 1 (1993), 45–67.

"My raspolagaem samymi luchshimi kadrami: Zapiski o poslevoennom ustroistve armii," in *Istochnik: Dokumenty russkoi istorii*, no. 2 (1996), 132–52.

Semin, Iu. N., Sigachev, Iu. V. and Chuvashin, S. I. "Na linii fronta: Dokumenty Tsentral'nogo arkhiva Ministerstva oborony RF. 1941–1945 gg.," in *Istoricheskii arkhiv*, no. 2 (1995), 40–85 and no. 3 (1995), 21–62.

Zhuravlev, V. R., Anufriev, A. S. and Emel'ianova, N. M. "Pervye dni voiny v dokumentakh," in *Voenno-istoricheskii zhurnal*, no. 5 (1989), 42–51.

Newspapers, journals, and periodicals

Argumenty i fakti
Istochnik: dokumenty russkoi istorii
Istoricheskii arkhiv
Izvestiia
Izvestiia TsK KPSS
Kommunist
Kommunist Vooruzhennykh Sil
Komsomolskaia pravda
Krasnaia zvezda
Literaturnaia gazeta
Novosti
Pravda
Sovetskii voin
Soviet Military Review
Soviet Soldier
Vestnik
Voenno-istoricheskii arkhiv
Voenno-istoricheskii zhurnal

INDEX